THE
FIRST
OF
EVERYTHING

THE FIRST OF EVERYTHING

A Compendium of
Important, Eventful, and Just-Plain-Fun Facts
About All Kinds of Firsts

DENNIS SANDERS

Research coordinated by
LEONARD LOVALLO

DELACORTE PRESS/NEW YORK

Published by
Delacorte Press
1 Dag Hammarskjold Plaza
New York, N.Y. 10017

Material in "Feminine Firsts: Women in Government" and "Women in a Man's World" is adapted from *The Women's Book of World Records and Achievements,* edited by Lois Decker O'Neill. Copyright © 1979 by Information Books, Inc. Reprinted by permission of Doubleday & Co., Inc.

Material in "Sexy Firsts" is in part adapted from *Simons' Book of Sexual Records* by G. L. Simons. Reprinted by permission of W. H. Allen, Ltd. Copyright © 1977 by G. L. Simons.

Designed by Giorgetta Bell McRee

Library of Congress Cataloging in Publication Data

Sanders, Dennis, 1949–
The first of everything.

Includes index.
1. Curiosities and wonders. I. Title.
AG243.S244   031'.02   81–2222

ISBN 0–440–02576–1   AACR2

For GBR,
first in so many ways

ACKNOWLEDGMENTS

Many have contributed in ways large and small to *The First of Everything*. First of all, thanks to Martha Kinney, who conceived the project, and thanks and love to Jane Rotrosen, who got the ball rolling. Special thanks and deep appreciation to my editor, Sandi Gelles-Cole, for her unflagging support, ideas, and much-welcome and necessary patience.

The project would not have been possible without the incomparable help of Len Lovallo in research; thanks are due as well to Don Cleary of the Jane Rotrosen Agency, and to Ken Harkins for keeping an eye out for obscure firsts.

A great debt of gratitude is owed to the librarians and staff of New York City's great Public Library system, and especially to the men and women at the Lincoln Center and the 40th Street research libraries. And special thanks to Gerry Geddes for making his own research facilities available to us.

And last, but not least, thanks to all the men and women who have done something for the first time.

CONTENTS

CONTENTS

ENTERTAINING FIRSTS

FIRST WORDS

FIRST THINGS LAST: PREHISTORIC AND PROGRESSIVE FIRSTS

FIRST THINGS
FIRST

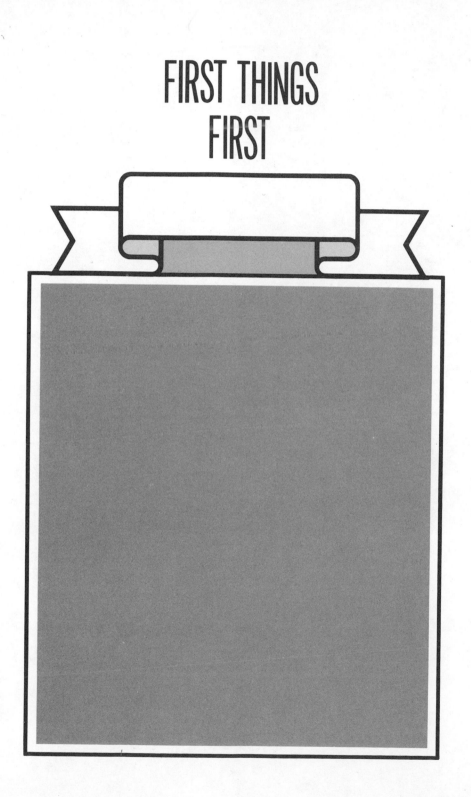

INTRODUCTION

This is not the first book of firsts, nor is it likely to be the last. Man has been interested in setting down his beginnings, his roots, his initial accomplishments, for a long time. After all, Genesis is a major compilation of firsts, as are the Hindu Vedas, and a number of other ancient writings. More recent are Kane's *Famous First Facts,* an admirably encyclopedic collection of American firsts, published originally in 1933, and Patrick Robertson's detailed *Book of Firsts* from 1974. And the reader can hardly pick up an issue of *The New York Times* or *National Geographic* without reading that something, somewhere, has been done by someone for the first time.

The problem with firsts is that there are so many of them—the devils seem to effortlessly keep pace both with the world population and the inflation rate. And, given the right context, almost *anything* can be made into a first. (If this isn't the first time you've read this sentence, it's probably the first time you've reread it, etcetera.) Faced with this sea of firsts, the author has to decide how to give his readers a *book,* as opposed to a computer printout of all available data. To this end, I have followed Lytton Strachey's philosophy of biographical writing, which applies equally well to a collection of firsts. Strachey writes in his preface to *Eminent Victorians* that if an author is wise, "He will attack his subject in unexpected places; he will fall upon the flank, or the rear; he will shoot a sudden, revealing searchlight into obscure recesses, hitherto undivined. He will row out over that great ocean of material, and lower down into it, here and there, a little bucket, which will bring up to the light of day some characteristic specimen, from those far depths, to be examined with a careful curiosity."

Here, then, is a collection of what my little bucket has brought up from the great ocean of firsts. If your favorite specimen of first doesn't appear here, perhaps it will on another voyage out; in the meantime, I hope there are enough commonplaces, curiosities, facts, and follies to keep you informed, entertained, and amused.

DENNIS SANDERS

Key West, Florida
June 1980

EVERYDAY
FIRSTS

Your tax dollar at work: Mrs. Ida May Fuller, the first recipient of a Social Security check, celebrates her 100th birthday in Brattleboro, Vermont, in 1974. Mrs. Fuller, a widow, received the Social Security check numbered 000-000-001, for $22.54, mailed out by Uncle Sam on January 31, 1940. Before her death, she had been paid more than $20,000 in benefits.

THE AMERICAN WAY OF LIFE:
Firsts That Make Life Worth Living

THE UNKINDEST CUT OF ALL

The first income tax in U. S. history was levied starting on August 5, 1862, to raise funds for fighting the Civil War. Incomes above $800 a year were taxed at 3 percent. In 1881 the Supreme Court ruled that the 1862 tax law was unconstitutional, and the tax was abolished. A second income tax was slipped into the Wilson-Gorman tariff act of 1894, and taxed incomes above $4,000 at a 2 percent rate. However, the constitutionality of the feds taxing incomes was still debatable, and it took the Sixteenth Amendment, which went into operation on February 25, 1913, to give the Government power to tax incomes without question.

The amendment reads, "The Congress shall have power to lay and collect taxes on incomes, from whatever source derived, without apportionment among the several States, and without regard to any census or enumeration."

Enter the IRS.

DO YOU TAKE PLASTIC?

In 1950 Ralph Schneider started Diner's Club, the first credit card organization, which charged members an annual fee in exchange for charge privileges at businesses. The first cards were given to two hundred subscribers who could use them at twenty-seven New York

7

area restaurants. The first bank card, the BankAmericard, was introduced by Bank of America in 1958.

ONE SLICE TO GO, WITH EVERYTHING

The first pizzeria opened at 53½ Spring Street, New York City (in present day Soho) in 1895.

DR. *SPOCK* SAYS . . .

Benjamin Spock, whose name was to become a household word, first published his *The Common Sense Book of Baby and Child Care,* written while he was a doctor in the Navy Medical Corps, in 1946. The book has sold to date over 23 million copies, and children raised on Dr. Spock are raising their children on Dr. Spock.

REDEEMING VALUE

In 1896 Thomas Sperry and Shelly Hutchinson of Jackson, Michigan, started the Sperry & Hutchinson Company, which issued the first trading stamps to customers, one stamp for every dollar of purchases. The idea of pasting stamps in books and then redeeming them for merchandise at premium parlors caught on big with consumers, and by 1914, 6 percent of all retail purchases in the United States were sold with trading stamps.

HOLD THE PICKLES, HOLD THE MAYO

New Haven, Connecticut, lunch-counter owner Louis Lassen invented the hamburger in 1900. The customers at "Louis' Lunch" were presented with ground lean beef, broiled, then served between two slices of toast.

BEER CAN POLKA

Kreuger Beer, brewed in Newtown, New Jersey, became the first beer sold in cans in 1935.

FOGGED WINDOWS

The future of sexual behavior among America's youth was forever changed with the opening of the first drive-in theater on June 6, 1933, on Wilson Boulevard, Camden, New Jersey.

AISLE FOUR, NEXT TO PAPER TOWELS

The first supermarkets resembling those of today were the Piggly Wiggly stores, owned by Clarence Saunders of Memphis, Tennessee. Saunders's first store, which featured self-service and check-out counters, opened at 79 Jefferson Street, Memphis, in 1916.

CARTWHEELS

As supermarkets got bigger, and customers' purchases more numerous, hand-held baskets weren't very handy for carting around all those brand-name, packaged products. To solve this problem, Sylvan Goldman, a Humpty Dumpty store owner in Oklahoma City, on June 4, 1937, introduced his shopping cart. The cart was converted from folding chairs mounted on wheels. The seat was moved to hold a basket above and below it, and was pushed around the aisles by the back of the chair.

NOT TURKEY AGAIN?

C. A. Swanson and Sons sold their first "TV Brand Dinners" in 1954.

BAKE IT OFF!

The Pillsbury Bake-Off was held for the first time in 1948. Mrs. Ralph E. Smafield of Rockford, Illinois, won for her "Water-rising Twists." For the first time in 1968 contestants were allowed to use Pillsbury mixed and refrigerator doughs in their recipes as well as Pillsbury flour.

VERY DRY, WITH A TWIST

The martini was invented by Jerry Thomas, a bartender at the Occidental Hotel, San Francisco, in 1860. It is not recorded who enjoyed the first three-martini lunch.

IT'S IN THE BAG

Merchants have been wrapping goods in paper for a long time, but the familiar square-bottomed paper bag was first made in the United States by Luther C. Crowell, who patented his design and the machine to make it in 1872.

FILL 'ER UP!

The gas station, that all-too-familiar fixture on the American landscape, was actually pioneered in France, where a Monsieur Borol opened an establishment for servicing automobiles at 41 rue St. Claire, Bordeaux, in December, 1895.

NICKEL AND DIME

Twenty-seven-year-old Frank W. Woolworth opened his first store selling only nickel items at Utica, New York, in 1879, and though the store failed within three months (and the four-hundred-dollar capital lost), Woolworth tried again at Lancaster, Pennsylvania, with success, and expanded to five-and-dimes at Harrisburg, Philadelphia, New York City, Newark, Scranton, Erie, and other northeastern cities.

VERY FUNNIES

Single-panel cartoons have been around for a long time, and were a regular feature of many nineteenth-century periodicals. But the classic "strip" originated on Sunday, October 24, 1897, with Frank Outcault's "The Yellow Kid," which appeared in the color Sunday supplement of the *New York Journal.* The Kid had originally been a single-cartoon character, but the multipanel strip proved popular, and many imitators soon followed.

WE'RE NUMBER ONE

In 1918, a used-car lot in Chicago started renting out twelve vehicles to drivers, the first car-rental firm. The lot was bought in 1923 by John D. Hertz, president of the Yellow Cab Company of Chicago, who renamed the fledgling operation The Hertz Drive-Ur-Self System.

LADY LOVELORN

Esther Pauline Friedman Lederer of Chicago published her first confidential column "Ann Landers Says" in the *Chicago Sun-Times* in 1955.

THE GREAT CRUSADES

Though he began his evangelical career in 1944 for the American Youth for Christ movement, the first real Billy Graham campaign was in Los Angeles in 1949, where he gained national attention for converting, among others, an Olympic athlete and an underworld mobster.

SINGING IN THE SHOWER:
Firsts Found in the
Smallest Room of Your House

ASPIRIN

Acetylsalicylic acid was produced for the first time in 1899 by German chemists Felix Hoffman and Hermann Dreser, who manufactured the pain killer and fever reducer from coal tar. In 1905, aspirin was marketed for the first time by Bayer Aspirin, and soon became the largest selling over-the-counter, nonprescription drug in the world.

KLEENEX

The Kimberly-Clark Company manufactured the world's first disposable handkerchief in 1924 under the name Celluwipes. The product was later renamed Kleenex 'Kerchiefs, and eventually shortened to Kleenex.

THE FLUSH TOILET

English poet John Harrington invented a practical flushing water closet in 1595, but the device made no inroads against the common chamber pot. In 1775 Alexander Cummings, an English inventor, received the first patent for a flush toilet, and in 1778 Joseph Brahama, age thirty, invented the valve and syphon-type flushing mechanism which became the model for all future toilets. However, the chamber pot remained firmly entrenched until the end of the nineteenth century, when the rich began discovering the joys of indoor bathroom plumbing.

THE TOOTHBRUSH

The toothbrush is said to have been invented in China in 1498, though they didn't become commonplace in Europe until the seventeenth century. The first nylon bristle brush was marketed in the United States in 1938 as Dr. West's Miracle Tuft Toothbrush. The bristles were made of Du Pont nylon. Squibb manufactured the first electric toothbrush in 1961.

BAND-AIDS

Johnson & Johnson of New Brunswick, New Jersey, introduced the Band-Aid—essentially unchanged today—in 1920.

ALKA-SELTZER

In 1931 Miles Laboratories of Elkhart, Indiana, introduced a tablet (containing sodium bicarbonate, monocalcium phosphate, aspirin, and citric acid), which fizzled in water. The product, Alka-Seltzer, would sell in excess of 2.5 billion tablets a year by the 1970's.

MERTHIOLATE

Eli Lilly Company introduced tincture of Merthiolate for cuts and scratches in 1930, though the product was not successful until Lilly added dye to make it stain the skin and alcohol to make it sting.

THE SAFETY RAZOR

King Camp Gillette patented the safety razor in 1901, and started his Gillette Safety Razor Company in Boston the same year. The new razors went on sale in 1903, when a grand total of 51 razors and 168 blades were sold.

MOUTHWASH

The Lambert Pharmaceutical Company of St. Louis introduced Listerine (named after Dr. Joseph Lister, discoverer of antiseptic surgical procedures) in 1880. However, the "it-kills-germs-by-the-millions-on-contact" slogan wouldn't make Listerine a household word until a massive marketing and advertising campaign was started in 1922.

KOTEX

During World War I, German-American chemist Ernst Mahler, thirty-one, developed a wood-cellulose substitute for cotton, called cellucotton, which helped alleviate a critical shortage of bandages when introduced in 1918. The Kimberly-Clark Company of Neenah, Wisconsin, which manufactured cellucotton bandages, learned that Red Cross nurses at military hospitals were using the bandages as sanitary napkins, and decided they were onto a good thing. In 1921 they introduced their modified cellucotton bandage as the world's first commercial sanitary napkin under the name "Kotex."

WHAT'S COOKING?
Kitcheny Firsts

GAS STOVE

James Sharp, a gas company executive in Northampton, England, designed and built the first practical gas stove for his own kitchen in 1826, and started manufacturing the stoves commercially in 1836.

ELECTRIC OVEN

The first known electric oven was installed by an unknown inventor in a Swiss hotel in 1889, and by 1891 the Carpenter Electric Heating Manufacturing Company of St. Paul, Minnesota, offered the first electric ovens for sale. However, during the "gaslight" era, electricity was an expensive power source, and electric ovens and stoves did not become popular with the public until the cheap electricity era of the 1930's.

POP-UP TOASTER

Charles Strite, an American inventor, patented the first pop-up electric toaster in 1918; the famous Toastmaster was first marketed by the Elgin Illinois Company of McGraw Electric in 1930.

REFRIGERATOR

The first commercial home refrigerator was the Domelre, manufactured in Chicago in 1913, which retailed for a costly nine hundred dollars. The first Kelvinator was made in 1918, and the first Frigidaire in 1919. Early refrigeration was not a runaway success with homemakers, and annual sales didn't exceed ten thousand units until 1920. General Electric's famous "monitor" top refrigerator (the first with a hermetically sealed compressor) went on the market in 1927 and soon became the most successful model sold.

BLENDER

The blender was invented by Fred Waring, well-known band leader of the thirties and forties, in 1936, and revolutionized food preparation and bartending.

DISHWASHER

Invented by Mrs. W. A. Cochran, a Shelbyville, Indiana, housewife, 1879–89.

WASHING MACHINE

The Hurley Machine Company of Chicago introduced the "Thor" —the first self-contained electric clothes washer—in 1907.

MICROWAVE OVEN

Microwave cooking was accidentally discovered by Percy Le Baron Spencer of the Raytheon Company, who found that microwave signals melted a candy bar in his pocket; Raytheon developed Spencer's discovery into a commercial microwave oven which they marketed in 1947. The first compact microwave oven was introduced by Amana in 1967.

ALUMINUM SAUCEPAN

Henry Avery of Cleveland produced the first aluminum saucepan in 1890, which Mrs. Avery used until 1933.

TEFLON

Roy J. Plunkett, a Du Pont chemist, discovered polytetrafluoroethylene, or Teflon, by accident in 1938, and the nonstick surface was soon being used for cooking utensils as well as industrial wiring.

TUPPERWARE

Earl W. Tupper, a former Du Pont chemist, started his own company to manufacture airtight plastic kitchen storage bowls and boxes in 1945.

TIN CANS

The tin can was patented in 1810 by Peter Duran of England, but the handmade cans were expensive (one tinsmith could cut, mold, and solder only about sixty cans a day); machine-stamped cans were introduced in 1847. In 1865 tins were made of thinner steel, allowing the first can opener to be made—prior to that, tin cans had been opened with a hammer and chisel.

ALUMINUM AND TAB-TOP CANS

American manufacturers introduced aluminum cans for soft drinks in 1960; the tab-top can, sponsored by Alcoa, was tested in Pittsburgh in 1962, and introduced on Schlitz beer nationally in February, 1963. By 1970, 90 percent of all beer was being sold in tab-top cans.

BRAND-NAME FIRSTS:
Sixty Famous Foods,
and the Year They Went on the Market

1. Crisco Shortening, 1911
2. Morton Salt, 1885
3. Campbell's Chicken Noodle Soup, 1933
4. Welch's Grape Jelly, 1927
5. Kellogg's All-Bran Cereal, 1919
6. Oreo Cookies, 1911
7. Life Savers, 1913
8. Wheaties, 1924
9. Maxim Freeze-Dried Coffee, 1964
10. ReaLemon Concentrated Lemon Juice, 1935
11. Spam, 1933
12. Kellogg's Sugar Frosted Flakes, 1952
13. Dannon Yogurt, 1942
14. Hellmann's Real Mayonnaise, 1911
15. Skippy Peanut Butter, 1932
16. Peter Pan Peanut Butter, 1928
17. Animal Crackers, 1902
18. Aunt Jemima Pancake Mix, 1889
19. Kellogg's Corn Flakes, 1906
20. Bisquick, 1931
21. Pepperidge Farm Bread, 1937
22. Quaker Oats, 1901
23. Jell-O, 1896
24. Minute Tapioca, 1894
25. Ritz Crackers, 1933

26. Kellogg's Rice Krispies, 1928
27. Campbell Pork and Beans, 1904
28. Pepsi-Cola, 1898
29. Gold Medal Flour, 1880
30. Quaker Puffed Rice and Puffed Wheat, 1913
31. Wise Potato Chips, 1921
32. French's Worcestershire Sauce, 1930
33. Maxwell House Instant Coffee, 1942
34. Lay's Potato Chips, 1939
35. Reddi-Wip, 1947
36. Sweet 'n Low, 1958
37. Cracker Jack, 1896
38. Log Cabin Syrup, 1887
39. Coca-Cola, 1886
40. Dr Pepper, 1886
41. Hires Root Beer, 1886
42. Lipton Tea, 1890
43. Wesson Oil, 1899
44. Eskimo Pie, 1921
45. Shredded Wheat, 1893
46. 7 Up, 1933
47. Frito-Lay Corn Chips, 1932
48. Diet-Rite, 1962
49. Sanka, 1903
50. Canada Dry Ginger Ale, 1904
51. Thomas' English Muffins, 1880
52. Cocoa Puffs, 1958
53. Sara Lee Cheesecake, 1949
54. Tab, 1963
55. Diet Pepsi-Cola, 1965
56. Grape Nuts, 1896
57. Velveeta, 1915
58. Popsicle, 1924
59. Wonder Bread, 1927
60. Hostess Twinkies, 1930

STICKY-FINGER FIRSTS:
Famous Candy Bars' Debuts

HERSHEY BAR, 1894

Milton S. Hershey, a Lancaster, Pennsylvania, caramel maker, introduced the Hershey Bar: 45 percent sugar, 16 percent cocoa beans, 14 percent liquid chocolate, 25 percent milk solids.

TOOTSIE ROLL, 1896

Leo Hirschfield, a twenty-nine-year-old Austrian-American candy maker, introduced the first candy wrapped in paper—a chewy, cigar-shaped chocolate. He named it after his six-year-old daughter, Clara "Tootsie" Hirschfield.

MOUNDS, 1921

Peter Paul Inc., founded in New Haven, Connecticut, by Armenian-American Peter Paul Halijian, manufactured a bittersweet chocolate and coconut candy bar created by chemist George Shamilian.

BABY RUTH, 1921

Otto Schnering, who had founded the Curtiss Candy Company four years earlier in a room over a Chicago plumbing shop, and given the company his mother's maiden name, introduced a nickel caramel, fudge, peanut, and chocolate concoction which he named after President Cleveland's daughter, Baby Ruth Cleveland. The candy's popularity was not hurt, however, by the growing fame of Babe Ruth in the 1920's, and the candy bar is usually said to be named after him.

BUTTERFINGER, 1923

The Curtiss Candy Company added a relative of Baby Ruth. The manufacturer's favorite publicity gimmick was dropping Baby Ruths and Butterfingers over cities from airplanes. In Pittsburgh, a massive traffic jam was caused by people rushing into the streets to grab the candy bars; the stunt was repeated in forty cities.

MILKY WAY, 1923

Frank Mars, thirty-nine, a Minnesota confectioner, created the Milky Way out of milk chocolate, corn syrup, sugar, milk, vegetable oil, cocoa, malt, butter, and egg whites. By his second year, the candy bar sold $792,000 worth.

SNICKERS, 1930

Mars Inc.'s second big hit, and profits hit 2.3 million dollars that year.

3 MUSKETEERS, 1932

Another Mars item, retailing for a nickel.

M & M's, 1940

Mars Inc. created the candy that "melts in your mouth, not in your hand" for the United States military. The "quick energy" sugar-coated candy was intended to hold up in GIs' pockets and rucksacks, and to keep their trigger fingers from getting sticky.

ALMOND JOY, 1947

Peter Paul Inc. added almonds to their famous Mounds recipe.

FAST FOOD FIRSTS

McDONALD'S HAMBURGERS

Movie-theater owners Maurice and Richard McDonald turned their hamburger stand near Pasadena, which they opened in 1940, into a self-service restaurant in 1948. By 1952 they were so successful in southern California that restaurant equipment entrepreneur Ray Kroc persuaded them to let him sell nationwide franchises; by 1960, when there were two hundred outlets, Kroc bought out the Mc-Donalds for 2.7 million dollars.

BASKIN-ROBBINS

The owners of two small chains of southern California ice-cream stores decided to merge their businesses in 1948, and Burton "Butch" Baskin and Irvine Robbins found their "100-plus flavors" a hit with the public, and started selling franchises worldwide.

SHAKEY'S PIZZA

World War II army buddies Sherwood "Shakey" Johnson and Edward Plummer invested $850 each in a Sacramento, California, pizza parlor in 1954. By the 1970's the chain grossed in excess of 100 million dollars.

KENTUCKY FRIED CHICKEN

When Harland Sanders's Corbin, Kentucky, restaurant business was hurt by a new highway bypassing the premises in 1955, the sixty-five-year-old took to the road in an old car, living off his $105 monthly Social Security check, convincing restaurateurs to use his secret recipe for "finger lickin' good" fried chicken, along with the Kentucky Fried Chicken name. Sanders got 3 percent of the gross, and by 1964 had built a chain of more than six hundred franchises, which he sold for 2 million dollars plus an annual salary for promoting the name and product.

PIZZA HUT

The first Pizza Hut opened in Kansas City in 1958; it grew to be the largest franchise pizza chain in the country, overtaking Shakey's, and by the mid-70's was doing 115 million dollars in business.

AFTER FIG LEAVES, WHAT?:
When Things Were First Worn

BIFOCALS

Benjamin Franklin (1706–90) described his new invention, bifocal eyeglasses, in a letter written in Passy, France, on May 23, 1784. The seventy-eight-year-old statesman created them to help with his own vision problems.

BIKINIS

French designer Louis Reaud revealed his new tiny two-piece swimsuit at a Paris salon showing on July 5, 1946, which became an immediate success in postwar Europe, though not popular (except in fantasy) in America for another fifteen years.

NYLON STOCKINGS

In 1938, after a decade of research, E. I. Du Pont de Nemours and Company introduced their new synthetic monofilament, nylon, suitable for brush bristles. In 1940, they introduced multifilament nylon yarn for manufacturing hosiery, and the first nylon stockings went on sale on May 15, 1940. With the cutoff of silk supplies from the Orient during the war, silk stockings became a relic of the past.

ZIPPERS

The first slide fastener was invented and demonstrated at the Chicago World's Fair in 1893 by American inventor Whitcomb Judson, who called it the "Clasp Locker or Unlocker for Shoes." In 1913 Gideon Sundback, a Swedish-American inventor, added the familiar metal teeth, and in 1926 this was dubbed the "zipper" by British novelist Gilbert Frankau who, after seeing the marvel demonstrated at a luncheon, remarked, "Zip! It's open. Zip! It's closed." Elsa Schiaparelli was the first designer to use the zipper in her clothing line, and in 1931, when the early patents expired, it became a familiar part of dress backs, pants flies, and outerwear.

THE LACOSTE SHIRT

The French clothing firm, Izod, which contracted with French tennis star René LaCoste to use his name and alligator trademark after he won the Davis Cup for France in 1927, imported their chic, status-symbol tennis shirt to the United States for the first time in 1951.

CHANEL NO. 5

The world's most popular fragrance was introduced by French designer Coco Chanel in 1920.

LEVI'S JEANS

San Francisco merchant Levi Strauss shrewdly combined an overstock of heavy-duty cotton sailcloth with the need of California Gold Rush miners for sturdy, durable trousers, and went into the pants-making business. He patented his famous riveted construction in May, 1873, and the basic pants have changed very little since.

BRASSIERES

The first record of a halter replacement for the stiff, boned corsets of the nineteenth century is a design made by Charles Debevoise, a

French clothing designer, in 1902. His innovation didn't catch on.

In 1910, Otto Tizling, a German-born American who worked in his uncle's corset factory, made the first halter-bra for Swanhilda Olafson, a young opera singer who found it difficult (and painful) to sing with her exceptional endowment pushed out of place by stayed corsets. The Tizling bra did catch on with the women's dress revolution in the war years, and he can be said to be the father of the modern bra.

The first elastic bra was made ca. 1913–14 by Mary Phelps Jacobs, a New York debutante, who improvised the article to wear under a ball gown, using two handkerchiefs, ribbon, thread, and elastic. The backless bra got enough attention that Mary started getting orders from friends; she patented the design in 1914, and went into production. When business proved too slow, she sold the patent to Warner Brothers Company (the corset, not the film, firm) who made millions from the product.

MINISKIRTS

Fashion reached new heights with the introduction of the first miniskirt by British designer Mary Quant in December ("It was in the chill December") of 1965.

CONTACT LENSES

A milestone in the history of vanity, the contact lens was first invented by A. E. Fick, a Swiss physician, in 1887, though the heavy lenses which covered the entire surface of the eye were problematic at the very least. The first plastic lenses were made by Theodore Obrig in 1938 (using newly discovered Plexiglas or Lucite). But the full-cover lenses had limited wearing time. The first truly comfortable lens, the corneal type still worn by millions of men and women, was introduced in 1950.

EVERYBODY INTO THE SECRETARIAL POOL: Firsts in the Office

NINETY WORDS A MINUTE

Man has been trying to come up with a substitute for writing by hand for a long time—the printing press was one solution—and the early typewriters were not much different in principle from the printing press. In 1808, for example, Pellegrino Turri of Italy built a writing machine for his blind friend Countess Fantoni. The machine, which didn't survive, was apparently operated by pushing down plungers with carved letters on them against a carbon or inked paper. Later inventors (such as Charles Thurber of Worcester, Massachusetts, with his chirograph in 1840) made wheeled or hemispherical machines which turned or rotated one letter at a time to impress a character on a sheet—not unlike today's wheeled plastic label makers.

The first typewriter that bore any resemblance to today's machine (and its direct ancestor) was built by Christopher L. Sholes of Milwaukee in June, 1872. The big breakthrough with the Sholes machine was its keyboard, with the letters arranged in alphabetical order. In November, 1872, Sholes (who got his backing from one James Densmore) tried a model with a keyboard arranged like the letters in a typesetter's case, and it's this keyboard that is used with only slight modifications by millions of typists today.

In March, 1873, Sholes signed a contract with the Remington Arms Company, and the Sholes and Glidden typewriter went into production, selling for $125, in July, 1874. In 1876, this became the

Remington No. 1 Type-Writer, a name that is still found in offices around the world.

SUBMIT IN TRIPLICATE

Carbon paper was invented by Ralph Wedgewood of England, and patented in October, 1806. Wedgewood's paper was soaked in ink and dried, which means it would have given an impression on both sides—leaving a "negative" print on the back of the original.

AND IT'S STILL WRITING!

The ballpoint pen was patented in 1938 by Hungarian chemist George Biro and his proofreader brother, Ladislao. The Biro patent was acquired by two Englishmen, Henry Martin and Frederick Miles, who began production in 1943 and sold pens to the R.A.F. because they didn't leak at high altitudes like fountain pens. The first commercially available pens were made in the United States by Milton Reynolds, and went on sale at Gimbels department store on October 29, 1945, where the $12.50 pens quickly sold out. Reynolds made a profit of $500,000 in the first month of business alone and by 1946 the ballpoint was well on its way to pushing out the fountain pen.

THE RUBBER BANDWAGON

The first elastic fasteners were patented in March, 1845, by Stephen Perry of Messrs. Perry and Company, London, and available for sale the same year.

DITTO

The mimeograph machine, that bane of purple-fingered secretaries, was invented by Thomas Edison, who patented his waxed-paper stencils for duplicating in 1875. Edison didn't pursue his invention, however, and sold the patent to A. B. Dick of Chicago, who developed the Diaphragm Mimeograph machine in 1887. In the meantime, however, the same principle had been used by David Gestetner, a Hungarian immigrant living in London, and marketed in 1881; he also introduced the first typewriter stencil.

ENDLESS REPETITION

Chester Floyd Carlson, thirty-one, a pre-law student, discovered the dry duplicating process which he called xerography (*xeros* is the Greek word for "dry") using powder and electrostatic charges on a metal plate, in 1937. He obtained the first true images in October, 1939, and patented the process in 1940. The rights to the process were bought in 1946 by the Haloid Company of Rochester, New York, and the first Xerox copiers were sold to the public in 1950.

TAKE THIS DOWN

The famous Pitman system of shorthand was devised by Sir Isaac Pitman (1813–97) while he was a schoolmaster in Gloucestershire, England, and was set forth in his book *Stenographic Soundhand* in 1837. It was the first successful system to use lines instead of words or letters to represent sounds. However, methods of notating language by "shortcuts" were known as long ago as Roman times, when Cicero's secretary Tiro took down the master's orations in his own shorthand. In 1558 Dr. Timothy Bright published the first known English system (which apparently wasn't very practical—it had more than five hundred characters, and would be almost as difficult to master as written Japanese). The Gregg system, the most popular rival to the Pitman system, was devised in 1888 by American Robert Gregg (1867–1948).

SIGNED, SEALED, AND DELIVERED

A postage stamp was licked and pasted to a letter for the first time on May 1, 1840, when the "Penny Black," the first adhesive stamp, went on sale. The stamp, with the head of Queen Victoria, was valid for postage after May 6. The first postage meter was produced by Pitney Bowes Inc. in 1920, after Congress passed a law making metered mail legal; one of the company's founders, Arthur Pitney, had developed a prototype meter in 1901 after seeing fellow employees at his company steal stamps.

THANK GOD, IT'S FRIDAY

The history of checking off days and weeks to keep track of things goes back at least as far as 34,000 B.C., during the ice age, when prehistoric man etched symbols for the phases of the moon on antlers, bones, and stone. The discovery that man was keeping calendars thousands of years before he was traditionally credited with inventing writing or notation of any sort was made by Alexander Marshack of the Peabody Museum, Harvard, in 1964, though it was fifteen years before his discovery gained any credence with archaeologists.

WHEN THE BIG HAND IS ON THE FIVE . . .

The great office pastime of clockwatching is as least as old as labor itself. The predecessors of the mechanical clock, the sundial and water clock (or clepsydra), date back to the early days of society. The water clock was in use in Egypt as early as 2000 B.C., and the first sundials are perhaps older. The earliest extant sundial is from Egypt, circa 1500 B.C., but numerous ancient stone structures, such as Stonehenge (ca. 1500 B.C.) and the great Pyramid of Cheops (ca. 2680 B.C.) all can be used to measure time due to the way they cast shadows.

The geared, mechanical clock, the ancestor of our watches, wall clocks, and kitchen timers, dates from about A.D. 1000. Various men are credited with building the first one: Gerbert, a monk who later became Pope Sylvester II, is said to have invented a mechanical clock ca. A.D. 996; likewise the Archbishop of Verona, Pacificus, is given credit for a weight-driven clock in the ninth century; there is also a written description of a thirty-foot-high mechanical clock with gears and a water-driven mechanism from China (from the Imperial tutor Su Sung) dating from A.D. 1088.

GAMES PEOPLE PLAY, AND WHEN THEY PLAYED THEM FIRST

CHESS

First played in India, then spreading to Persia and the Levant in the sixth and seventh centuries A.D., and introduced to Europe by the Muslims, chess was played throughout Europe by the thirteenth century.

Françis André Danican, known as Philidor, French composer and chess master (who died in 1795), is usually credited with being the first man to play (and win) chess blindfolded. However, as early as the eleventh century, Arab and Persian chess virtuosos would blindfold themselves while playing against less talented opponents to give the other guy a fighting chance.

The first modern international chess tournament was held in Britain in 1851, with Adolph Anderssen of Germany the winner.

BACKGAMMON

The first evidence of backgammon, dating from ca. 2000 B.C., was discovered in Babylon, and the game has been played virtually unchanged since.

CHECKERS

First played in Europe in the sixteenth century, checkers (or draughts) was known in ancient Greece, Rome, and the Near East.

MAH-JONGG

The basic game has been played in various versions in China for centuries using tiles, sticks, and a board. The modern, Western version originated in 1920 with Joseph Babcock, a United States citizen living in Shanghai who brought back the game with standardized rules and equipment of his own devising. The game took America by storm, and Mah-Jongg parties (sometimes complete with Chinese costumes) were big during the twenties.

POKER

Believed to have originated in the Orient, poker was first played in the United States in the nineteenth century, probably introduced by seamen.

BRIDGE

Whist, the "parent" game of bridge, was first played in England in the sixteenth century (where it developed out of earlier games). Bridge grew out of whist in England in the nineteenth century. Auction bridge was first devised by the British in India, ca. 1904, and contract bridge, the current game, was invented by Harold S. Vanderbilt while on a Caribbean cruise in 1925.

SCRABBLE

In 1948 James Brunot of Newtown, Connecticut, copyrighted Scrabble, developed from "Criss Cross," a spelling game with wood tiles and a board originated by Alfred M. Butts in 1931. The first Scrabble games were produced by Selchow & Righter of Bay Shore, Long Island, starting in 1952.

MONOPOLY

Charles B. Darrow, an unemployed engineer from Germantown, Pennsylvania, invented Monopoly in 1933, naming the properties on his capitalism game after Atlantic City streets where he and his family had spent vacations in more prosperous times before the Depression. Parker Brothers initially rejected the game as "too long and complicated"—but finally produced the game in 1935. The unexpected success of Monopoly made Darrow a millionaire, and Monopoly the most popular board game in America.

KID STUFF:
Toyish Firsts

THE TEDDY BEAR

Morris Michtom, a Brooklyn candy-store owner, and his wife, saw a cartoon in the *Washington Evening Star* on November 18, 1902, showing President Theodore Roosevelt sparing the life of a female bear with cubs while on a hunting trip. Teddy's kindness inspired them to name their new fuzzy brown toy the "teddy bear."

THE RAGGEDY ANN DOLL

In 1915 John Gruelle, a political cartoonist for the *Indianapolis Star,* found a handmade rag doll in his attic, which he gave to his daughter Marcella, who suffered from tuberculosis. The doll was named Raggedy Ann after "Little Orphan Annie" and "the Raggedy Man," characters from stories by James Whitcomb Riley, a friend and neighbor. Raggedy Ann soon became the character in stories Gruelle told his invalid daughter, and in 1916 she died while holding the doll. In 1917 Gruelle published a book of his stories along with more Raggedy Ann dolls to promote the book. The idea caught on, and in 1918 the first Raggedy Anns were offered for sale to the public.

THE POGO STICK

Patented by George B. Hansburg, age thirty-two, in 1919, the pogo stick became an American rage during the faddish twenties.

ROLLER SKATES

A Belgian musical instrument maker named Joseph Merlin invented roller skates to wear to a costume party at Carlisle House, Soho Square, London, in 1759. Merlin intended to roll into the party while playing his violin. However, he neglected to master the art of stopping on skates and crashed into a mirror on his entrance, breaking both mirror and violin, and cutting himself badly in the process.

The first four-wheeled skates with brake pads (Merlin's only had two wheels each) were patented by James L. Plimpton of New York in 1863, making "modern" roller-skating possible, and creating a nationwide fad during the 1860's and 1870's.

FERRIS WHEEL

Designed by American engineer George Washington Gale Ferris, the first Ferris wheel was installed at the World's Columbian Exposition, Chicago, in 1893; the huge amusement machine, costing $300,000, had a wheel 250 feet in diameter with thirty-six cars holding forty people each.

THE KEWPIE DOLL

Rose Cecil O'Neill, a Greenwich Village illustrator and author, patented her celluloid, pointy-headed Kewpie doll in 1909. Kewpie went into production in 1913 and made O'Neill 1.5 million dollars.

SILLY PUTTY

In the late 1940's, General Electric researchers came up with an experimental substitute for natural rubber. The silicone substance, which stretched, bounced, molded, and was generally pliable, had no real industrial value. But a New Haven advertising man named Peter

Hodgson bought $147 worth of the stuff from G. E., hired a Yale student to separate it into one-ounce globs that were then packaged in plastic cubes, and sold them in a 1949 toy catalogue which Hodgson was preparing for a New Haven store. Silly Putty became an overnight sensation, at least among kids and nervous executive types. Mothers found that it did less damage to walls and furniture than bubble gum, though it did tend to turn up in unlikely places, get caught in the kid's braces, and collect cat fur.

THE FRISBEE

The Wham-O Manufacturing Company of San Gabriel, California, introduced the plastic Frisbee in 1957 after one of the company's executives had observed Yale students tossing metal pie plates to one another on the campus grounds. The plastic model, which launched a craze that has now become an established sport, was named after the pie tins favored by Yalies: those manufactured by the Frisbie Company of Bridgeport, Connecticut.

THE BARBIE DOLL

Ruth Handler, one of the founders of toy-manufacturing giant Mattel Inc., designed the first Barbie Doll for her daughter, who enjoyed making clothes for "grown-up" dolls. Mattel produced the first Barbies in 1958, selling for five dollars, and Barbie's sophisticated wardrobe, svelte contours, and grown-up ways (Ken was to be introduced a few years later), made her a big hit. By 1980, she was enough of a classic for a New York fashion designer to recreate Barbie's fashion wardrobe for real, life-size Barbies.

THE HULA-HOOP

In 1958, Richard P. Knerr and Arthur K. "Spud" Melvin, owners of the Wham-O Manufacturing Company of San Gabriel, California, introduced the Hula-Hoop, which became the biggest toy fad in history. The dollar ninety-eight plastic hoops (which cost fifty cents to produce) sold 20 million units by September of the same year, and Wham-O is reputed to have eventually made 45 million bucks off the gimmick.

The swinging nun: When the first Hula-Hoops were sold in the United States, in 1958, the Benedictine Sisters of Christ King Convent in Oklahoma City found the fad a welcome diversion from daily devotions. WIDE WORLD PHOTOS

Knerr and Melvin took the idea from Australian gym teachers, who had been using wooden hoops to keep their pupils in shape. In 1957 the Australian hoops had reached California, and the entrepreneurs made their own experimental models from scrap wood, which were tested by their kids.

By November of 1958, the *Wall Street Journal* was able to predict that the fad was dying, and headlined, "The Hoops Have Had It."

LIFE HAS ITS UPS AND DOWNS:
Druggy Firsts

ALCOHOL

Wine grapes were grown by peoples of the Indus valley by 4000 B.C.

OPIUM

The Sumerians of Mesopotamia were deriving opium from poppies by 4000 B.C.

COFFEE

In 850 B.C., according to legend, an Arab goat herder named Kaldi noticed that his goats were livelier than usual after eating berries from a certain wild bush. He tried some himself, and discovered coffee beans—and the stimulant, caffeine.

TOBACCO

Roderigo de Jerez and Luis de Torres, of Christopher Columbus's 1492 expedition to America, reported that Indians on shore "drank smoke"—and promptly picked up the nicotine habit. Roderigo later was imprisoned by the Inquisition for tobacco smoking.

MORPHINE

German pharmacist Frederich Seturner isolated a narcotic derivative from opium and called it Morphium, after Morpheus, the Greek god of sleep, in 1803.

COCAINE

The alkaloid cocaine, the chief ingredient in coca leaves, was first isolated in 1844 by Heinrich Emmanuel Merck of Darmstadt, Hesse (South and Central American Indians had been chewing coca leaves for centuries), and Merck began commercial production of cocaine in 1862. However, little attention was paid to the substance until 1883, when the German Army physician Dr. Theodor Aschenbrandt bought a supply from Merck and issued it to Bavarian soldiers on fall maneuvers. He reported the cocaine had a beneficial effect on their ability to endure fatigue. Dr. Aschenbrandt's report was read —and heeded—by young Sigmund Freud, the first illustrious user of cocaine, who described the "most gorgeous excitement" after an injection of coke.

MARIJUANA

Cannabis sativa has been cultivated for centuries for its strong fiber as well as its strong intoxicating effect. It was in use in China, according to one ancient treatise, before 2700 B.C., and is mentioned in the Indian Atharva Veda of 2000 B.C. The Greek historian Herodotus describes the Araxians, who "meet together in companies," and throw a plant on a fire, "and by inhaling the fruit that has been thrown on, they become intoxicated by the odor, just as the Greeks do by wine; and the more fruit is thrown on, the more intoxicated they become, until they rise up and dance and betake themselves to singing."

The first definite record of marijuana in the New World is from A.D. 1545, when the Spaniards brought it to Chile; the Jamestown settlers brought it with them to Virginia in 1611. Hemp was a major crop in the Colonies, and was grown by George Washington at Mount Vernon. Though primarily a fiber crop, the physiological qualities were not unknown to Americans. Thomas Jefferson grew it for the use of his slaves.

AMPHETAMINES

Amphetamine was first synthesized in 1887, but it was not used until 1927, when doctors discovered that it raised blood pressure, dilated the bronchial passages, and stimulated the central nervous system. In 1932 the first amphetamine was put on the market, when Smith, Kline, and French introduced the Benzedrex inhaler, which contained Benzedrine—an amphetamine—which was used by cold and sinus sufferers to open clogged nasal passages, and to get an unexpected "lift."

BARBITURATES

Barbituric acid, from which all barbiturates are derived, was first synthesized by German chemist Adolf von Baeyer in 1864. From it eventually came Seconal, Nembutal, Pentothal, Amytal, and Lumital. The first of the commercially manufactured barbiturates was Veronal, introduced in 1903, followed by Luminal in 1912. By 1940 it was estimated that one billion grains of barbiturates were being taken every day in the United States.

MILTOWN

Meprobamate, considered a "minor" tranquilizer by medical science though its effects are similar to (if less pronounced than) barbiturates, was first marketed in 1954 as Miltown by Wallace Laboratories, and as Equanil by Wyeth labs, the same year. Miltown was the first, and best known, of the "minors" until the sixties.

LSD

Hallucinogens have been used by society for centuries, notably peyote by the North and South American Indians, and the fly agaric mushroom in Europe during the Middle Ages (where witch covens may have hallucinated flying while on a "trip"). But the properties of LSD (lysergic acid diethylamide) were discovered on April 16, 1943, by Dr. Albert Hoffman, a chemist at Sandoz Laboratories in Basel, Switzerland, who was "seized with a feeling of great restlessness . . . I lay down and sank into a not unpleasant delirium, which was characterized by extremely excited fantasies." Dr. Hoffman had taken the first acid trip—having unwittingly swallowed a small amount of the LSD-25. He and an associate had isolated LSD five years before, but had for the most part ignored it when the chemical had no apparent effect on test animals. Soon after Hoffman's trip, LSD was being tested by psychiatrists, the military, and even the CIA. It was not until 1962 that federal law restricted Sandoz—the legal manufacturer—in the distribution of the substance to doctors, psychiatrists, and researchers.

LIBRIUM

Chlordiazepoxidehydrochloride, or Librium, was first marketed by Roche Laboratories after FDA approval on March 24, 1960; the tranquilizer was developed by Polish-American scientist Leo H. Sternbach, and soon became more popular than the Miltown and Equanil of the 1950's.

VALIUM

Diazepam, developed by Leo H. Sternbach of Roche, the father of Librium, was marketed as Valium by Roche Labs in 1963. Valium soon became the most widely prescribed tranquilizer in the world (making Roche one of the richest drug companies). Today, in the United States alone, intake of Valium numbers in the billions of tablets per year.

IT'S ALL DOWNHILL FROM HERE:
A Quiz About When Things Went from Better to Worse

---

1. In _____ for the first time Americans consumed more margarine than butter.
    1898
    1918
    1929
    1957
    1965

2. In _____ for the first time heart disease killed more Americans than tuberculosis, the previous leading cause of death in the nation.
    1865
    1890
    1914
    1921
    1933

3. In _____ for the first time Americans drank more vodka than whiskey.
    1913
    1933
    1946
    1961
    1973

4. In _____ Baltimore, Maryland, became the first city in which more hours were spent watching television than listening to radio.
>   1948
>   1950
>   1953
>   1957

5. In _____ for the first time the United States Government derived more revenue from income taxes than from customs duties.
>   1913
>   1917
>   1929
>   1933
>   1941

6. In _____ for the first and only time the United States Government was free from debt.
>   1789
>   1835
>   1860
>   1917
>   1929

7. In _____ for the first time the urban population of the United States exceeded the rural population—54 million to 51.5 million.
>   1898
>   1920
>   1935
>   1950
>   1970

ANSWERS: (1) 1957; (2) 1921; (3) 1973; (4) 1950; (5) 1917; (6) 1835; (7) 1920.

44

INVENTIVE, EXPLOSIVE, AND DEADLY FIRSTS

United Air Lines on May 15, 1930. The flight attendants, in their now classic profession, were trained nurses who had a great deal more authority than today's employees.

Coffee, tea, or first aid: The world's first airline stewardesses began service for United Air Lines on May 15, 1930. The flight attendants (as they are now called) were required to be registered nurses. Note that most—but not all— wore sensible shoes.

BETTER MOUSETRAPS:
Revolutionary Inventions and Discoveries

THE TELESCOPE

Man's concept of the universe was revolutionized in 1609 when Galileo Galilei (1564–1642), Italian astronomer, built the first refracting telescope, after having heard a description of a "magnifying tube" invented by a Dutch spectacle maker, Hans Lippershey, in 1608. The first reflecting telescope, which focuses the image on a mirror, rather than passing it through lenses directly to the viewer, was built in 1672 by Sir Isaac Newton (1642–1727).

THE MICROSCOPE

The man generally credited with inventing the microscope is Zacharias Janssen, a Dutch spectacle maker who discovered compound, or multiple lens magnification, ca. 1590.

Italian astronomer Galileo Galilei also claimed to have invented the microscope in 1610. *His* microscope was developed as an outgrowth of his telescope experiments (both instruments use compound lenses), and it's not known if the Italian knew of Janssen's invention. However, there may have been an indirect connection with Janssen's and Galileo's microscopes by way of the "magnifying tube" built in 1608 by Dutchman Hans Lippershey. Galileo did know of the Lippershey tube, and Lippershey and Janssen, being countrymen, contemporaries, and spectacle makers, may well have been aware of each other's work.

THE LOOM

The simplest loom is not much more than a frame used to hold threads while being woven together, and it's been in use since about 4400 B.C. The automatic fly shuttle, which greatly speeded up the weaving process, was invented in 1733 by John Kay of England, and in 1785 Edmund Cartwright patented the first practical power loom. The first Jacquard loom was perfected in 1804; the Jacquard process, which makes use of punched paper patterns which are "read" by the loom to automatically weave complicated designs, had far-reaching implications for the eventual development of the computer punch card.

THE COTTON GIN

Eli Whitney (1765–1825), a twenty-seven-year-old Yale graduate, invented the cotton gin in 1792 while visiting Mulberry Grove Plantation on the Savannah River, Georgia. Whitney had noticed the difficulty with which seeds were separated from short-staple cotton bolls, and built a simple turning cylinder device with saw teeth made from bird cage wire which caught the seeds as the cotton fibers were pulled through by the rotating teeth. The Whitney device enabled one slave laborer to clean as much as fifty pounds of cotton a day, as opposed to the one pound which had been average with manual cleaning. In the decade after Whitney's gin was invented the agricultural economy of the United States had radically changed, with the 140,000 pounds of cotton produced in 1792 increasing to a staggering 35 *million* pounds by 1800.

THE STEAM ENGINE

The first crude steam engine was invented in 1698 by Thomas Savery, an English engineer. Called the "miner's friend," it was used to pump water from coal mines. In 1705 Thomas Newcomen, an English blacksmith, built the first steam engine with a piston driven by condensed steam. James Watt of Scotland, usually credited with the "invention" of the steam engine, built his famous machine in 1765. Watt's steam engine greatly improved the efficiency of the Newcoo men model by adding a condenser chamber.

THE SEWING MACHINE

The first sewing machine was built in 1829 by Barthelemy Thimmonier, a tailor in the town of Amplepuis in the Rhone district of France. Though built for his own use, Thimmonier received an order for eighty of his machines from a Paris uniform factory two years later, and the inventor himself was hired by the company. Unfortunately, the other employees felt their livelihood was threatened by the mechanization of hand sewing, and an "anti-sewing-machine mob" destroyed all but one of the machines, which was saved by Thimmonier. In 1845 the ill-starred Thimmonier got backing from a businessman, went into production, and once again had his sewing machines destroyed by an angry mob. The French sewing-machine business somehow never seemed to get off the ground.

The first sewing machine built for home use was the famous Singer model, invented by Isaac Singer in 1850 and patented and manufactured in 1851 at a Boston factory. Later Singer had to pay royalties to Elias Howe of Spencer, Massachusetts, who had patented his own machine in 1846, which was used by tailors in the United States and Britain. But the Singer model went on to become the first common labor-saving machine in the average American household.

THE ELEVATOR

Pulley-and-weight mechanisms have been in use for a long time for lifting freight and sometimes people (Louis XV had a "lift" to carry him upstairs from his suite at Versailles to that of his mistress, in 1743). But the revolution in the urban landscape wrought by the elevator began in 1852 in Yonkers, New York, where Elisha Graves Otis, then aged forty-one, invented the safety elevator, which had teeth and ratchets to prevent the platform from falling should the rope break. Otis himself dramatically demonstrated this in 1853 at the Crystal Palace exhibition when, before a dubious crowd, he had himself hoisted above the floor, then deliberately cut the ropes. The audience gasped and screamed, but Otis's gears held, and the proud inventor stepped safely to the ground, taking a bow.

The Otis elevator was soon in production. The first to be installed in a hotel went to the Fifth Avenue Hotel, New York, in 1859; the first in a commercial business went into the famous cast iron Hagwout Department Store at Broadway and Broome Street (still standing) in 1857. The Hagwout elevator was the first to have a completely enclosed passenger car.

BESSEMER STEEL CONVERTER

In 1856 Henry Bessemer, a British engineer, patented his converter, which made the production of high quality, low-cost steel possible by decarbonizing pig iron with a blast of cold air. The Bessemer process would make steel widely available for construction; cheap steel, when combined with the Otis elevator, would father the modern skyscraper.

THE PHOTO CAMERA

In the eighteenth century scientists discovered that silver salts darkened under light; in 1802 Thomas Wedgwood, the physician son of the famous potter, Josiah, took the world's first photograph when he spread moist silver nitrate on a piece of paper, then projected an image onto the sheet. The image "took," but Wedgwood had no way to fix the "image" and it soon faded. The first permanent photo was made in 1822, when J. N. Niepce and his seventeen-year-old cousin, Claude, discovered a method of producing fixed images on glass treated with bitumen.

Though cameras had been commercially available since 1839 when the french firm of Alphonse Giroux offered a large box camera for sale for four hundred francs, photography remained largely in the hands of professionals until 1895 when the first pocket camera developed by George Eastman was introduced by the Eastman Kodak Company of Rochester, New York. The even more successful Brownie camera was introduced in 1900, at a price of one dollar, putting photography in the grasp of amateurs for the first time.

The first color photograph was made in 1861 by Scotch physicist James Maxwell, who developed a technique of taking black-and-white photos through three color filters, then projecting them on a screen through the same filters (red, blue, and green) to give a color image. This early experiment in the three-color process didn't give a final color print—only a "slide projection." In 1868, however, Louis Ducos de Hauron of France made the first true color photographic print—of his home village ot Agen—by taking the three-color separation process of Maxwell and devising a method of transferring the three screens to one print in three dye steps.

Color photography remained complicated and difficult (though some of the early images that have survived are quite beautiful), and it wasn't until 1935 with the development of the Kodachrome process that color photography became readily available to the public.

THE OIL WELL

Man has been using petroleum for thousands of years for coating boat hulls, cementing bricks, occasionally as a flaming weapon, or, as by the American Indians, for body paint. But the oil age was born in 1859 when an unemployed forty-year-old railroad conductor named Edwin L. Drake successfully drilled the world's first oil well at what is now Titusville, Pennsylvania. The seventy-foot well hit oil-bearing shale using salt-well drilling equipment on August 28, and was soon producing two thousand barrels a day. The oil was used mainly in the production of kerosene for lamps. The first commercial oil refinery was opened in June, 1860, at Oil Creek valley in Pennsylvania, where only kerosene was extracted from the crude oil. (Kerosene was first extracted from oil in 1855 by Abraham Gesner of Newtown Creek, now part of Queens, New York, who named the liquid "Keros," after the Greek word for wax, and promoted it as a patented medicine!) At the Oil Creek valley refinery the by-products of the kerosene refining, including gasoline, had no use and were dumped into Oil Creek, creating the first environmental pollution by the oil industry.

THE ELECTRIC LIGHT

The first practical incandescent light bulb was demonstrated for the first time on December 20, 1879, by Thomas Alva Edison, who had constructed the bulb with a carbonized cotton filament after thirteen

51

months of experiments at his Menlo Park, New Jersey, laboratories; the cotton filament bulb was first built by Edison on October 21 of that year. A year earlier, however, British inventor and chemist Joseph Swan had demonstrated *his* carbon filament bulb to the Newcastle-on-Tyne Chemical Society (December 18, 1878). But the Swan bulb was not completely successful, and though he later perfected the bulb and went into production in 1881, the slightly "younger" but workable Edison bulb overtook the Swan design, and the modern electric industry developed from the Edison Company.

THE NUCLEAR REACTOR

The world's first controlled, self-sustaining nuclear reaction was achieved on December 2, 1942, at Stagg Field, University of Chicago, by a team headed by Enrico Fermi, Edward Teller, and Leo Szilard; their work led directly to the Manhattan Project in Los Alamos, New Mexico, which produced the first atomic bomb. After World War II, the application of atomic reactions to produce something other than destructive energy led to the first reactor, built in 1951 by the Atomic Energy Commission. Peaceful atomic energy remained largely experimental until 1956, when the first full-scale atomic-powered electric turbine went into operation at Calder Hall in England (August 20) and began supplying power to the British electric system on October 17 of the same year.

The first commercial nuclear reactor (that is, privately built and operated for energy production) was opened in 1963 by New Jersey Power and Light at Oyster Creek, New Jersey; the first serious nuclear reactor accident occured on March 28, 1979, when the Three Mile Island reactor in Pennsylvania suffered a series of systems breakdowns causing the contamination of the central core room, a shutdown of the plant, the release of radioactive gas into the atmosphere (intentionally, to lower radiation levels in the reactor room), and the evacuation of area residents.

RADAR

The first practical radar device was developed by Rudolph Kuhnold, Signals Research Chief of the German Navy, and demonstrated at

Kiel Harbor on March 20, 1934. Kuhnold bounced signals from his seven-hundred-watt transmitter from a battleship anchored six hundred yards away; this and subsequent tests were so successful that the German Government appropriated money to develop the device, which has had a dramatic impact on warfare, auto traffic, and even geologic research and other scientific applications.

THE COMPUTER

The first known mechanical computing device—or computer—is none other than the abacus, which was in use in China as early as (and probably earlier than) the sixth century B.C., and in Greece and Rome of ancient days. This most basic computer is still in use in parts of the Orient.

The first complex, modern computer was conceived, designed, and partially built by Charles Babbage (1792–1871), a British mathematician, who began building his computer in 1822. The Babbage machine (which was never completed because the sheer complexity of its moving parts was beyond the technology of the day) utilized many features and principles of the modern computer, including the punch card, borrowed from the famous Jacquard loom punch cards of 1804. Babbage's first concept, the "analytical engine," was put forth in 1822; the second and more complex, the "difference engine," was designed in 1833 and, had it been finished with sufficient technical accuracy, would have worked as well as early digital computers of the twentieth century.

The first electronic computer (actually a tabulating machine) was built by Dr. Herman Hollerith for the U. S. Census Bureau in 1889 for the 1890 census. The Hollerith machine made use of punch cards with eighty columns, which became part of the IBM system, and the card today bears Hollerith's name.

The first digital computer was the Mark I, completed in 1944 by Professor Howard Aiken of Harvard. The Mark I used both electronic and mechanical parts for operation. The first electronic computer was the Electronic Numerical Integrator and Computer (ENIAC), completed in 1946 at the University of Pennsylvania. ENIAC, which contained some eighteen thousand vacuum tubes and diodes, weighed thirty tons, and was used by the U. S. Army to solve artillery problems.

The modern computer industry began in 1951 with the introduction of UNIVAC, the first mass-produced computer available to private enterprise.

THE LASER

The first laser was built in 1960 by Theodore Maiman of the Hughes Research Laboratory, Malibu, California, based on work patented by physicists Charles Townes and Arthur Schwarlow. The term *laser* (light amplification by stimulated emission of radiation) was first coined by R. Gordon Gould of Columbia University in 1957, but Gould's leftist political activities in the 1940's caused his work on lasers to be hampered by the Defense Department and research agencies.

The first laser used a ruby rod surrounded by a flash tube to agitate chromium atoms in the ruby's lattice crystal to an excited state, producing pulses of red light with coherent waves.

The laser, thought of by the public as a twenty-first-century tool, has found numerous applications in holography, surgery, physics, and even astronomy.

CONCEPTUAL FIRSTS:
Five Ideas That Revolutionized Thinking

THE HELIOCENTRIC SYSTEM

Aristarchus of Alexandria, in the middle of the third century B.C., theorized that the Earth moved around the Sun, but his idea was ignored until revived by Copernicus in 1530. Though Copernicus (1473–1543) made errors, like assuming that planets have circular orbits, his destruction of the concept that the Earth is the center of the universe had a profound effect on later scientists like Newton and Kepler, and deflated traditional theological theories about man's place in things.

EVOLUTION

In 1859 Charles Darwin published *Origin of Species,* the mammoth culmination of years of travel and research, which led to his formulation of his theory of organic evolution. His ideas, such as the slow development of new and varied species through an interaction of chance and environmental adaptation, was heresy to theologians, but radically changed man's understanding of how he came to be. Ironically, Alfred R. Wallace of England developed an almost identical theory of evolution independently, at the same time as Darwin, and they jointly published their preliminary papers in 1858.

PSYCHOLOGY

Heraclitus, the Greek philosopher, was the first to say that dreams are not supernatural encounters but journeys into a personal world, in the fifth century B.C. But this concept was not to come to fruition until Sigmund Freud developed his theories of dreams, the subconscious, and sexuality beginning with his papers *On the Psychical Mechanism of Hysterical Phenomena* and *Studies in Hysteria* (written with early colleague Joseph Breuer) in 1893 and 1895. By 1900 Freud had written his *Interpretation of Dreams,* and within a few years men, women, and children were talking in terms of their egos, repression, Oedipal conflicts, and the subconscious.

THE DIVISIBILITY OF THE ATOM

From the time of Democritus in 330 B.C., the atom had been considered the smallest particle of matter (the word is Greek for indivisible or indestructible) until 1897 when Joseph John Thompson, a British physicist, put forth a model of the atom with nucleus orbited by electrons. The discovery that the atom was itself made up of smaller, moving particles revolutionized scientific thinking about the nature of matter—it suddenly had positive, negative, and neutral charges—and physicists are still discovering more and more obscure and curious subatomic particles every decade.

RELATIVITY

Albert Einstein revolutionized physics in 1905 with the introduction of his special theory of relativity, which made time the fourth dimension. One of the many aspects of the theory is that mass and energy are equivalent, a basic concept leading to the development of nuclear fission and the atomic bomb. The bomb demonstrated most impressively the divisibility of the atom (see above). However, it may someday render the concepts of psychology, evolution, and the heliocentric system irrelevant, since there may be no one left to psychoanalyze, nothing to evolve, and nothing left to revolve around the sun but radioactive dust.

It's all relative: The man who first made us aware of the fourth dimension reminds us that everything depends upon how you look at it.

THE BETTMANN ARCHIVE, INC.

SPEAK UP:
Communications Milestones

DOT-DOT-DASH-DOT

On May 24, 1844, Samuel F. B. Morse, a successful painter-turned-inventor, transmitted the famous first message, "What hath God wrought" from the U. S. Capitol in Washington to his assistant, Alfred Vail, at the Mount Clare station of the B. & O. Railroad in Baltimore, the first long-distance telegraph message.

Morse had begun developing his apparatus in 1832, while a professor of art at New York University, and had given the first public demonstration in 1837, the year he took out a patent on the telegraph. The same year Vail devised the Morse code to replace the cumbersome numbered system he and Morse had used up to that time.

Prior to Morse, British inventor Francis Ronald had devised an electric telegraph in 1822, which failed to get off the ground due to lack of Government interest. And two other British inventors, Charles Wheatstone and William Fothergill Cooke, patented *their* telegraph in 1837, the same year Morse gave his first demonstration. In 1831 Joseph Henry demonstrated an electromagnetic telegraph in Albany, New York, but failed to patent or promote the device, thus losing out to Morse—who made a fortune from his telegraph. Wheatstone and Cooke were more fortunate—the British telegraph system grew out of their patented invention, which they sold for a whopping £168,000 in 1846.

UNDER THE OCEAN AND THROUGH THE WOODS

Cable service from New York to Chicago began in 1848. The English Channel cable was completed in 1850; the transamerican cable from New York to San Francisco was completed (despite Indians' objections) in 1861, putting the Pony Express out of business; and a major communications first came in 1866 when Cyrus W. Field completed the first transatlantic cable, allowing instantaneous communication between two continents for the first time.

ELEMENTARY, MY DEAR WATSON

On March 10, 1876, Alexander Graham Bell spoke the first sentence to be transmitted over wire at 5 Exeter Place, Boston, when he said, "Mr. Watson, come here, I want you." The first practical telephone was an improved version of the machine built in 1875, when Bell discovered by accident that a telegraph transmitter using harmonic frequencies in matching receivers could transmit matching sounds (June 2, 1875). Bell was only twenty-nine at the time he called Thomas Watson, who was twenty-two.

THE NEXT BEST THING TO BEING THERE

The first long-distance phone call was placed in October, 1876, when Boston lawyer Gardiner Hubbard, future father-in-law of Bell and an early promoter of the phone, took two of young Bell's telephones, hooked them up to a telegraph wire running from Boston to the Cambridge Observatory across the Charles River, and spoke to Thomas Watson for over three hours.

HELLO, CENTRAL

The first telephone was sold by Bell in May, 1877, to the Cambridge Board of Waterworks. By August there were eight hundred in service. The first switchboard was installed in the offices of the Holmes Burglar Alarm Company of Boston, at 342 Washington Street, who used their existing burglar alarm lines from a client's premises as phone lines during the day and burglar alarms at night. Bell loaned twelve of his phones to Holmes, and Holmes in turn didn't charge clients for the phone service.

The first commercial phone exchange was opened in New Haven, Connecticut, by the District Telephone Company on January 28, 1878, with twenty-one customers subscribing to the service. The first telephone operator was George W. Coy, who answered calls with shouts of "Ahoy!"

SORRY, WRONG NUMBER

The first telephone in a private home was installed on April 4, 1877, in Somerville, Massachusetts, in the home of Charles Williams, Jr., at the corner of Arlington and William streets. Mr. Williams was also the first to manufacture Bell phones commercially. Since the first phone exchange had yet to be installed, Williams had to have a line run to his office in Boston so there would be someplace to call.

THAT WILL BE FIVE CENTS, PLEASE, FOR THE NEXT . . .

William Gray, an inventor from Hartford, Connecticut, installed the first coin pay phone in the Hartford Bank in 1889 and began widespread installation in 1891. The cost of a call was a nickel, making a pay call one of the most stationary prices of modern times.

DIAL "U" FOR UNDERTAKER

The first automatic telephone, the precursor of today's dials and touchtones, utilized three keys which were depressed to register the number through a mechanical, operatorless central switchboard. It was patented in March, 1889, and went into service at La Porte, Indiana, on November 3, 1892. The inventor was Almon Strowger, an undertaker in Kansas City, who was moved to create the device because he was convinced that one of Kansas City's operators, who happened to be the wife of one of his chief rivals in the funeral business, was diverting calls for undertakers to her husband's establishment.

THEY TOLD MARCONI WIRELESS WAS A PHONY

Wireless telegraphy was developed between 1894 and September, 1895, by Guglielmo Marconi at his family's country house, the Villa Grifone, at Pontecchio near Bologna. Marconi, whose mother was British, took his device to Britain, where he demonstrated how electronic signals could be transmitted through the air, over hills, and around obstacles—privately in September, 1896, on Salisbury Plain and publicly on December 12 at Toynbee Hall in London.

Ironically, the wireless, which has made Marconi famous, was apparently demonstrated first by an American, Mahlon Loomis of Washington, in 1866. Unfortunately, Loomis was a bit ahead of his time, and that, in combination with financial setbacks, prevented his wireless from getting off the ground.

Marconi was more fortunate, and formed the Wireless Telegraph Company Limited in July, 1897, for the manufacture and sale of his equipment. Though wireless telegraphy would find many applications (the *Titanic* used wireless to signal that she was going down in 1912), Marconi's invention would be even more important than the beginning of radio.

LOOK, MA, NO WIRES!

The first transatlantic wireless message was sent from Poldhu, Cornwall, on December 12, 1901, and received in Newfoundland by Marconi, using a wired kite as a receiving antenna. The message received consisted of the letter *S*.

YOU SOUND LIKE YOU'RE JUST NEXT DOOR

Transcontinental phone service began January 25, 1915, when Alexander Graham Bell in New York called Thomas Watson in San Francisco and repeated their famous message of 1876. The call took twenty-three minutes to get through, and cost $20.70. (Presumably Mr. Bell put it on his expense account at Bell Telephone, but that's what a paying customer would have forked out.)

LET YOUR FINGERS DO THE WALKING

The first true dial phones were introduced November 8, 1919, in Norfolk, Virginia. Dial mechanisms had been available earlier, but A.T. & T. hadn't been interested until a potential operators' strike threatened to stop phone service.

PLEASE DEPOSIT SEVENTY-FIVE DOLLARS FOR THE FIRST THREE MINUTES

Intercontinental long-distance service began January 7, 1927, between New York and London.

AFGHANISTAN? I WAS TRYING TO DIAL ARKANSAS

The first direct-dial long-distance service began on October 10, 1951.

LONG, LONG DISTANCE

A.T. & T. launched Telstar, the first private communications satellite, on July 10, 1962, to relay television programs globally. On April 6, 1965, the Communications Satellite Corporation (Comsat) launched Early Bird, the first of a projected network of commercial satellites designed to provide almost unlimited global telephone and telegraph communications.

DEADLY FIRSTS:
Weapons from Hands to H-Bombs, and Beyond

PUT 'EM UP

Human hands, the first weapons and still the most common, were used for defense and attack long before man learned to use his hands to make even deadlier weapons. And, if behavior among the other primates in the wild and among humans in barroom brawls is any indication, teeth, feet, and elbows would have been used in a prehistoric free-for-all as well.

STICKS AND STONES

During the period from 3,000,000 to 1,000,000 B.C., the major predecessor of the species *Homo* evolved. Aside from walking upright and perhaps using some form of simple language, *Australopithecus* began using tools—albeit very simple ones—on a regular basis. The first and simplest was a rock, used to break open something—like a hard nut, or an irritating neighbor's head. Later, *Australopithecus* also learned, probably from picking up a naturally broken rock, how to chip one rock with another to make a sharp edge. *Voilà,* a cutting edge for scraping hides—or slicing open that of a stranger who wanted to hang out in one's territory.

THE RAZOR'S EDGE

Ingenuity has been around a lot longer than Yankees, so it's hardly surprising that as soon as bronze was discovered by the early Sumerians, about 3600 B.C., they started making spear and arrow points from the new edge-holding metal, even though the stone-pointed weapons that had been around for centuries had been efficient enough to kill foes as formidable as furry mastodons and fellow Mesopotamians.

THE BOW AND ARROW

Archery for hunting and fighting developed even before metallurgy, and dates from the Paleolithic era in Asia, Africa, and Europe, and was probably developed from slings used to throw spears. The first arrow points were made from burned, hardened wood. Stone (especially flint) and metal points were used later. The bow and arrow deserve a special place in weaponry since they have been used for so many centuries in warfare. Even after the introduction of guns to Europe, longbows and crossbows were widely used, since early guns were so inaccurate and took so long to reload.

BLOWUP

The explosive mixture of saltpeter, sulfur, and charcoal we call gunpowder was known in China in the ninth century A.D., where it was used for fireworks. Its first use in Europe is more obscure. English philosopher and scientist Roger Bacon made the first known European mention of gunpowder in a letter he wrote in Oxford in 1249. Bacon, who wrote down a formula for gunpowder in 1256, probably learned the recipe from Eastern Europeans who had fled the Mongol invasions of Russia in 1237. It's known that the Chinese used bombs to resist the Mongols in 1235, and that the Mongols in turn used gunpowder to conquer Russia, Hungary, and Poland during 1237 to 1241.

By 1325 gunpowder was being used to power newfangled weapons called cannons.

BANG! BANG! YOU'RE DEAD

Early artillery proved so useful that weapon craftsmen were soon making portable models that could be carried and used by one man. Early handguns, which first came into use at the end of the fourteenth century, were little more than portable cannons—muzzle loaded and lighted with a match held to a touchhole (the matchlock gets its name from this). These muskets and matchlocks, though they did the job, were notoriously inaccurate and slow to reload. A big improvement came with the rifle, invented in the early eighteenth century by German gunsmith August Kotter, who introduced a rifled bore in the barrel of the gun, causing the bullet to spin rapidly on firing. This lead to greater accuracy and distance. The rifle was first extensively used by German colonists in the 1730's.

BREECH-LOADING GUNS

The long-standing problem of reloading time in muzzle-loading guns was finally solved in 1841 by Prussian gunsmith Johann Dreyse, who made the "needle-gun" the first successful breech-loading rifle. The success of breech-loaders would change the course of combat, and would be especially important in the American West, where Indians had consistently been able to shoot arrows faster and more accurately (even from horseback) than whites with muzzle-loading rifles.

THE COLT REVOLVER

Samuel Colt patented his breech-loading revolver in 1836, and went into business the following year in Paterson, New Jersey. The business failed, but a Government order for the revolvers for Army use in the 1847 Mexican War put Colt back in business and inaugurated the era of rapid-fire, repeating guns.

THE GATLING GUN

The grandfather of all machine guns, the Gatling gun was invented by Richard J. Gatling (1818–1903) of St. Louis, an inventor and manufacturer of agricultural equipment. Gatling's gun, the first rapid-fire repeating weapon with large bullet capacity, might have been used in the Civil War: He offered it to the Union side in 1862, but the Ordnance Department didn't get around to buying the machine until 1866. Once adopted by the Army, the Gatling was in use until gradually replaced by more modern and efficient designs in the twentieth century.

CHEMICAL WARFARE

With the invention and development of accurate artillery well underway, there weren't any major innovations in weapons until World War I, when Germany took advantage of the great strides made in chemistry during the nineteenth century to became the first nation to use chemicals as a weapon. (Though as early as the fifth century B.C. the ancients were using catapults to throw burning pitch or other flammables into enemy cities or battalions, these were used mainly to start fires.) On April 22, 1915, the Germans released chlorine gas against the Allied forces at the second battle of Ypres. They used the famous mustard gas later in the war, July, 1917, again at Ypres, Belgium. The mustard gas took a high toll, both in deaths from pulmonary edema due to inhalation, and in blindness. The gas was dispersed by firing a gas-filled aerosol shell into enemy positions.

ROCKET WARFARE

World War I was a technologically innovative war, in that it saw the first widespread use of aerial bombing and dogfights, and the use of land and sea mines, all of which had been used in one form or another in earlier wars. World War II brought a new age of weaponry into battle—the unmanned missile.

The V-1, the first aerial rocket, was a long-distance, propeller-driven missile developed by Germany, which could easily be fired from positions on the French coast toward southern England.

Even more deadly was the first long-range, jet-propelled rocket, the notorious V-2, also developed in Nazi Germany during World War II. The first V-2s were built at a plant in Peenemünde, Germany, in 1942, and stood 46 feet high, weighing 27,000 pounds. The rocket was powered by liquid oxygen and alcohol, carried a 2,200-pound payload, and had a flight range of about 210 miles. When the first V-2 hit England on September 8, 1944, it became the first liquid-fueled rocket used in warfare. All together, about 3000 V-2s were manufactured, and 1500 hit England between 1944 and March 27, 1945, when the last one fell on Orpington, Kent. An estimated 2500 people were killed by the rocket payloads.

The V-2 was developed under Wernher Von Braun, and the program cost Germany an estimated two hundred million dollars. After the war, American troops captured the V-2 plant at Nrohaousen, and sent 100 of the rockets to the United States, along with Dr. Von Braun. The first of the captured V-2s was fired at White Sands Missile Range, New Mexico, in January, 1946, and reached a record height of 244 miles. Others were subsequently used for high-altitude research. The captured V-2s, and the German scientists who began working for the United States after the war, became the backbone of the American rocket development program.

NAPALM

Though, as we mentioned, flammable substances have been in use in warfare for centuries, the twentieth century truly ushered in the era of better killing through chemistry. Napalm, for example, was developed during World War II by Harvard scientists working with the U.S. Army. Napalm is basically a mixture of gasoline (or gasoline and other petroleum agents) combined with a thickening agent. This thickening agent gives napalm the advantage of flowing under pressure (but not scattering or evaporating like gasoline), and it sticks to the target, somewhat like flaming molasses. Though it was used first in World War II, napalm really came into its own during the Vietnam "conflict" when it often wound up sticking to civilian targets instead of military ones.

THE ATOMIC BOMB

The first atom bomb, developed in intense secrecy by the Manhattan Project at Los Alamos, New Mexico, was exploded in the early morning of July 16, 1945, at White Sands Proving Ground, near Alamogordo, New Mexico. The bomb remained a secret until August 6 of that year, when the B-29 bomber *Enola Gay* dropped the first A-bomb used in warfare on Hiroshima. The bomb, dropped

Small but powerful: The first atom bomb being lifted to its testing tower at Alamogordo, New Mexico, July, 1945. When the bomb went off, the heat at this spot reached 100 million degrees—ten times hotter than the surface of the sun. WIDE WORLD PHOTOS

from 32,000 feet, exploded 660 feet above the center of the city, completely devastating four square miles, killing 100,000 people instantaneously and injuring another 100,000 seriously enough so that they died within days or weeks of burns or radiation sickness.

WARFARE OF THE FUTURE

Weapons whose first use has yet to come:

The first hydrogen bomb was exploded at Eniwetok Island in the Pacific Ocean by the United States on November 1, 1952.

The neutron bomb is a nuclear fusion device (like the H-bomb) that produces minimal heat and shock waves along with a hail of invisible, deadly neutrons. Net result: Buildings will remain standing, but all life will be destroyed or seriously hurt.

In November, 1969, President Richard Nixon banned the production of a number of substances that were being studied as possible "germ-warfare" agents, among them anthrax, Rocky Mountain spotted fever, and botulism. Though firing a canister of bubonic plague bacteria into an enemy position might effectively wipe out the enemy, the near-impossibility of containing the intentional plague bodes ill for bacteriological and viral warfare. Yet, in 1979 and 1980, Russia came under attack from the United States for allegedly training troops in germ-warfare techniques.

HIT THE ROADS, TURNPIKES, AND HIGHWAYS

THE FIRST ROADS

Man built the first roads in southwestern Asia in the areas bounded by the Caspian Sea, the Black Sea, the Persian Gulf, and the Mediterranean—roughly, the area where agricultural civilization developed. These earliest roads were nothing more than the smoothing out and leveling of paths that had been worn naturally from walking to and from trade or supply centers. The first wheeled vehicles were built in this area, ca. 3000–3500 B.C.

PAVE THE WAY

The cities of Assur, Babylon, and Tell as-Asmar all had paved streets of burnt brick and stone set in mortar, dating from the early Sumerian civilization, ca. 3000 B.C.

THE FIRST LONG-DISTANCE ROAD

The Persian Royal Road, which was in use from 3500 to 300 B.C., ran from Shushan, on the Persian Gulf, to Smyrna (in modern Turkey), on the Aegean Sea, a distance of 1775 miles. According to Greek historian Herodotus, writing in the fifth century B.C., the journey took ninety-three days.

ALL ROADS LEAD TO ROME

The first great road builders were the Romans, and they were the first civilization to build an extensive road system along scientifically engineered lines, including cutting through hillsides and laying solid foundations with good drainage. Of the twenty-nine military roads leading from Rome, the first and most famous was the *Via Appia,* the world's first long, paved roadway. It was begun in 312 B.C., and ran 410 miles from Rome to Hydruntum on the Adriatic coast. The 35-foot-wide road was built with two center lanes paved with a flint gravel set over a stone and gravel foundation, and separated from two outer one-way lanes by stone curbs.

THESE ROADWAYS ARE FOR WALKING

From ca. A.D. 1200 to 1532, when the Spaniards arrived in South America, the Incas of Peru and Ecuador built a remarkable network of highways in excess of 4000 miles long—the first great American road system. The 1650-mile Andes road, for example, was 25 feet wide and had many cuts through steep mountainsides, sections carved into sheer cliff faces, retaining walls hundreds of feet high, and wool or rope suspension bridges up to 200 feet long. Even more remarkable, the system was constructed only for walking or running from town to town—the Incas had no wheeled vehicles. Parts of the roadway are still in use today.

"MODERN" ROADS

When commerce and travel boomed in the eighteenth century, Europe found itself with a woefully inadequate highway system (there was nothing systematic about it) that had hardly changed since the Middle Ages. In 1716 France became the first nation to have a "highway department" with the founding of the Departement des Ponts et Chausees—the Department of Bridges and Roads—to oversee road transport. In 1747 the department opened an engineering school which began developing the kind of modern highway engineering in use today, which stresses a paved surface over a load-bearing subsurface, unlike the rigid-surface roads built by the Romans. The most influential of the new school of engineers were

71

Frenchman Pierre Trésaguet and John McAdam (who gave his name to paved roads).

WHAT'S IN A NAME?

In 1657 a street in the colonial town of New York was paved with stones, making New York the first city in North America after the European settlement to have paving. It was cleverly named Stone Street.

PAY AS YOU GO

In October, 1785, the General Assembly of Virginia appointed nine commissioners to erect tollgates on the Little River turnpike between Alexandria and Snicker's Gap, Virginia, the first "pay" road in America. The tolls were to be used to "keep in repair said roads."

PRIVATE ENTERPRISE

In 1795 the Lancaster (Pennsylvania) turnpike was finished—the first extensive paved road in the United States (sixty-two miles worth). It was surfaced with gravel and hand-broken stone, and was built with $465,000 in private funds.

UNCLE SAM STEPS IN

The first—and for more than a century the only—Federally financed highway project was the National Road (or Great National Pike, or Cumberland Road), which was authorized and surveyed in 1806. Construction began in 1811, in Cumberland, Maryland, and the first section, to Wheeling, West Virginia, opened in 1818. By 1838, the road had been extended to Springfield, Ohio, and reached Vandalia, Illinois, in 1840. Total cost was about $6,825,000. The road, paved with broken stones compacted into a hard surface, was maintained by Federal funds and tolls collected by the states.

GO WEST, YOUNG MAN

The Oregon Trail was the first transcontinental route consistently used by settlers moving west, and grew up out of Indian and buffalo trails centuries old. But by 1842 there was enough traffic to warrant a Government survey, taken by John Charles Frémont (1813–90), who mapped out the route to be taken by thousands of covered wagons from Independence, Missouri, to Oregon.

SMOOTH GOING

The first asphalt paving was laid in Newark, New Jersey, in 1870, and the first concrete pavement in Bellefontaine, Ohio, in 1894.

COAST TO COAST

On September 13, 1913, the famous Lincoln Highway, the first paved transamerican highway, was completed from New York to San Francisco.

THE FIRST PARKWAY

The first parkway, that is, a four-lane, divided highway designed mainly for car traffic, with landscaped right-of-way and limited access, was the Bronx River Parkway in New York, completed in 1923.

ROME UPDATED

The German autobahn system—the first national network of integrated highways designed for modern, fast vehicles with multiple lanes and medians, was conceived in 1926 and begun with the Cologne-Bonn roadway in 1926 (opened in 1932). When Hitler came to power he rushed the system to completion, and about 2500 miles of modern roads—clearly designed to handle military traffic in large volume in speeds in excess of 100 mph—was completed in only two years.

THE FIRST AMERICAN SUPERHIGHWAY

The model for today's freeways was the Pennsylvania Turnpike, begun in 1937 and finished in 1940. Built on the wide, almost flat bed of an abandoned railroad track, the four-lane divided highway featured overpasses and underpasses for cross traffic, and access limited to interchanges.

TIERRA DEL FUEGO, HERE I COME

In 1923 the Conference of American States proposed a highway—the Pan American—to run the length of North and South America, from Alaska to Chile, a distance of 16,000 miles. Except for a section between the Panama Canal and northern Colombia, the highway today is complete, though some sections are impassable except in good weather. The route goes through tropical jungles, 15,000-foot mountain passes, and large desert regions.

ROLLING IN CLOVERLEAFS

On June 29, 1953, Congress passed the Federal Aid Highway Act, authorizing the construction of a 42,500-mile interstate freeway system—the first American interstate system. The project was budgeted at 33.5 billion dollars, 90 percent to be paid for by Uncle Sam. The target completion date of 1972 was missed, though 38,000 miles were finished by 1978, at a cost considerably over the budget. The interstate system was the biggest transportation subsidy since the building of the railroads in the nineteenth century, and ironically contributed much to the decline in the passenger rail business.

OVERDRIVE:
The Automobile from
Pressure Cooker to Edsel

1690 · Denis Papin (1647–1712), French physicist and inventor of the pressure cooker ("steam digester"), proposed a road vehicle driven by piston engine.

1769 · Nicholas Joseph Cugnot (1725–1804) took the first ride in a self-propelled, steam-driven vehicle of his own invention. The vehicle, which attained a speed of about 2½ mph, also resulted in the first auto accident. Cugnot knocked down a wall in Paris, where the experiment took place.

1801 · Englishman Richard Trevithick (1771–1833) invented and built the first successful steam vehicle, which he test ran—at a speed somewhere between 4 and 9 mph—in Cambourne, Cornwall. When the first model went up in flames, a veritable auto-da-fé, Trevithick rebuilt his vehicle, which in 1803 made the first cross-city trip, from Leather Lane to Paddington, London, by way of Oxford Street.

1805 · Isaac de Rivaz built the first vehicle powered by an internal-combustion engine, which, unfortunately, only made it a few yards. Since this was the first internal-combustion auto, it was also the first to pollute the air with carbon monoxide.

1829 · Goldsworth Guerney made the first long-distance auto journey, from London to Bath, in his eighteen-seater, six-wheeled steam

75

coach. The size of Guerney's vehicle should also qualify him as the first bus driver, and the trip as the first bus tour. The distance traveled was about eighty miles.

1831 · The world's first scheduled "bus" service operated for a few months between Gloucester and Cheltenham, England, using three Guerney steam carriages.

1860 · Belgian-born inventor Jean Joseph Étienne Lenoir (1822–1910) built the world's first successful internal-combustion-engine vehicle—a "gas carriage"—using an engine he first constructed the previous year. By 1863 a second Lenoir vehicle traveled from Paris to Vincennes, a distance of six miles, in three hours—giving an average speed of one-half mile per hour.

1864 · The first auto export in history: Lenoir sold one of his internal-combustion-powered carriages to Czar Alexander II of Russia.

1865 · Karl Benz of Germany (1844–1929) designed and built a three-wheeled gas-driven vehicle, the first to be designed and built as a motor vehicle, rather than converted from a carriage. The Benz had its first test runs in 1886.

1888 · John Dunlop (1840–1921) "invented" the pneumatic tire (or, rather, tyre), marking the beginning of the modern tire industry. Curiously, another Scotsman, R. W. Thomson, took out a patent on pneumatic tyres in 1845. But Dunlop got all the credit.

1891 · French inventor Ferdinand Forest built the first four-cylinder gas engine with mechanical valve operation; a few years later he built the first six-cylinder engine. Ironically, Forest's inventions—which became the standard for millions of automobiles—were first used in boats, and he failed to be recognized for his contribution when they were later used in automobiles.

1893 · Brothers Charles Edgar and James Frank Duryea (1861–1938, 1869–1967) built the first "motor buggy" in Springfield, Massachusetts. Other motor vehicles had been built in the United States before the Duryeas', but theirs is recognized as the first practicable automobile built in the United States.

1894 · Henry G. Morris and Pedro Salom open the first automobile factory in the United States in Philadelphia. The product: the Electrobat.

1896 · Henry Ford (1863–1947), Ransom Eli Olds (1864–1950), C. B. King, and Alexander Winton—all major pioneers in the American auto industry—built and tested their first models. In France, Léon Bollée offered his *voiturette* (little car), the first with pneumatic tires a standard feature.

1899 · Ransom Eli Olds began production of the first Oldsmobiles.

1901 · Cannstatt-Daimler of Germany introduced the first Mercedes, named after the teen-aged daughter of Emil Jellinek, one of Daimler's first customers.

1902 · Dr. Lehwess Panhard made the first attempt to drive around the world, but his auto caravan *Passe Partout* didn't get past Ninji, Novgorod, Russia.

1903 · Henry Ford founded the Ford Motor Company in Detroit, Michigan. The same year, H. M. Leland founded the Cadillac Motor Car Company in the same city.

1906 · Sir (Frederick) Henry Royce (1863–1933) of England, who built his first Royce car in 1904, organized an auto manufacturing business with C. S. Rolls, and the first Rolls-Royce was born.

1908 · William C. Durant (1861–1947) founded General Motors Company, and Henry Ford produced the first Model T Ford, perhaps the most famous single model car ever built. The first year, eight thousand Model T's were built.

1909 · In France, De Dion Bouton produced the first important production-line auto with a V-8 engine.

1911 · Ford opened its first overseas factory at Trafford Park, Manchester, England. The same year Cadillac was the first manufacturer to feature electric lights and starters on their models.

GENTLEMEM OUR COUNTRY

HENRY FORD AND HIS FIRST CAR.

For Ford and country: Sitting at the helm of his first car, complete with Stars and Stripes superimposed, this early public relations photograph of Henry Ford in retrospect makes a point about the impact of Detroit on the American Way of Life. THE BETTMANN ARCHIVE, INC.

1913 · Henry Ford used conveyor belts in his assembly lines for the first time, but only for assembly of the magneto. In 1914 Ford produced the first cars completely assembled on conveyor belts, reducing the time required to build a car from twelve and one-half hours to one and one-half hours, revolutionizing American industry.

1915 · Because sales had surpassed annual target figures, Ford Motor Company offered the first rebate—fifty dollars—to anyone who purchased a Model T.

1918 · For the first time, car registrations in the United States exceeded 5 million.

1922 · In the United States, Trico introduced the electric windshield wiper.

1924 · Walter P. Chrysler (1875–1940) produced the first Chryslers.

1934 · The Chrysler Corporation produced the first Airflow cars—streamlined vehicles that were to have a revolutionary impact on auto design. Airflow also featured the first overdrive transmissions.

1936 · The Nazi Government financed the development and manufacture of the first Volkswagens, the design of which remained virtually unchanged to the 1970's.

1939 · The Lincoln division of Ford Motor Company produced the first Lincoln Continental and Mercury models.

1948 · Rover of Great Britain introduced the first four-wheel-drive Land-Rovers.

1950 · Rover pioneered the first gas-turbine engine car.

1956 · Ford Motor stock sold to the public for the first time since Henry Ford bought out all Ford shareholders in 1917. In the 1917 stock buy-back, Henry Ford paid 105 million dollars to buy out other shareholders, which gave a return of 12 million dollars on an investment of five thousand dollars in Ford stock made in 1908. From 1917 to 1956 the Ford family retained full control of the giant business.

The Ford Foundation, which offered the stock for sale in 1956, netted some 643 million dollars from the transaction, 500 million dollars of which it gave away within the next eighteen months.

1957 · Ford produced the first Edsel—Detroit's first major flop.

RAILROADING FIRSTS:
From Iron Horse to Amtrak

Sixteenth century · The first recognizable railways were built in mines in central Europe, when flanged wooden tracks were used to carry wheeled ore cars pulled by horses or men. By 1767 the first iron rails were in use at Coalbrookdale, England.

May 21, 1801 · British Parliament okayed the Grand Surrey Iron Railway, the first rail line incorporated to haul goods for the public. The line, with horse-drawn cars, opened a route from Wandsworth to Croydon on July 26, 1803.

February 6, 1804 · British engineer Richard Trevithick test ran the first steam locomotive, which he converted from a steam hammer by adding a wheeled chassis. The trial run was on the Penydarren Railway near Merthyr Tydfil, Wales.

June 29, 1804 · The Oystermouth Railway was incorporated in England. It became the first to carry fare-paying passengers on March 25, 1807. The fare for the seven and one-half mile trip was one shilling. The line, which opened in 1806, first hauled cars by horsepower, and later by steam and electric engines. The line (modernized, of course) remained in service until 1960.

August 13, 1812 · Steam engines built by Matthew Murray of England were used for the first commercial steam-engine rail service on the Middleton colliery railway, Leeds, England.

May 24, 1830 · The first public railway in the United States, the Baltimore and Ohio Railroad, opened for passenger and freight service between Baltimore and Ellicott's Mills, Maryland. Passenger tickets were nine cents for a ride on the horse-drawn cars.

September 15, 1830 · The Liverpool-Manchester Railway opened, the first line in the world with all-steam service. At the opening ceremonies the first railroad fatality occurred when William Huskisson, a member of Parliament, was struck down by a steam locomotive. The ceremonial train had stopped at Parkside to take on water and Honorable Mr. Huskisson was standing beside the train engaged in conversation with the Duke of Wellington. Despite the duke's warnings, Huskisson failed to notice a locomotive approaching on the parallel track behind him and he was struck down and killed.

January 15, 1831 · The first regular steam-locomotive service began on the South Carolina Railroad out of Charleston. The locomotive, The Best Friend of Charleston, was also involved in the first railroad fatality in the United States on June 17, when the engine's fireman negligently held down the boiler safety valve while the train was stationary, causing the boiler to explode, killing him.

November 9, 1833 · The first railway passenger deaths occurred in the United States, when an axle on the Camden and Amboy line in New Jersey broke, overturning a passenger car. Two passengers were killed, and twelve seriously injured. One of the injured was Cornelius Vanderbilt, who would one day become one of the most powerful railroad magnates in America.

May 15, 1835 · The first nationally planned, built, and operated railway opened in Belgium with service from Brussels to Mechlin.

August 24, 1835 · President Andrew Jackson witnessed the arrival of the first train into Washington, D.C., on the Baltimore and Ohio Railroad.

May 8, 1842 · The first major rail disaster occurred when the axle on the locomotive of the Versailles-Paris express broke, causing a pile-up of the cars. Because the passenger compartment doors were locked, fifty-three passengers were killed in the ensuing fire.

1857 · Robert F. Mushet installed the first experimental steel rails at Derby Station on the Midland Railway in England; within a few years steel rails had replaced the old iron types.

September 1, 1859 · Twenty-eight-year-old George Mortimer Pullman, a former cabinetmaker, converted a conventional rail coach to the first sleeping car, and put it into service between Bloomington, Indiana, and Chicago. The success of the converted prototype enabled him to build the famous Pioneer sleeping car a few years later—the first modern sleeper and a major innovation in rail travel.

1867 · The Great Western Railway of Canada began the first dining-car service (along with sleeper accommodations), though in 1863 the Philadelphia, Wilmington, and Baltimore Railroad had offered hot box lunches to passengers in a stand-up "buffet car."

May 10, 1869 · The first transcontinental track was completed at Promontory Point, Utah, with the driving of a ceremonial gold spike into the last rail joining the Union Pacific and Central Pacific railroads. The monumental task, accomplished by more than 10,000 workers, many of them Chinese "coolie" laborers working in virtually uninhabited territory in the West, was seen as the final blow to the rugged Old West and a major step in the settling of the continent. The rail companies received huge grants of land and cash subsidies from the Government, and it was later revealed that the project was riddled with graft and profiteering.

September 18, 1871 · The Montcenis tunnel under the French-Italian Alps was completed—the first of the great rail tunnels. Built between 1857 and 1871, it is eight and a half miles long—eight times longer than any previous tunnel, and was built using manual digging, compressed-air drills, and black blasting powder.

October 5, 1883 · The Orient Express, created by Belgian railroad promoter Georges Nagelmackers, began full service from Paris to Istanbul. It was destined to become the most famous and luxurious train in the world.

October 1, 1964 · Japan inaugurated the Tokyo-Osaka high speed line, the first rail service designed to run at speeds in excess of 100 mph.

May 1, 1971 · The first passenger trains began operating under the management of the National Railroad Passenger Corporation (Amtrak), the Government-sponsored attempt to save the United States' dying railroad passenger service.

BALLOONATICS AND BLIMPS: Lighter-than-Air Firsts

TRIAL RUN

The first known hot-air balloon flight took place on August 8, 1709, when Father Bartholomeu de Gusmão (1695–1724) launched his small model in an indoor test at the Casa de India, Terreiro do Paco, Portugal.

HOT-AIR PETTICOATS

On April 25, 1783, the Montgolfier brothers, Joseph Michael (1740–1810) and Jacques Étienne (1745–99), launched the first hot-air balloon capable of carrying a man. The French brothers, who inherited their father's paper factory in Annonay, first tested small paper and cloth bags; they then tried a one-hundred-foot-diameter balloon, made of linen. According to one story, Jacques' wife hung a petticoat over a fire to dry. The hot air inflated the garment, giving them the idea for the hot-air balloon.

BAA! QUACK! COCK-A-DOODLE-DOO!

On September 19, 1783, the Montgolfiers launched a sheep, a duck, and a rooster in one of their balloons, making the trio the first animals to fly under something other than their own power. Had the flight failed (which it didn't) two passengers were equipped with bail-out equipment—the sheep would have been out of luck.

BIRD'S-EYE VIEW

Pilâtre de Rozier became the first man to fly in a balloon on October 15, 1783, when his Montgolfier balloon, tethered to the ground, ascended to a height of eighty-four feet.

ALL TIES SEVERED

The first manned free-flight in a hot-air balloon took place on November 21, 1783; the balloon covered a distance of six miles over Paris at an altitude of three hundred feet. The two men in the balloon were Pilâtre de Rozier and the marquis d'Arlandes.

ANY REQUESTS?

The first womanned free-flight in a balloon took place on June 4, 1784, in a Montgolfier balloon. The woman on board was Elizabeth Tible, who ascended over Lyons, France, while singing operatic arias. The balloon was christened *La Gustave* in honor of King Gustav of Sweden, one of those observing the ascent.

WE'VE GOT GAS!

The British scientist Henry Cavendish demonstrated that hydrogen was seven times lighter than air in 1766. By 1783, at the same time the Montgolfier brothers were working on hot-air flights, the Frenchman J.A.C. Charles and associates ascended for the first time in a hydrogen balloon on December 1; they traveled twenty-seven miles.

DROP YOUR DRAWERS!

J. P. Blanchard of France and an American physician, Dr. John Jeffries, made the world's first aerial sea voyage and channel crossing. They flew from France to England on January 7, 1785.

This historic flight across the channel had two other firsts, one of them unplanned. One of the observers was Benjamin Franklin, who had witnessed the earlier first untethered flight. Old Ben posted the first airmail letter via the balloon, from England to France. The channel crossing was also, unexpectedly, the first nude flight. En route from Dover to Calais, Jeffries and Blanchard began to lose altitude and were in danger of landing in the channel. First they jettisoned all loose objects on board. Then they stripped and threw their clothes overboard. Finally, they managed to lighten the payload by urinating in the channel (another first?) and were welcomed with open arms by the admiring Frenchmen on the other side.

HOT AIR!

The first manned balloon flight in America took place on January 9, 1793, at Philadelphia. The hydrogen-powered balloon was manned by French balloonist J. P. Blanchard.

THE SPY BALLOON

On June 26, 1794, the French Army launched a balloon at the battle of Fleurus (Belgium), which they used for observation of enemy troops. The French won the battle against the Austrians—a decisive victory in the French Revolution.

DOWN TO EARTH

French aeronaut J. P. Blanchard claimed the invention of the parachute in 1785, but the first major test did not come until October 22, 1797, when Blanchard's countryman André Jacques Garnerin jumped from a balloon at the height of three thousand feet and landed safely on the ground.

AERIAL DESTRUCTION

On August 22, 1849, Austria launched unmanned balloons carrying bombs with time-delay fuses against rebellious Venice—the first use of aircraft in warfare.

THE FIRST TRANSOCEANIC BALLOON FLIGHT

On August 11, 1978, the *Double Eagle II* left Presque Isle, Maine, with a crew of three. One hundred and thirty-seven hours and six minutes later they touched down at Eureux, France, about 3,500 miles away—almost two hundred years after the first Montgolfier ascent. The crew members were Ben Abruzzo, Max Anderson, and Larry Newman, all of Albuquerque, New Mexico.

KITTY HAWK, OFF TARGET

On Monday, May 12, 1980, Max Anderson, age forty-five and a veteran of the record-breaking transatlantic flight of 1978, and his son Kris, twenty-three, successfully made the first balloon crossing of North America, from San Francisco, California, to the Gaspé Peninsula of Quebec, on a journey of more than 3,100 miles. The *Kitty Hawk* was originally charted to land at the place of that name in North Carolina where the Wright brothers had made their first flight, but strong winds carried the Andersons far north of their course. The balloonists departed just after midnight on May 8 and touched down at 7:25 A.M., May 12, in a field outside Matane, Quebec.

THE BIG GASBAG

The dirigible, a cigar-shaped balloon with a propulsion system and a box or cabin for passengers or cargo, was first built and tested on September 24, 1852, by French inventor Henri Giffard. The ship was 144 feet long and contained 88,300 feet of coal gas.

ELECTRIFYING

On August 9, 1884, *La France* made its maiden flight. Built by Charles Renard and Artur Krebs, the hydrogen-filled dirigible contained electric storage batteries, making it the first electric-powered airship.

TEUTONIC RIGIDITY

Count Ferdinand von Zeppelin of Germany (1838–1917) invented and tested the first rigid-frame lighter-than-air ship on July 2, 1900, at Friedrichshafen, Lake Constance, Germany. The first zeppelin, with its metal-frame construction, lightweight skin containing hydrogen-filled bags, and cabins and propeller motors on the underside, became the prototype for the giant and famous airships of the early decades of this century.

BOMBS AWAY

On January 19, 1915, a German zeppelin dropped a bomb on England, the first time an airship had been used in attack. On May 31, the first bomb was dropped on London from a zeppelin.

TRANSATLANTIC STOWAWAY

On July 2, 1919, Britian's *R-34* dirigible left Scotland for the first transatlantic flight. Captained by Major G. H. Scott, the 665-foot airship arrived after battling rough weather at Montauk, Long Island, on July 6, with only two hours of fuel remaining. The *R-34* also carried the first stowaway on a transatlantic flight—a ship's rigger who resented having been left off the crew roster after working on the construction of the ship. The *R-34* was the first large airship seen in the United States, attracting huge crowds during its stay. On departure on July 9 the ship circled the Empire State Building and arrived back in England in the fast time of seventy-five hours and three minutes.

GOING MAGELLAN ONE BETTER

From August 8 to 29, 1929, the *Graf Zeppelin* piloted by Dr. Hugo Eckener made the first and only circuit of the globe in an airship. The *Graf,* which had been built in 1926–27, was designed with passenger comfort and luxury in mind, but at a price: A first-class ticket for the twenty-thousand-mile journey was a staggering nine thousand dollars!

SAFE, BUT NOT THAT SAFE

The *Shenandoah,* completed in 1923, was the first American-built airship, and the first dirigible to use helium gas instead of hydrogen. Helium has less lifting power than hydrogen, but has the big advantage of being nonflammable. Though the *Shenandoah* was safe from the fiery fate that overtook airships like the *Hindenburg,* which exploded and burned at Lakehurst, New Jersey, in 1937, it was nevertheless wrecked and destroyed in a severe storm in 1927.

FLYING FIRSTS:
Man and Woman Get Off the Ground

HOP, SKIP, JUMP

Though the Wright brothers have (deservedly) gained lasting fame for their first flight, it was Clement Adler (1841–1925) who was the first man to get off the ground in a winged, engine-driven machine. On October 9, 1890, the French aviation pioneer made a short hop into the air in his bat-winged monoplane *Eole.*

NO FEAR OF FLYING

At 10:25 A.M. on December 17, 1903, at Kill Devil Hill, Kitty Hawk, North Carolina, Orville Wright (1871–1948) took off in the *Flyer I,* a 12-horsepower plane designed and built by himself and his brother Wilbur (1867–1912). The flight lasted twelve seconds and attained an air speed of approximately thirty to thirty-five miles per hour. The *Flyer* made two other flights that day, including an impressive haul of 852 feet with Wilbur at the controls.

EARLY WHIRLYBIRDS

The ancient Chinese and medieval Europeans had rotary-winged toys, and sketches for a helicopter-type vehicle appear as early as the *Notebooks* of Leonardo da Vinci (1452–1519). However, it was not

91

until November 13, 1907, that French aviation designer Paul Cornu made the first, brief flight in a twin-bladed rotary-powered machine at Lisieux, France.

ACROSS THE CHANNEL

Louis Blériot (1872–1936) made the first crossing of the English Channel on July 25, 1909, in the Blériot XI monoplane of his own design. The daring feat earned Blériot a £1,000 prize offered by the *London Daily Mail,* as well as a fortune in orders for his burgeoning aircraft company. The flight took thirty-seven minutes, which was about the capacity his 25-horsepower engine had for running without stopping, and the landing on the Dover cliffs was little short of a crash landing. After Blériot's flight the military began to take notice of the potential of the airplane for warfare. On August 2 of that year, the U. S. Army bought its first plane from the Wright brothers.

THE RED BARONESS

On March 8, 1910, the French aviatrix Madame la Baronne de Laroche became the first certified woman pilot in the world. She was also the first woman involved in a plane crash, in July, 1910. "La Baronne" was an assumed title.

DO YOU READ ME?

On August 27, 1910, James McCurdy made the first radio transmission from a plane in flight to the ground while on a round-trip flight from New York to Philadelphia. His first words: "Another chapter in aerial history is hereby written in the receiving of this first message ever recorded from an airplane in flight."

SEABORNE, AIRBORNE

On November 14, 1910, Eugene Ely piloted a Curtiss biplane which took off from a platform that had been specially built on the U.S.S. *Birmingham,* anchored in Chesapeake Bay. The plane landed on the ground, but on January 18 of the following year Ely, also in a Curtiss biplane, made the first landing on a ship, the U.S.S. *Pennsylvania,* in San Francisco Bay.

BETTER LUCK NEXT TIME

In 1911 American pilot Calbraith P. Rodgers made the first transamerican flight in an attempt to win the $50,000 prize offered by newspaper magnate William Randolph Hearst for the first pilot to do so. The flight, in a Wright biplane, required a total of eighty-two flying hours in eighty-two stages over a period of forty-nine days. Rodgers crashed no fewer than nineteen times during the flight, but thanks to a special train which followed him with spare parts, his wife, and his mother, he was able to patch up the aircraft every time and take off again. He got to California on November 5 but didn't get the full prize money—the contest had specified a flying time of thirty days!

SPY IN THE SKY

On October 22, 1911, an Italian pilot, one Capitano Piazza, flew a Blériot monoplane on a one-hour reconnaissance flight to observe Turkish positions at Aziza, near his home base at Tripoli. Capitano Piazza also flew the first plane in actual combat three days later, in the battle of Sciara-Scut, when he flew over the battle and directed Italian gunfire on the Turkish troops from a battleship and on-land gun emplacements. These two flights marked the first use of an airplane in warfare.

THE FIRST AIRPLANE TO DROP A BOMB

During the Italo-Turkish war (1911–12) three 4½-pound bombs were dropped on a Turkish encampment at Ain Zara, near Tripoli, from an Etrich monoplane piloted by Lieutenant Guilio Gavotti. This first airplane bombing brought immediate protests that the Italians were violating the Geneva convention.

IS PARIS BURNING?

The first major city to be bombed by airplane was Paris, on August 30, 1914. The Germans did the dropping.

NOW BOARDING

On January 1, 1914, the Benoist Company began its flight from St. Petersburg to Tampa, Florida, the first regularly scheduled airline service. The twenty-mile flight across Tampa Bay was in a Benoist air-boat and cost five dollars. The service lasted for four months, with two flights daily.

The world's first scheduled daily international commercial airline service began August 25, 1919, when Aircraft Transport and Travel, a British company, began their London-Paris route.

The first American international airplane service began on November 1 of that year when Aeromarine West Indies Airways began flying from Key West, Florida, to Havana, Cuba. The infant company eventually became Pan American World Airways, the world's largest airline.

ACROSS THE ATLANTIC OR BUST

In 1919 the U.S. Navy began an ambitious program to make the first transatlantic flight. They arranged for three Curtiss NC-4 flying boats (one of the largest planes built up to that time) to make the attempt, with Navy destroyers, spaced at 50-mile intervals across the entire ocean route, to come to their rescue in event of an emergency. Two of the planes *were* wrecked, but the third, piloted by Lieutenant Commander A. C. Read, made it. The NC-4 left Newfoundland on May 8, made two refueling stops—in the Azores and in Portugal—and eventually arrived in England on May 31. The flight covered a record 3925 miles in fifty-seven hours and sixteen minutes flying time at an average airspeed of 78.8 mph.

CLOSE ENCOUNTERS

An even more remarkable flight took place the following month, when Captain John Alcock and Lieutenant Arthur Brown, two British airmen, flew nonstop from Newfoundland to Ireland in a Vickers Vimy bomber which had been outfitted with extra fuel tanks. Their flight, which began on June 14, was chock full of close scrapes: The plane was so loaded with fuel it almost didn't get off the runway; while flying blind in a cloudbank they lost control of the aircraft and went into a spin, recovering only a few feet above the water; at one point the engine intakes became so clogged with ice that navigator Brown had to climb out onto the biplane wings and scrape off the ice. The final crisis came on landing, when they chose what turned out to be a peat bog for a landing site: The plane crash-landed on its nose. Both men survived, though, and their remarkable crossing of 1,890 miles had been made in sixteen hours and twenty-eight minutes. Both men were knighted by King George V. Unfortunately Alcock was killed the following December in a crash in France.

IF IT'S TUESDAY, IT MUST BE SAN DIEGO

The first coast-to-coast, nonstop flight in America took place on May 2–3, 1923. Lieutenants O. G. Kelly and J. A. McReady, two American pilots, flew from Long Island to San Diego nonstop in a Fokker T-2 monoplane. They flew the 2,516 miles in twenty-six hours and fifty minutes. (On September 4, 1922, the famed James Doolittle had made the first coast-to-coast flight in one day [twenty-one hours and nineteen minutes], from Florida to San Diego, but he made one refueling stop in Texas.)

AROUND THE WORLD IN LESS THAN EIGHTY DAYS

The first round-the-world flight was made in 1924. The U. S. Army sent four Douglas Aircraft World Cruisers on an attempted round-the-world flight. Two of the planes, with open cockpits and single engines, made it—25,345 miles in 363 hours and 7 minutes flying time.

NO SANTA IN SIGHT

American pilot Floyd Bennett (1890–1928) and Admiral Richard E. Byrd (1888–1957) were the first men to fly over the North Pole, on

May 9, 1926, flying in a Fokker FVIIA-3M. The base for the flight was Spitsbergen, Norway.

WHICH WAY IS UP?

On November 28, 1929, Admiral Byrd, pilot Bernt Balchen, and two crew members left the base at Little America on the Ross Ice Shelf of Antarctica and flew eighteen hours and fifty-nine minutes over an almost totally uncharted ice cap to fly over the South Pole.

LUCKY LINDY

Of all the early, record-setting flights, none captured the public's attention more, or has become as famous, as Charles Lindbergh's (1902–74) solo crossing of the Atlantic in the *Spirit of St. Louis* on May 20–21, 1927. Six pilots had died in earlier attempts to win the $25,000 prize offered by Raymond Orteig for the first to make the flight. Lindbergh's flight was fraught with close calls: The takeoff runway was muddy; the plane was overloaded with fuel and barely missed electric wires at the end of the runway; the plane went into a spin in mid-Atlantic (like Alcock and Brown on their first nonstop transatlantic); and, with no forward visibility due to the special gas tank that had been installed where the windshield should have been, Lindbergh had difficulty landing in the dark field at Le Bourget, outside Paris—where thousands had jammed the airport anticipating his arrival.

Lindbergh became an instant international hero, and the *Spirit of St. Louis,* which was never piloted by another man, was enshrined in the Smithsonian Institution. Lindbergh later became a tragic hero, with the kidnap-murder of his infant son in New Jersey in 1933, and something of an antihero in the late 1930's with his unpopular pacifist and pro-German sentiments.

COFFEE, TEA, OR ME

On May 15, 1930, Boeing Air Transport (a forerunner of United Airlines) hired eight trained nurses in a three-month experiment to see if women attendants on passenger flights would work out. The idea of women attendants was sponsored by Ellen Church, a nurse and one of the original eight. The women, in addition to helping passengers on and off planes and serving box lunches and refreshments, were required to help move planes in and out of hangars, load luggage, and sometimes even refuel tanks. The original flight was from San Francisco to Chicago, and the women were paid $125 a month for 100 hours of work time.

A LADY ALOFT ALONE

The great Amelia Earhart (1898–1937) made the first solo Atlantic crossing by a woman on May 20–21, 1932, piloting a Lockheed Vega monoplane; she also made the first solo flight from California to Hawaii (January 11–12, 1935) and was making an attempt at the first woman's solo round-the-world flight when she disappeared over the Pacific in 1937.

WILEY AND WINNIE MAE

The one-eyed Texan, Wiley Post, completed the first global solo circuit from July 15–22, 1933, piloting a Lockheed Vega called *Winnie Mae*. The 15,596-mile flight took seven days and eighteen hours. Post was killed in 1935 while flying near Point Barrow, Alaska, with comedian Will Rogers.

GIVE 'EM HELICOPTERS

On June 6, 1936, the German Focke-Wulf FW-61 helicopter made its first flight. It was the first successful rotary-winged aircraft ever built.

JET PROPELLED

On August 27, 1939, the jet age began with the successful first flight of the German Heinkel 78, the first aircraft to fly solely under power of a gas turbine (or jet) engine; by April 5, 1941, the Heinkel He-280 —the first jet plane equipped as a fighter—made its maiden flight.

FAST AND NASTY

The Germans developed the Heinkel 178, the first jet aircraft, in 1939; by 1942 the Messerschmidt 262A, the world's first fully operational jet fighter, was test flown (July 18, at Leipheim). Production models were delivered by German aircraft factories in May, 1944. The first Messerschmidt to engage in combat was over Munich on July 25, 1944, when the German jet engaged a British plane piloted by Flight Lieutenant Evelyn Wall. Wall evaded several firing passes before eluding the jet fighter.

RATTLE MY WINDOWS

On October 14, 1947, a Bell X-1 rocket-powered aircraft piloted by Major Charles Yeager of the U.S. Air Force, was launched from under the wing of a B-52 bomber and succeeded in breaking the "sound barrier," that is, traveling more than 659.78 m.p.h. Thus, on October 14, the first "sonic boom" was heard.

NO TOUCHDOWNS

In March, 1949, a Boeing B-50 Superfortress captained by James Gallagher, with a crew of 18, flew 22,500 miles around the globe nonstop at an average speed of 235 m.p.h. The *Lucky Lady II* was refueled four times in flight: over the Azores, Saudi Arabia, the Philippines, and Hawaii.

FOLLOW ME, BOYS

In 1957, three Boeing B-52 bombers flew nonstop around the world in formation, with four in-flight refuelings. The 24,325-mile flight took forty-five hours and nineteen minutes—or less that half the time of the first nonstop global circuit in 1949. To one of the tail gunners on the flight goes the distinction of being the first man to fly around the globe facing backward.

THE FASTEST WOMAN ALIVE

In 1948 Jacqueline Cochrane, piloting an F-86 Sabre jet, became the first woman to achieve Mach 1, the speed of sound. Her flight took place on May 18. Her death in the summer of 1980 was a great loss to aviation.

THE JET SET

On May 2, 1952, British Airways (BOAC) inaugurated their Haviland Comet 1, the first jet passenger service, from London to Johannesburg, South Africa. On July 15, 1954, the first American jet passenger flight took off in a Boeing 707.

BIGGER IS BETTER

On February 9, 1969, the Boeing 747 flew for the first time, inaugurating the age of jumbo, wide body, and stretched jets.

SOVIET SONICS

Russia test flew its Tupolev TU-144 prototype on December 31, 1968, the first supersonic plane designed for commercial use.

LA CONCORDE

On March 2, 1969, the British-French Concorde prototype *001* made its first test flight at Toulouse, France. It was not until January 21, 1976, after considerable controversy and protest over the cost, efficiency, and environmental impact of the plane, that the Concorde SST went into regular commercial service simultaneously for Air France and British Airways.

THIS IS YOUR CAPTAIN SPEAKING

In 1953 Maria Atanassova of the USSR became the first woman in the world to fly a large commercial aircraft. In 1956 she was made a full pilot for Aeroflot, the Soviet airline. Her first landing at Heathrow airport in 1966—the first time a woman had piloted a large jet aircraft at a non-Russian airport—created a sensation. The first commercial female pilot in the United States was Emily Howell, a flying instructor, divorcée, and mother of three, who was hired by Frontier Airlines in January, 1973.

DEATH IN THE AIR

LUCK WAS ON THE WRIGHT SIDE

Lieutenant Thomas Selfridge became the first airplane fatality when he was killed on September 17, 1908, while flying in a biplane with Orville Wright at Fort Myers, Florida. Wright survived.

NEXT TIME TAKE THE TRAIN

On Tuesday, December 14, 1920, a Continental Air Services liner with six passengers and two crew members crashed at Golders Green, North London, shortly after takeoff from Cricklewood Aerodrome. The plane struck a house and fell into the garden. Four passengers managed to jump clear of the wreckage before it hit the ground; the crew and two passengers died.

JET LAG

On March 3, 1953, a Canadian Pacific Comet Jet crashed at Karachi, Pakistan, killing eleven on board—marking the first commercial passenger jet crash.

MOUNTING STATISTICS, PART I

The first plane crash to kill more than 100 people occurred on June 18, 1953, when a U.S. Air Force C-124 crashed and burned near Tokyo. Killed were 129 crew members and troops being transported.

MOUNTING STATISTICS, PART II

The first commercial crash to kill more than 100 people occurred on June 30, 1956, when a Lockheed L-1049 carrying 64 passengers and 6 crew members and a Douglas DC-7 with 53 passengers and 5 crew members collided in midair over the Grand Canyon, Arizona. All 128 were killed.

MIDAIR MAYHEM

On the night of December 16, 1960, a United DC-7 jet and a TWA Super-Constellation collided over New York City, killing all 128 on board and 6 on the ground. It was the first jet crash with more than 100 fatalities.

THE FIRST SINGLE PLANE JET CRASH TO KILL MORE THAN 100 PEOPLE

An Air France Boeing 707 jet crashed on takeoff from Paris on June 3, 1962, killing 130 passengers and crew.

SONIC SHAKEUP

A Soviet Supersonic Tu-144 became the first supersonic craft to crash when it exploded in midair outside Goussainville, France, on June 3, 1973, killing fourteen on board.

DC-10 DEATH AND SCANDAL

March 3, 1974: A Turkish DC-10 crashed just before landing in Paris when a cargo door blew out due to a faulty locking mechanism, causing the plane's subfloor and hydraulic system to fail. All 346 persons on board were killed. It was the first jumbo jet crash—and the first crash with 300-plus fatalities.

SUFFER THE CHILDREN

On October 13, 1976, a Bolivian 707 cargo jet with a crew of three crashed into a school in Santa Cruz, Bolivia, killing three crew members and ninety-seven on the ground, mostly children—the first major crash to kill more children than adults.

TRAGEDY AT TENERIFE

The worst air disaster of all time occurred on March 27, 1977, at Tenerife, Canary Islands, when a KLM 747 and a Pan Am 747 collided on the runway, killing 581 people. It was the first crash to kill 500-plus and the first between two jumbo jets.

SEXY
FIRSTS

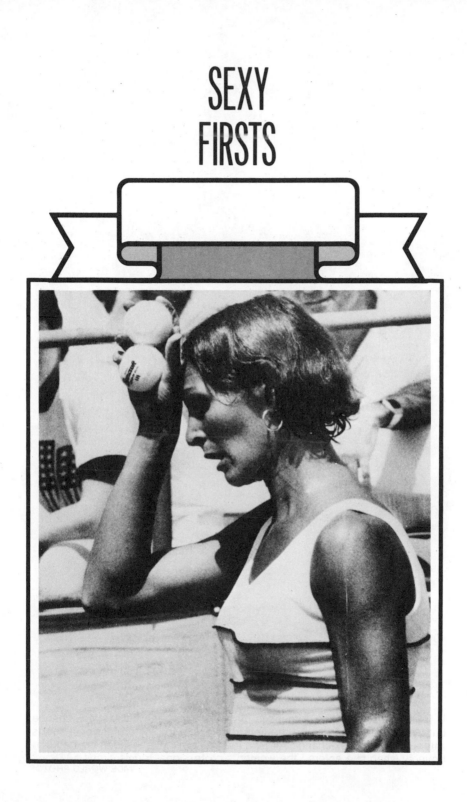

It takes balls: Christine Jorgenson may not have been the first sex change, but Dr. Renee Richards was the first transsexual to play professional sports. After undergoing sex-change surgery, the California eye surgeon created controversy when she entered the women's professional tennis circuit.

SEX AND SCIENCE:
Fifteen Firsts from Algae to Clones

MICROSCOPIC SEX

One billion years ago algae began sexual reproduction—the first living things to do so. Instead of reproducing by simple cell division, they began to form spores which joined with other spores to create a new individual. This simplest of sex acts is still going on by the billions every year in ponds and oceans around the world.

ONE PICTURE IS WORTH A THOUSAND WORDS

Humans have been drawing and sculpting sex organs since the beginning of time, but the first known drawings—and the first to survive —of human sexual organs in coitus, with a scientific point of view, were done by Leonardo da Vinci in his *Notebooks,* ca. 1500. In his cross-section drawing of a penis inserted in a vagina he included a tube joining the breasts and the uterus.

THE WAY I SEE THINGS . . .

Gabriel Fallopius (1523–62), Italian anatomist, made the first accurate description of human oviducts (which were named Fallopian tubes in his honor). He also gave us the first accurate (professional) description of the clitoris and of fetal skeletal structure, laying the foundation for modern understanding of reproduction.

WHAT'S IN A NAME?

In 1662 a Dutch anatomist named Van Horne coined the term ovary (from Latin *ova,* or eggs) to replace the rather silly term "female testicle," which had been used to that time by medical men.

SPERM SIGHTED

In 1677 in Delft, Holland, a student of microscope pioneer Anton van Leeuwenhoek discovered small animals swimming around in a sample of semen he'd examined under his microscope. The student's name isn't exactly known—Hamm, van Hamm, or von Hamen; neither is his nationality—he has been claimed by the Dutch and the Germans. Nor has history recorded if he looked at his own sperm first. But in any case, he got a shock for, in his master's words, "I am much astonished . . . in a bit of matter no longer than a grain of sand more than fifty thousand animalcules were present [moving] about with uncommon vigor." Scientists were mystified by the strange animals and thought they might be parasites. Not until the nineteenth century did science figure out what these creatures were doing in semen.

IN THE NAME OF SCIENCE

In 1855 a French doctor, Felix Roubaud, was the first to observe men and women having sex with an eye to scientifically and medically analyzing what went on. He published his findings in *Traité de l'Impuissance et de la Sterilité chez l'Homme et chez la Femme (Treatise on Impotence and Sterility in Men and Women).*

The first scientific observations by an American doctor would today probably have landed the observing physician a lawsuit from the patient. On August 7, 1872, Dr. Joseph R. Beck of Fort Wayne, Indiana, was fitting an intrauterine device to a female patient to correct a medical problem. The patient apparently warned Dr. Beck to be careful on insertion of the device lest she have an orgasm. In the spirit of scientific observation, Dr. Beck instead, "swept my right forefinger quickly three or four times across the space between the cervix and the pubic arch when almost immediately orgasm occurred. . . ." Dr. Beck wrote about his observations in the September, 1872, issue of the *St. Louis Medical and Surgical Journal.*

BABY, IT'S COLD OUTSIDE

In 1866 the Italian physiologist, Paolo Mantegazza (1831–1910), successfully froze human semen to −17°C, then thawed it out and noted that the sperm cells had survived.

WISH YOU WERE HERE!

In 1880 French anthropologist Vacher de Lapouge achieved the first long-distance animal fertilization. He later wrote, "Semen can be transported; in one of those idiotic experiments which Darwin recommends I obtained in Montpelier the fertilization of a rabbit with semen sent from Beziers by post."

AN ANGORA IN THE WOODPILE

In a remarkable experiment that would have wide implications for the animal breeding business, and eventually for human "breeding," Walter Heape of Cambridge University successfully transferred fertile eggs from one rabbit to another in April 27, 1890. A female Belgian hare, who had been impregnated by a male of the same breed, had two fertilized ova, which had been removed from an Angora rabbit, implanted in her fallopian tubes. When she came to term, four of the rabbits were Belgians, and two Angoras.

HORMONES DISCOVERED

On January 16, 1902, Ernest Starling of University College, London, discovered what he called the "chemical messenger," or hormone (from the Greek *hormon,* to set in motion). Though Starling's discovery was of a hormone involved in digestion, it was soon discovered that hormones (especially testosterone and estrogen) play a tremendous role in sexuality and reproduction, and are the basis for many modern methods of contraceptive and fertility drugs.

YOU CAN BANK ON IT

By the 1960's scientists had few worries about producing healthy offspring from stored semen, and the demand for artificial insemination from couples where the "father" was sterile had grown. To meet the demand, in 1964, two sperm banks opened—in Tokyo and Iowa City, Iowa.

OUTSIDE ACTIVITY

In 1945 Dr. Gregory Pincus, one of the pioneers in the development of the birth control pill, claimed to have united a human egg and sperm outside the body and to have watched the test-tube cell divide three times. Other researchers had difficulty in duplicating his feat. However, in 1961 Italian researcher Dr. Daniele Petrucci at the University of Bologna gave irrefutable proof that he had fertilized not one, but as many as twenty human ova in vitro: He took films of the fertilizations and subsequent cell divisions. In the words of *Newsweek*, "So bizarre did the idea of test tube babies appear to most scientists and laymen that the research was either ignored or greeted with outraged disbelief."

BE A CLONE

In 1966 a team of Oxford University scientists announced the first successful cloning of an animal—a frog. They had extracted a fertile egg from a female frog, removed the nucleus of the cell—containing the genetic material—then replaced it with the nucleus of a body cell from a tadpole. The egg, with a complete set of genetic blueprints from the tadpole, was then replaced in the female frog and allowed to develop as if it had never been removed. The result was a tadpole identical to the donor tadpole—and not at all genetically related to the female who provided the egg.

OUT OF THE "TEST TUBE"

At 11:47 P.M. on July 25, 1979, a daughter named Louise was born to Lesley and Gilbert Brown at Oldham General Hospital in England. The five-pound twelve-ounce baby achieved overnight fame as the world's first test-tube baby—conceived outside her mother's body. The feat, which created a stir in scientific and religious circles, was accomplished by Drs. Patrick Steptoe and Robert Edwards, who removed an egg cell from Mrs. Brown, thirty-one (who could not conceive due to damaged Fallopian tubes), fertilized the egg in vitro, that is, in a test-tube culture, with sperm from Mr. Brown (a thirty-eight-year-old truck driver), and reimplanted the fertile egg in Mrs. Brown's uterus. Nine months later Louise was born, delivered prematurely by Caesarean section. Steptoe and Edwards got special attention, not all of it favorable, because the procedure had not previously been done on any animals higher up the evolutionary scale than rabbits and rats.

THE "FIRST" HUMAN CLONE

In 1979 the New York publisher Lippincott published *In His Image: the Cloning of a Man* by David Rorvik, which claimed to be the true account of a secret cloning of an American millionaire who "commissioned" a scientist to secretly duplicate him in a baby boy. Major newspapers ran banner headlines, but within a day of the announcement of the book, the scientific community had universally denounced the book as a hoax—or misrepresented fiction. However, the controversy did bring one point home to the public: The first human clone isn't far away.

TABOO FIRSTS:
Sex Versus Society

LOVE FOR SALE

The history of the oldest profession without doubt predates written history, and there is anthropological evidence that behavior that in our modern eyes constitutes prostitution may have evolved along with the human species: A female baboon, for example, will sometimes offer herself sexually to a male who is in possession of food; while he mounts her, she steals some of his food—but if he sees her doing so, he allows her to.

HANDS OFF!

The first known written condemnation of masturbation appears in the Egyptian Book of the Dead (1550–950 B.C.).

THE BEST LITTLE WHOREHOUSE IN ATHENS

Though religious-administered temple prostitution is very ancient, the Greeks take credit for the first secular brothel. It was organized by Solon (ca. 639–559 B.C.), the progressive and liberal Athenian political leader. The brothel was opened in 550 B.C., staffed by slaves, and was praised as a place where "you can have them without fear, day or night. . . ."

FASTEN YOUR CHASTITY BELTS, PLEASE

The chastity belt, a very ancient device, may date to the earliest years of civilized man—the concept of women as men's property having developed alongside settled, agrarian society. In any case, it was certainly known in ancient China and the Middle East; it made its appearance in Europe probably around A.D. 1150. Though the vogue peaked in the Middle Ages, chastity belts were popular in some circles in the nineteenth century, and have even been made in recent years.

IT'S SOMETHING I READ IN A BOOK

The Handbooks of Sex date to the reign of the legendary Huang-ti (2697–2598 B.C.), the Yellow Emperor, who is traditionally credited with originating sexual practices and beliefs, along with the other basic elements of civilization. The legend notwithstanding, *The Handbooks* are a five-thousand-year-old ancestor of *The Joy of Sex*.

TICKLED PINK

In the thirteenth century, Tibetan lamas turned the Chinese emperors on to what they called a "happy ring" or "the goat's eyelid." When a goat was slaughtered, the eyelids and eyelashes were removed intact. They were then put into quicklime to be dried and preserved, then steamed in a bamboo basket for twelve hours or more. The process was repeated several times. The ring, with hardened but flexible eyelashes, was then slipped onto the penis during sex to give the woman what would in later centuries be called a "French tickle."

DOWN, BOY!

Among the excesses of sex and violence that were popular in the heyday of the Roman arena, in the first four hundred years A.D., were exhibitions of sex between humans and animals. The bestiary included dogs, apes, giraffes, boars, bulls, zebras, horses, jackasses, and even cheetahs and leopards. The animals were trained to their task, and their human partners were either willing or unwilling.

Take the "A" train: The construction of the first elevated railroads in New York City in the nineteenth century gave rise to a new discipline of the oldest profession: the first railway hookers. This 1885 woodcut was captioned "Working the elevated—Man-fishers on Sixth Avenue, New York City—Siren games they play to rope in trade." The illustration doesn't make clear exactly what is written on the cards these women of the elevated are holding: address, price, or house specialty. THE BETTMANN ARCHIVE, INC.

THE FIRST PROSTITUTES REQUIRED BY LAW TO GO TOPLESS

In the fifteenth century the city fathers of Venice ordained that local prostitutes should wear bare breasts while plying their trade at open windows overlooking the city's famous canals and walkways. The ruling was designed to separate the city's "professional" women from the general female citizenry, and to encourage young men to purchase the prostitutes' wares—lest the men fall into the unspeakable sins of masturbation and homosexuality!

I'M IN A STEW

Henry II (1133–89), the remarkable king who lay claim to the throne through his mother Matilda, and who founded the Plantagenet line of royalty, was born in France, where he inherited the vast provinces of his father, the count of Anjou. From there he invaded England in 1133 and forced King Stephen to hand over the disputed crown to him, and from then on ruled half of what is modern France and England itself. When this busy king wasn't wedding Eleanor of Aquitaine (in 1152) and plotting the murder of Thomas à Becket (in 1170), he introduced "the stews"—public bathhouses where sex was available to customers. The first stews—which derived from a much older French tradition of public bawdy houses and court brothels dating back to the days of Charlemagne—were opened in 1161. Brothels of all types have been operating in England ever since, and were, naturally, exported to the Colonies centuries later.

BUT WHAT'S IT FOR?

Thomas Nash (or Nashe) (1567–1601) is credited with the first description of an artificial penis in the English language. Nash, a satirist and anti-Puritan, wrote *The Choise of Valentines or the Merie Ballad of Nash his Dildo.*

DOCTOR'S ORDERS

An anonymous treatise of 1644, *Hippolytus Redivivus,* suggested masturbation as a way for men to avoid the temptations of women.

SMALL BUT PERFECT

According to early medical authority Durston, writing in 1731, a mastectomy—the first on record—was performed ca. 1671 in England on a woman with breasts "of prodigious bigness." In the days before modern surgery and anesthetics the case must have been exceptional to warrant such a major operation.

POPULATION CONTROL—THE HARD WAY

In 1933 Germany passed a law "for the Prevention of Hereditary Disease to Posterity," and the statute went into effect in January, 1934. The list of diseases included mental deficiency, schizophrenia, epilepsy, hereditary blindness and deafness, physical deformity, and even alcoholism. From 1934 to 1945 somewhere between 200,000 and 2,000,000 men, women, and children were sterilized (estimates vary), making Germany the first and last country to practice sterilization on a large scale.

BOB AND CAROL AND TED AND . . .

In 1957 *Mr.* magazine, published in New York, carried the first article on the subject of wife-swapping; this led to reader correspondence, a long series of articles in other magazines, personals columns, and, within a few years, a widespread interest in the heretofore taboo subject—and presumably, a widespread interest in the activity itself.

ENJOY BEING A GIRL

On December 2, 1952, *The New York Times* carried a story—as did most other American newspapers—on Christine, formerly George, Jorgenson, the daughter, formerly son, of a Bronx carpenter, who had undergone sex-change surgery in Denmark under the direction of Dr. Christian Hamberg and a team of surgeons.

Christine, who, as George, had been a clerk in the U.S. Army, was reported as being "happy, although scared to be facing the world as a female."

Christine Jorgenson, who returned to America to become something of a celebrity, is usually credited with being the first transsexual. And certainly Christine deserves credit as being the first to get any attention for sex-change procedures. However, as reported in *The New York Times Magazine* article on Christine, Danish doctors were understandably blasé about the American press interest in the Jorgenson case, since "the Danish press had covered at least one such case before—the 'transformation' into a woman of the artist Lily Erbe back in the '20s."

MY MOTHER GAVE IT TO ME

The Manchester Guardian reported in 1973 that a young woman in Salonika, Greece, who had been born without a vagina, had received a vagina-transplant from her fifty-year-old mother in 1970; the doctors reported that there were no signs of tissue rejection after three years. The woman, whose first marriage had been annulled because of her deformity, was reported to have a boyfriend.

NEXT!

In 1966 the Erickson Educational Foundation provided funds for the world's first gender-reversal clinic. The clinic, which provided applicant screening, psychological evaluation and counseling, and sex-change surgery for individuals, operated at Johns Hopkins Hospital with a committee of nine doctors, headed by a plastic surgeon. Two applicants were accepted each month for the program. The clinic announced in early 1980 that they would no longer provide gender-changing services, though since 1966 a number of other hospitals worldwide have begun similar programs.

IT'S JUST AFTER FUCHSIA BUT BEFORE FUCOID

The first dictionary to include the word *fuck* was John Florio's *A World of Wordes,* an Italian-English dictionary, published in 1598. Included was "the word" along with, of course, its Italian counterpart.

SO THAT'S WHAT THEY CALL IT!

Derived from the Latin *impotentia,* meaning lack of power, the word *impotence* had found its way into English as early as Thomas Hoccleve (1370–1454), who used it in his poem "De Regimine Principium." But it wasn't used in a sexual sense until 1655, when Thomas Fuller wrote in his *A Church History of Britain:* "While Papists crie up this, his incredible Incontinency; others unwonder the same by imputing it partly to Impotence, afflicted by an affirmity." Fuller was talking about Henry VIII.

OUT OF THE MOUTHS OF BABES

Sigmund Freud shocked the medical establishment and revolution-ized thinking about human sexuality when he published his *Three Essays on the Theory of Sexuality* in 1905. One of the shocks was his discussion of "innocent babes" being sexual creatures from the mo-ment they are born—the first discussion of infant sexuality.

A POX ON YOU

The history of syphilis, or "the pox," is a complicated one. Some writers believe that the disease existed in Europe during ancient times, but died out (or at least became very rare) during the Dark and Middle Ages. However, what is clear is that between 1492 and 1497 a major epidemic of syphilis swept through Europe, reaching as far as Russia by 1499, India in 1498 (with Vasco da Gama and his sailors), and China by 1506. The outbreak is attributed to none other than Christopher Columbus, whose crew contracted it from the American Indians and brought it back to Europe instead of the gold and spices for which they'd hoped.

Whether syphilis was dead or dormant in Europe will probably never be known for sure; but the men of the *Pinta, Niña,* and *Santa Maria* did apparently catch a virulent and deadly strain of the bacil-lus: The disease soon became known as the great pox—as opposed to another killer disease, the small pox.

NOW YOU SEE IT

The first national magazine to reveal pubic hair in photographs was *Penthouse* magazine (published by Bob Guccione) in April, 1970.

YOU WON'T FIND IT IN THE *ENCYCLOPAEDIA BRITANNICA*

Though it was not intended as an encyclopedia, but as a daring assault on societal conventions through the medium of explicit cataloguing of every conceivable type of sexual act, the Marquis de Sade's *120 Days of Sodom,* written while the notorious Frenchman was in jail during the French Revolution, is encyclopedic in scope. It lists and describes hundreds of sex acts, from simple copulation to incest, homosexuality, gerontophilia, corporphilia, urolagnia, sadism, masochism, and a few that don't even have names. The massive work was never completed, though de Sade outlined the entire book.

UP IN FLAMES

The first organization for study and research in human sexuality was founded by Magnus Hirschfeld in Berlin in the 1930's. The Institut für Sexual Wissenschaft (Institute for Sexual Studies) was destroyed by the Nazis in 1939 and much of the rare, painstakingly assembled library burned; the director escaped to Switzerland.

LIKE FATHER, LIKE SON

In a pioneering 1955 study, American researchers Money, Hampson, and Hampson studied seventy-six children who were born hermaphroditic—that is, with genitals of both sexes. In most of these cases, the parents had to decide which sex their child would be raised as. In all but four cases, the doctors found that infants who were raised and treated as boys grew up seeing themselves as boys: playing boys' games and with "male" toys, eventually having male sexual fantasies and sexual attraction to females—even though they themselves had female genitals as well as male, or a combination of both. Hermaphrodites who were raised as girls likewise took on female gender roles, even though biologically they were equally male as female.

GOD IS WATCHING:
Firsts in Sex and Religion

ROCK HARD

The first evidence of phallic worship is found in Norwegian rock carvings from the Old Stone Age, or Paleolithic period, the earliest period of human development, dating from as early as 40,000 B.C.; their phallic nature is quite unmistakable.

PUT YOUR CONTRIBUTION IN THE COLLECTION BOX

Temple prostitutes—women, and sometimes men, who offered themselves to the devout in exchange for religious sacrifices or donations —are mentioned first in Mesopotamia, ca. 2300 B.C., though the institution no doubt predates the first written record, and, incidentally, survived in ancient Egypt, Babylon, Greece, and Rome.

THE GOOD BOOK

The first sex in the Bible is found in Genesis 1:22, God creates animals, saying, "Be fruitful, and multiply. . . ." By Genesis 4:1, Adam and Eve have eaten the forbidden fruit and been expelled from the garden, where "Adam knew Eve his wife; and she conceived, and bore Cain, and said I have gotten a man from the Lord."

THE FIRST RAPE IN THE BIBLE

Again, in Genesis, Chapter 34, Dinah, daughter of Leah and Jacob, is out visiting "the daughters of the land" (Canaan), when she is spotted by Shechem, son of a local ruler, who "took her, and lay with her, and defiled her." But Shechem also fell in love with Dinah, and, "though they were very wroth" due to Dinah's defilement, he went to her father and brothers to ask her hand in marriage.

I'VE STILL GOT RHYTHM

St. Augustine (A.D. 354–430), in his treatise *Marriage and Concupiscence,* was the first Christian writer to condemn the use of "poisons of sterility." He proclaimed that couples who use an "evil deed" or an "evil prayer" to prevent conception are "married in name only."

STOP THAT RIGHT NOW!

In A.D. 305 the Council of Elvira (Spain) ruled that all men involved in performing rites of priesthood should abstain from women—even their wives—or forfeit their priesthood. It was the first such celibacy for Christian priests.

WHAT A DRAG!

The first Christian condemnation of transvestites came in the fourth century A.D., when St. Asterius, Bishop of Amasia in Cappadocia (modern Italy), railed against the men in his diocese for celebrating New Year's Eve by dressing up "in long robes, girdles, slippers, and enormous wigs."

THIS IS GOING TO HURT ME MORE
THAN IT HURTS YOU

St. Peter Damian (A.D. 1007?–72), a rigorously ascetic Camaldolese Dominican father—who, among other things, fought against the application of reason in theology—was the first to organize groups

The joy of sects: The first flagellant sects were organized in the eleventh century, and as this fifteenth-century illustration shows, the sinful were still (literally) whipping themselves into a religious frenzy 400 years later.

THE BETTMANN ARCHIVE, INC.

of lay flagellants in the mid-eleventh century. St. Pete's flagellants whipped themselves and one another to atone for sins. Whipping had been popular with the priesthood for some time, but with the introduction of flagellation to the flock, the whipping movement began in earnest. By 1260, processions of voluntary scourgers walked through Europe, chanting and scourging as they walked. The Black Death added to the growing movement, and by 1349–50, according to one authority, "Europe was criss-crossed from end to end by hordes of desperate men, women, and children scourging themselves for the Glory of God."

THE DEVIL, YOU SAY?

In 1275 Angela de Labarthe of Toulouse, France, gave birth to a monster with a wolf's head and a snake's tail. The church-state authorities were on to Angela: She had cohabited with the Devil, who was the father of the monster. To put a stop to any such foolishness in the future, they burned her at the stake—the first woman to die for sleeping with Satan.

THE GOOD DIRTY BOOK

Pioneer American lexicographer and editor Noah Webster, father of the *Webster's Dictionary,* undertook in 1833 to purge the Good Book of its more offensive words and passages—the first Bible censorship. For example, "to give suck" became "to nurse" or "to nourish"; "whore" became "lewd woman"; "teat" became "breast"; "fornication" became "lewdness." Even whole passages of the Holy Scriptures were blue-penciled out because "Many words and phrases are so offensive, especially to females, as to create a reluctance in young persons to attend Bible classes and schools in which they are required to read passages which cannot be repeated without a blush."

BETTER SAFE THAN SORRY:
Firsts in Birth Control

WHAT'S THAT CROCODILE DOING IN YOUR PURSE?

In 1899 fragments of papyri were found at Kahun, El Fayum, Egypt, describing contraceptives used by Egyptian women in the twelfth dynasty (ca. 2000–1786 B.C.), the earliest known reference. During this period, a well-to-do Egyptian woman—even then, contraceptives were less available to the lower classes—used a pessary, or vaginal suppository, made of crocodile dung, to prevent pregnancy. Or, for an alternative, they employed a vaginal douche of honey and natron (a naturally occurring sodium carbonate), or inserted a suppository of some natural gumlike substance.

The crocodile-dung method was in use for almost three thousand years, though later and in certain locales elephant dung was substituted. Since human sperm survive best in an acid-based solution, the alkaline chemical base of the crocodile dung would tend to inhibit sperm in the vagina—in fact, this is the basis for many modern-day vaginal foams. The honey and natron douche packed a double whammy: The honey would tend to prevent sperm from moving freely in the vagina, and the carbonate natron—an alkaline —would reduce their effectiveness as well. The gum pessaries would have a similar effect.

THE UNKINDEST CUT OF ALL

The first and undoubtedly the most effective male contraceptive, even to this day, is castration, which was practiced widely by all ancient societies (and some not so ancient, such as twentieth-century Europe, and America in the 1930's). The practice probably predates recorded history.

Noted sex researcher Alfred Kinsey wrote that "the understanding and practice of castration may have begun as early as 7000 B.C. in the early neolithic age when animals were first domesticated." In most nations of the ancient world, a warrior was expected to collect the testicles of his fallen enemies as proof of his prowess, and in the Near East of biblical times, kings were often brought the foreskins or testicles, or both, of their slain enemies as proof of victory.

SAFETY FIRST

Though Italian anatomist Gabriel Fallopius (1523–62) is credited with "inventing" the condom, there is evidence that the Romans, and possibly the Egyptians, used animal bladders or lengths of intestine as sheaths for the penis to prevent venereal infection or pregnancy. But Fallopius can be considered the father of the "modern" condom, which he constructed out of linen and claims to have tested on over one thousand men without a single one contracting V.D. He wrote about his device, which covered only the head of the penis and was held in place by the foreskin, in *De morbo gallico,* published posthumously in 1564.

THE CONDOM CONUNDRUM

The condom is allegedly named after one Dr. Charles Condom (variously Conton or Condon), at the court of Charles II of England (1630–85), who is supposed to have "invented" the device that had been in use for many—perhaps many thousands—of years. What *is* known is that the word first appeared in an anonymous 1706 poem, "A Scot's Answer to a British Vision" in the lines, "Siringe and Condum/Come both in Request."

LEFT TO YOUR OWN DEVICES

The IUD—a small metal, plastic, or other nonorganic device inserted into the uterus to prevent conception—is first mentioned in medical literature in connection with one Dr. Möller, a German, who constructed an IUD from a flexible rubber tube and metal wire in 1803; by the mid-1800's, several experimenters had constructed their own versions of the IUD.

TAKE ONE A DAY, BEFORE BEDTIME

The first oral contraceptive, a combination of the hormones norethynodrel and synthetic estrogen, was marketed in 1960 under the trade name "Enovid"; the "Pill," as it soon become known, was developed in the 1950's by Drs. Carl Djerassi and Min Chueh Chang, and Gregory Pincus of the Worcester Foundation for Experimental Biology, and tested on a large scale in Puerto Rico in 1956; several years of further tests were made before FDA approval in 1960.

SORRY, ROVER

In 1823 Sir Astley Cooper (1768–1841), a pioneer British surgeon (and the man given the delicate task of removing a tumor from King George IV's head in 1820), performed an experiment on one of his dogs: He cut the vas deferens in one of the dog's testicles (the other testicle being atrophied due to another surgical procedure); the dog was kept for another six years, during which it was seen to engage in sex with females, but none conceived. When an autopsy was performed, Cooper found the testicle normal and healthy, but the vas deferens still severed; he concluded that this led to the dog's sterility.

YOU WON'T FEEL A THING

The first recorded human vasectomies were performed starting in 1883 by French surgeon Felix Gruyon, who believed that cutting the vas deferens concurrent with prostate operations reduced the chance of postoperative complications. He did not, apparently, recommend the operation for birth control.

The first American doctor known to perform vasectomies was Dr. Harry Sharp of Indianapolis, who first performed the surgery in October, 1899. Dr. Sharp's report, published in the *A.M.A. Journal* in December, 1909, is interesting. "This operation is very simple and easy to perform. I do it without administering an anesthetic, either general or local. It requires about three minutes time to perform the operation, and the subject returns to his work immediately, suffering no inconvenience, and is in no way hampered in his pursuit of life, liberty, and happiness, but is effectively sterilized.

"I began this work in October, 1899 and from 1899 to 1907 this operation was done on 176 men in the Indiana Reformatory on request. The request was solely for the purpose of relief from the habit of masturbation, and I will give as an illustration the story of my first operation in October, 1899.

"A boy nineteen years old came to me and asked that he be castrated as he could not resist the desire to masturbate. I first had him put in a cell with a fellow inmate, thinking that perhaps he would be abashed (!) and the sense of shame would prevent him. He came to me again still insisting on castration saying it was bad as ever. I did the operation [vasectomy] and two weeks afterward he came to me and said I was just fooling him, that I had not operated on him and he wanted the other operation [castration]. I told him to wait two months and then, if he was no better, I would perform castration. In two months time he came to me and told me he had ceased to masturbate and that he was all right. I asked him if he had lost any desire or pleasure of the gratification. He said, 'No, but I have the will power to restrain myself.' "

Dr. Sharp's article was titled, "Vasectomy as a Means of Preventing Procreation in Defectives."

Millions of men today know that vasectomies have no effect on sexual desire. But back in 1899, Dr. Sharp's patients believed the operation worked—a good example of the placebo effect.

FIRST
PERSONS

Hail to the Chief: Publicity-conscious Calvin Coolidge was the first President to have American Indian ancestry, as he was happy to remind his public.

FIRST CITIZEN:
Famous and Little-Known Firsts
About the Presidents of the United States

GEORGE WASHINGTON (1732–99) (served 1789–1797)

★ The first and only president to be elected unanimously by the electoral college, February 4, 1789. He received sixty-nine of the sixty-nine votes.

★ The first president with false teeth. General Washington had a long history of dental problems, and suffered greatly from toothaches; by his later years all his teeth had either fallen out or been removed, and he was fitted with a set of false teeth made from black wood, which accounts for his habit of smiling little.

★ The first to marry a wealthy woman. When George married Martha Custis in 1759, she was the wealthiest widow in Virginia, he an impoverished landowner. At the time of his death, the estate of $530,000 made the Washingtons one of the richest couples in America.

★ The first presidential inauguration took place on the afternoon of April 30, 1789, on the balcony of Federal Hall, at the corner of Broad and Wall streets in the then U. S. capital, New York City.

★ The first president to grow *Cannabis sativa,* or marijuana.

JOHN ADAMS (1735–1826) (served 1797–1801)

★ The first to occupy the White House (then known simply as the President's House or the President's Mansion). The cornerstone of Irishman James Hobart's design, based on the Duke of Leinster's Palace in Dublin, was set October 13, 1792; the Adamses took possession in '97.

131

★ Abigail Adams, famous for hanging the family wash in the unfinished East Room of the White House, was also the first president's wife to be criticized for running her husband's business. Her critics dubbed her "Mrs. President."

★ Adams was the first Harvard graduate to become president (Harvard has produced more Chief Executives than any other school or university.)

★ The first—and only—president to reach ninety years of age: 90 years and 247 days, to be exact.

THOMAS JEFFERSON (1743–1826 [died the same day as John Adams, July 4]) (served 1801–1809)

★ The first president to be inaugurated in Washington, D.C., March 4, 1801.

★ The first to be elected by the House of Representatives. Jefferson and his opponent Aaron Burr each received 73 electoral votes, and the House voted to break the tie; according to the constitutional rule then in effect, Burr then became Jefferson's vice-president, not the most congenial of arrangements.

★ The first presidential genius. Jefferson was a man of remarkable mental abilities, noted not only for his political and administrative talents, but as a writer (the Declaration of Independence), architect (his home, Monticello, and the University of Virginia are the best examples of his design), and as an inventor (the revolving chair, a pedometer, and many other practical devices).

★ The first known to have illegitimate children. When Jefferson's wife, Martha Skelton, died at age thirty-three (making him the first widower president) Jefferson kept his promise never to remarry. He *did,* however, have a relationship with Sally Hemings, one of his teen-age slaves. She bore five children, some—and possibly all—fathered by Jefferson.

★ The first to shake hands instead of bowing at official receptions. This "democratic" custom appeared first at a reception held July 4, 1801, in the Blue Room of the White House.

JAMES MADISON (1751–1836) (served 1809–1817)

★ The first short president. Adams was 5'7"—an average height in those days—but Washington and Jefferson had both been large men, Washington between 6'2" and 6'3½", and Jefferson 6'2½". The diminutive Madison stood only 5'4" and weighed less than 100 pounds.

★ The first and only president to engage in combat while in office. Madison was too frail to fight in the Revolution, but during the War of 1812—which he encouraged the United States to get involved in—he briefly took command of an artillery battery trying to stave off the British troops marching on Washington. When he saw that things weren't going well for the American forces, he wisely gave up command and exited the city to safety. Dolley, presumably, had already completed her famous rescue of George Washington's portrait before the British burned the city.

JAMES MONROE (1758–1821) (served 1817–1825)

★ The first presidential college dropout, Monroe left William and Mary College, Virginia, in 1776 to fight in the Revolution. He later studied law under Thomas Jefferson from 1780–83.
★ The first heavy drinker in the White House, Monroe allegedly learned boozing from General Stirling when he was the general's aide. Monroe took his drinking seriously, though apparently never lapsed into outright alcoholism.

JOHN QUINCY ADAMS (1767–1848) (served 1825–1829)

★ The first, and only, president to be descended from a president —his father.
★ The first president to publish his poetry, a 108-page volume in 1832. No president has done so since.
★ The first to receive fewer popular *and* electoral votes than an opponent. In the 1825 election, Andrew Jackson beat out Adams in the popular and electoral vote: Adams was second with eighty-four electoral votes to Jackson's ninety-nine, William Harris Crawford was third with forty-two votes, and Henry Clay fourth with thirty-seven. When Clay, who strongly opposed Jackson, released his votes to Adams, the House of Representatives then voted for Adams.

ANDREW JACKSON (1767–1845) (served 1829–1837)

★ The first born in a log cabin, March 15, 1767, along the North-South Carolina border, and the first not from the Virginia "aristocracy" or an Adams of Massachusetts.
★ The first subject of an assassination attempt. In 1835, an insane house painter who believed himself to be the rightful heir to the British throne fired two pistols at Jackson from about six feet away. Both misfired, and the president was unhurt.

★ The first bigamist president. Jackson married Rachel Donelson before her divorce was officially final. His enemies seized on this to attack Jackson, and he fought numerous duels to defend his wife's honor. The strain of the "scandal" eventually brought on her nervous breakdown and death shortly before her husband reached the White House.

MARTIN VAN BUREN (1782–1862) (served 1837–1841)
★ The first president born after the American Revolution.

WILLIAM HENRY HARRISON (1773–1841) (served 1841)
★ The first to die in office. Harrison delivered his two-hour inaugural address in a freezing rain, after which he contracted a cold and pneumonia. He was ill most of his thirty-one-day term, and thereby is the first president to have made no significant decision while in office.

JOHN TYLER (1790–1862) (served 1841–1845)
★ The first vice-president to succeed to the presidency through death.
★ The first president to remarry while in office. Tyler's second wife was the young Julia Gardiner, a famous Washington beauty. The bride was twenty-three, the groom fifty-two, and seven children resulted from the marriage, the last when Tyler was seventy.
★ Tyler was the first president to face a serious impeachment attempt, for "gross usurpation of power." The impeachment was voted down by the House, January 10, 1843, by a vote of 127 to 83.

JAMES KNOX POLK (1795–1849) (served 1845–1849)
★ The first dark horse candidate, Polk was nominated on the eighth ballot at the Democratic Convention at Baltimore (1844), as a compromise candidate against opponents of former President Van Buren and Lewis Cass.
★ President and Mrs. Polk were the first White House residents to ban dancing and drinking at the presidential mansion; even at their inaugural ball all such festivities stopped until the president and his devout Presbyterian wife left the party.

ZACHARY TAYLOR (1784–50) (served 1849–1850)
★ Taylor, who died from probable sunstroke after less than a year and a half in office, was the first president to openly despise politics, and the first who *never* voted in a presidential election.

MILLARD FILLMORE (1800–74) (served 1850–1853)

. . Fillmore is the first president who had no really interesting firsts in his life or career.

FRANKLIN PIERCE (1804–69) (served 1853–1857)

★ The first out-and-out alcoholic president, Pierce literally drank himself to death after the death of his three sons and his fanatically religious, near-insane wife, Jane. Fortunately, his worst drinking came after his tenure in the White House. It was said he was "the hero of many a well-fought bottle."

JAMES BUCHANAN (1791–1868) (served 1857–1861)

★ In a doggedness worthy of Richard Nixon, Buchanan sought the presidential nomination three times ('44, '48, '52) before finally clinching it—and winning—in 1856, making him the first and only candidate to win after three unsuccessful tries.

★ The first and only lifelong bachelor president, Buchanan is possibly the first homosexual president. During his term, Washington gossip linked him with Vice-President William Rufus De Vane King, who was nicknamed "Miss Nancy."

ABRAHAM LINCOLN (1809–65) (served 1861–1865)

. . The first president to be assassinated: April 15, 1865, at Ford's Theatre, by John Wilkes Booth.

. . The first Republican president: The party had been formed in the early 1850's, with John Frémont as its 1856 candidate.

. . The first major American leader to advocate extending the vote to women. In 1832 Lincoln, then a state legislator in Illinois, gave a newspaper a statement endorsing "female suffrage."

ANDREW JOHNSON (1808–75) (served 1865–1869)

. . The first president never to attend school. Johnson was a tailor's apprentice and tailor in his youth and teens, and was illiterate when he married at eighteen; his wife taught the future President to read and write.

. . The first president to be impeached by the House and tried by the Senate for misconduct; the House voted to try Johnson by a vote of 126 to 47, but Johnson was found not guilty by the Senate by vote of 35 to 54.

. . The first president to make all his own clothes: Johnson never lost his tailoring skills, and in fact was quite proud of his sewing.

ULYSSES S. GRANT (1822–85) (served 1869–1877)
★ The first West Point graduate to become president, Grant had graduated near the bottom of his class.
★ The first heavy smoker, Grant polished off upward of twenty cigars a day. He also died of throat cancer.

RUTHERFORD B. HAYES (1822–93) (served 1877–1881)
★ The first president to win by one vote (185 to 184) in the electoral college; at the last minute, 19 disputed votes were awarded to Hayes by the college, giving him a controversial win.

JAMES GARFIELD (1831–81) (served 1881)
★ Our first left-handed president.

CHESTER A. ARTHUR (1829–86) (served 1881–1885)
★ The first president born outside the United States. Two towns in Vermont claim to be Arthur's birthplace, but recent research supports his opponents' charges that he was born in Canada, and therefore not eligible to be president under the Constitution.
★ Arthur was the first to totally redecorate the White House (not counting the restoration after the fire of 1812). After auctioning off twenty-four carts of historically irreplaceable furniture from previous administrations, Arthur had the executive home redone in high Victorian clutter, which included the first "modern" tiled bathroom in the White House.
★ Arthur was also the first Phi Beta Kappa president.

GROVER CLEVELAND (1837–1908) (served 1885–1889 and 1893–1897)
★ The first and only president to be reelected after leaving office, hence the two numbers he is allotted in the chronology of Presidents.
★ The first president to be married while in office, Cleveland's bride was Frances Folsom, age twenty-one, the daughter of Cleveland's deceased law partner. On her father's death, Miss Folsom had become Cleveland's ward (at age eleven!), until she became his wife ten years later.
★ The first president to have cancer surgery, in 1893 (while in office). A portion of Cleveland's upper jaw was removed when a cancerous growth was discovered in the roof of his mouth, and a hard rubber artificial jaw was fitted for him. Surprisingly, be-

cause of the financial crash of '93, the operation was kept secret, to maintain the public's confidence in the presidency, and the president's secret surgery wasn't revealed until 1917.

BENJAMIN HARRISON (1833–1901) (served 1889–1893)
★ During Harrison's term, the White House was electrified. The marvel of electric lighting so baffled and frightened the Harrisons that they were afraid to touch the light switches, fearing they would get a shock. As a result, lights were often left blazing around the clock, with the presidential couple sound asleep in their brilliantly lit bedroom.

WILLIAM McKINLEY (1843–1901) (served 1897–1901)
★ The first president with an epileptic wife. Mrs. McKinley, who was scarcely fit for the rigors of public life, was kept constantly by the side of her devoted husband, who showed utmost concern for her well-being—where other men in his position would have found it easier to have her under professional nursing care.

THEODORE ROOSEVELT (1858–1919) (served 1901–1909)
★ The first cowboy president. Teddy, by far the greatest outdoorsman ever to inhabit the White House, worked as a cowboy on a ranch in the Dakota Territory while in his late twenties, in part to forget the tragic early death of his first wife. In addition to cowpoking, Roosevelt was an ardent camper, hiker, hunter, and fisherman, and his great interest in the outdoors led directly to the creation of the first national park, Yellowstone, during his presidency.
★ Roosevelt was also the first president to leave the continental United States during his term of office, when he traveled to Panama in 1906. However, he doesn't get credit for being the first to visit foreign soil in office, since the United States had seized Panama from Colombia in 1903, and at the time of Teddy's visit the country was a U.S. Protectorate.

WILLIAM HOWARD TAFT (1857–1930) (served 1909–1913)
★ The first and only man to hold the two highest offices in the U.S. Government: president from 1909–13 and chief justice of the Supreme Court from 1921 to his death in 1930.

★ The first president to weigh over 300 pounds. Though there have been numerous chief executives on the beefy side (including Roosevelt and Cleveland), to Taft goes the honor of being the first *really* fat president, weighing 325 pounds at the time he took office. He installed a now-famous bathtub in the White House, capacious enough for four average-size men.

★ Taft was also the first president in office to visit foreign soil, when he met with Mexican president Porforio Diaz in 1909.

★ Taft was the first in a long line of what have become presidential traditions: the first to play golf, the first to throw out the first ball of the baseball season, and the first to have a car provided at Government expense.

Ball one: William Howard Taft throws out the first ball of the season, June 10, 1911—inaugurating a presidential tradition.   THE BETTMANN ARCHIVE, INC.

WOODROW WILSON (1856–1924) (served 1913–1921)

★ Though predecessors had done postgraduate studies—usually in law—Wilson was the first president to hold a Ph.D. degree (in political science), from Johns Hopkins, 1885.

★ When Wilson suffered a paralytic stroke on September 26, 1919, his (second) wife, Edith Bolling Galt Wilson, became the de facto president of the United States. All her stricken husband's decisions were channeled through Edith, and the machinery of government, denied access to the president, had strong suspicions that many decisions were made by Mrs. Wilson, and that some documents may even have had *her* signature. Mrs. Wilson continued in her position of unofficial power practically until her husband left office early in 1921. Ergo: She was the first woman president.

WARREN G. HARDING (1865–1923) (served 1921–1923)

★ The first president to speak over the radio, at the Minnesota State Fair, September, 1920.

★ The first president to have had serious nervous breakdowns. The future leader of the nation suffered not one, but five mental collapses while in his twenties and early thirties, and spent time in sanitoriums while recovering.

★ The first president rumored, at least in his hometown of Corsica (Blooming Grove), Ohio, to have had black blood in his ancestry.

★ The first president rumored to have been poisoned by his wife. Florence Kling DeWolfe, known as "The Duchess," was a cold, forbidding woman, and it was no secret that she and Warren had a difficult marriage, and that he sought more congenial female companionship elsewhere. When Harding died suddenly in San Francisco while on a goodwill tour (August 2, 1923), rumors sprang up that Florence had slipped him poison. The fact that she forbade an autopsy didn't help dispel the talk.

CALVIN COOLIDGE (1872–1933) (served 1923–1929)

★ The first president born on the Fourth of July.

★ The first president with known Indian blood in his veins, though many generations back. One of the most famous photographs of the taciturn Cal shows him wearing an Indian feather bonnet.

HERBERT HOOVER (1874–1964) (served 1929–1933)

★ The first president born west of the Mississippi, in West Branch, Iowa, August 10, 1874.

★ The first president to enter office a self-made millionaire. Starting as a mining engineer, Hoover spent twenty years building a business fortune estimated at 4 million dollars at the time he took the oath of office.

FRANKLIN DELANO ROOSEVELT (1882–1945) (served 1933–1945)

★ The first and only president to serve more than two terms.

★ The first to leave the United States during wartime, when he conferred with Winston Churchill at Casablanca, Morocco, in January, 1943.

★ The first to host a foreign monarch—George VI and Queen Elizabeth of England, who spent the night at the White House.

★ The first to appoint women to high administrative posts: Frances Perkins, Secretary of Labor, and Ruth Bryan Owens, minister to Denmark.

★ The first and only crippled president, F.D.R. contracted polio in 1921 at age thirty-nine, and for the rest of his life depended on crutches and wheelchairs to get about. His persistence in a political career despite the handicap was and is seen as a strong contributing factor to his great popularity.

HARRY S TRUMAN (1884–1972) (served 1945–1953)

★ "Give 'em Hell, Harry" was the first though, regrettably, probably not the last president to authorize the use of atomic weapons in warfare: the bombs dropped on Hiroshima and Nagasaki, August 6 and August 9, 1945.

DWIGHT D. EISENHOWER (1890–1969) (served 1953–1961)

★ The first president to appear on national television (Roosevelt had appeared on early, nonpublic TV), the first to have a press conference covered by movie and television cameras (January 19, 1955), and the first to campaign for reelection on television (1958).

JOHN FITZGERALD KENNEDY (1917–63) (served 1961–1963)

★ The first president to be born in the twentieth century.

★ The first Roman Catholic president.

LYNDON BAINES JOHNSON (1908–73) (served 1963–1969)

★ The first Southern president since Andrew Johnson (both Johnsons succeeded assassinated presidents).

RICHARD MILHOUS NIXON (b. 1913) (served 1969–1974)

★ The first president to resign office, August 8, 1974; the resignation took place under imminent threat of impeachment and trial by Congress for Nixon's part in the Watergate scandal. He was also the first president to receive pardon for all crimes he might have committed as chief executive, the pardon granted by his successor Gerald R. Ford one month after Nixon's resignation.

★ The first president to visit all fifty states while in office.

★ The first to visit mainland China (1972).

★ The first born on the West Coast (Yorba Linda, California).

★ The first—as far as is known—to use the machinery of federal government to discredit, harass, and smear his opponents and their supporters for reelection.

GERALD R. FORD (b. 1913) (served 1974–1977)

★ The first president to have worked as a fashion model. In 1939, while studying law and coaching football at Yale, Ford dated Phyllis Brown, a sometime fashion model. Ford was photographed by a *Look* magazine photographer while on a ski weekend in Vermont, modeling ski clothes on the slopes.

★ In 1974, Ford said, "I am the first Eagle Scout president of the United States."

★ The first president never to have been elected to the presidency or vice-presidency. On the resignation of Spiro Agnew at the height of the Watergate affair (October, 1973), Nixon nominated Ford to be the new vice-president, and Ford was approved by Congress and sworn in by Chief Justice Warren Burger on August 9, 1974.

JIMMY CARTER (b. 1924) (served 1977–1981)

★ The first president to be born in a hospital.

RONALD REAGAN (b. 1911) (served 1981–)

★ Just for the record, the first film actor to be elected president. He is married to Nancy Davis (b. 1924), the first film actress to be first lady. Their first film together was *Hellcats of the Navy* in 1957.

FATHER OF OUR COUNTRY:
Firsts While Washington Was in Office

1. The first quorums, therefore the first official legislative sessions of the House of Representatives and the Senate, April 1 and April 6, 1789, respectively.

2. The first tariff act imposed on foreign imports to protect domestic goods and manufacturing, July 4, 1789.

3. The first Federal navigation act, imposing duty on the tonnage of vessels docking at U.S. ports, July 20, 1789.

4. The first Federal bond issue authorizing the funding of domestic and state debt, August 4, 1789.

5. Alexander Hamilton arranges the first loan by banks (in this case, New York banks) to the Federal Government, September 13, 1789. The loan was illegal according to statutes at the time.

6. The first session of the U. S. Supreme Court, February 1, 1790.

7. The first U. S. Census authorized, March 1, 1790. The results: The population of the U. S. in 1790 was 3,929,214.

8. The first patent law passed, April 10, 1790.

9. The first copyright law passed, May 31, 1790.

10. The first ten Amendments to the Constitution ratified (the Bill of Rights), December 15, 1791.

POWERS THAT HAVE BEEN:
First Holders of High Offices

WASHINGTON'S CABINET MEMBERS AND THEIR SALARIES

SECRETARY OF STATE: Thomas Jefferson (Virginia)

Department created: July 27, 1789
Assumed duties: March 22, 1790
Starting salary: $3,500
John Jay, who had held the position equivalent of secretary of state under the Articles of Confederation, acted as secretary of state at Washington's request until Jefferson assumed duties.

**SECRETARY OF THE TREASURY:
Alexander Hamilton** (New York)

Department created: September 2, 1789
Assumed duties: September 11, 1789
Starting salary: $3,500

SECRETARY OF WAR: Henry Knox (Massachusetts)

Department created: August 7, 1789
Assumed duties: September 12, 1789
Starting salary: $3,500

ATTORNEY GENERAL: Edmund Randolph (Virginia)

Post created: September 24, 1789
Assumed duties: September 26, 1789
Starting salary: $1,500

POSTMASTER GENERAL: Samuel Osgood (Kentucky)

Appointed: September 26, 1789
Starting salary: $1,500

The postmaster general and attorney general, though considered Cabinet members, did not head departments—in fact, the Post Office was a division of the Treasury Department until 1829 under Jackson.

THE FIRST SECRETARIES
OF CABINET POSTS CREATED
AFTER WASHINGTON'S TIME

SECRETARY OF THE NAVY: Benjamin Stoddert (Maryland)

Appointed by President John Adams, April 4, 1798

POSTMASTER GENERAL: William T. Barry (Kentucky)

Appointed by President Andrew Jackson, March 9, 1829

SECRETARY OF THE INTERIOR: Thomas Ewing (Ohio)

Appointed by President Zachary Taylor, March 3, 1849

SECRETARY OF AGRICULTURE:
Norman J. Colman (Missouri)

Appointed by President Grover Cleveland, February 2, 1889
(The Department of Agriculture was created on May 15, 1862, with
a commissioner at its head, who was not a Cabinet member.)

SECRETARY OF COMMERCE AND LABOR:
George B. Cortelyou (New York)

Appointed by President Theodore Roosevelt, February 14, 1903

SECRETARY OF COMMERCE:
William C. Redfield (New York)

Appointed by President Woodrow Wilson, March 4, 1913

SECRETARY OF LABOR: William B. Wilson (Pennsylvania)

Appointed by President Woodrow Wilson, March 4, 1913
(Both positions created when the former Department of Commerce
and Labor was split into two separate Cabinet departments.)

SECRETARY OF HEALTH, EDUCATION, AND WELFARE: Oveta Culp Hobby (Texas)

Appointed by President Dwight Eisenhower, April 11, 1953

SECRETARY OF HOUSING AND URBAN DEVELOPMENT: Robert C. Weaver (Washington)

Appointed by President Lyndon Johnson, January 1966. Weaver was the first black to serve in a Cabinet-level position.

SECRETARY OF TRANSPORTATION: Alan S. Boyd (Florida)

Appointed by President Lyndon Johnson, October 15, 1966

SECRETARY OF ENERGY: James R. Schlesinger (Virginia)

Appointed by President Jimmy Carter, August 4, 1977

THE FIRST SUPREME COURT

During George Washington's first term, it was his job to appoint the members of the Supreme Court, subject to congressional approval. Since Washington's term, no President has had the obvious political advantage of packing the Supreme Court with all his own choices, though many, notably Roosevelt and Nixon, have tried.

The first session of the Court began February 1, 1790, in the Royal Exchange Building on Broad Street, New York, and lasted for ten days.

FIRST CHIEF JUSTICE: John Jay, New York (1745–1829), September 26, 1789. *Salary, $4,000*

ASSOCIATE JUSTICES: *Salaries, $3,500.*

John Rutledge, South Carolina (1739–1800), September 26, 1789
William Cushing, Massachusetts (1732–1810), September 27, 1789
Robert H. Harrison, Maryland (1745–90), September 28, 1789
The first Justice of the Supreme Court to die while on the Court.
James Wilson, Pennsylvania (1742–98), September 29, 1789
John Blair, Virginia (1732–1800), September 30, 1789

FEMININE FIRSTS:
Women in Government

THE TOKEN SENATOR

In 1922, eighty-seven-year-old Rebecca Latimer Felton, a Democrat from Georgia and an outspoken suffragist, was appointed to fill a vacancy of one of her state's Senate seats, and served for the one day remaining in the term: November 21–22, making her the first woman in the Senate. On her appointment, Mrs. Felton—who had been appointed by the Georgia governor to appease women voters angered by his antisuffrage sentiments—said, "There are now no limitations upon the ambitions of women." She died in 1930 at the age of ninety-four.

MADAME PACIFIST

Jeannette Rankin, born in 1880 in Missoula, Montana, found herself the first woman elected to Congress in 1916—four years before American women were given the right to vote in national elections. Montana, however, had given the vote to women in state elections: Ms. Rankin won on the strength of her peace and women's rights platform. One of the most famous and ardent pacifists in American political history, she was the only member of Congress to vote against the entry of the United States into World War I. Her pacifist stand was a factor in her failure to be reelected, but she did win a second term many years later—in 1941—when she was once again the only member of Congress to vote against the entry of the United States into World War II.

A MIND OF HER OWN

After Rebecca L. Felton's token nomination to the Senate, it was a decade before Hattie Wyatt Caraway became the first woman to be elected into the Senate. The wife of an Arkansas senator, she was appointed to serve the remainder of her husband's term on his death in 1931—but only after promising the governor who appointed her that she wouldn't seek reelection. However, Mrs. Caraway changed her mind, ran for reelection, and won, in 1932. In the Senate, under the guidance of mentor Huey Long of Louisiana, she went on to become the first woman to chair a Senate committee, to preside over Senate sessions, and the first to conduct Senate hearings. Mrs. Caraway was elected three terms and was finally unseated by J. William Fulbright in 1944.

MINORITY BREAKTHROUGH

A former schoolteacher and day-care worker, Shirley Chisholm was elected to the House of Representatives from New York State in 1968, the first black woman in either house (there still has not been a black woman senator).

ANOTHER MINORITY BREAKTHROUGH

On January 4, 1965, Patsy Mink, Democrat of Hawaii, and of Japanese-American descent, became the first woman of a racial or ethnic minority to sit in the House of Representatives. She was elected for three terms, during which time she sponsored important legislation for equal rights for women, including the Women's Educational Equity Act of 1974.

THE FIRST FORMER FILM ACTRESS ELECTED TO CONGRESS

Though film folks who go into politics have a mixed record, there is no doubt about the success of Helen Gahagan Douglas (1900–80), who served as Democrat representative from California from 1945 to 1951, when she was defeated by Richard M. Nixon with a "soft-on-communism" smear campaign. She was an ardent and influential supporter of important New Deal, NATO, Marshall Plan, and civil liberty programs.

HEADS OF STATES

Two women were elected governors of their states on the same election day in 1924, thus sharing title of first woman elected governor: Nellie Taylor Ross (1876–1977) of Wyoming and Miriam A. "Ma" Ferguson (1875–1961) of Texas. Both followed their husbands into office, but for widely different reasons. Mrs. Ross's husband, William B., died while in office, and Democratic party leaders persuaded his widow to run for office. She reluctantly accepted, did no campaigning, and won largely because of the sympathy vote. She later went on to become the first woman director of the U.S. Mint (1933–1953).

"Ma" Ferguson, on the other hand, won because her husband, James Edward, elected to the Texas governorship in 1914 but impeached and removed from office for corruption in 1917, was still immensely popular with the poor tenant and independent farmers whose causes he championed. Husband James was barred from running, but "Ma" Ferguson ran in his place, took the election, and served three terms—not consecutive—with it an open secret that James really wielded the power behind the throne.

Mrs. Ross gets the title of first woman governor in office by a hair because she was inaugurated three weeks before Mrs. Ferguson.

IN NO MAN'S FOOTSTEPS

When she took office on January 8, 1975, Ella Tambussi Grasso of Connecticut became the first woman governor of a state whose husband had not previously held the same office. Governor Grasso

151

resigned on December 31, 1980, after fighting a losing battle with cancer, and died on February 5, 1981.

THE PIONEER

Kate Barnard, born in 1875 in Geneva, Nebraska, was elected Commissioner of Charities and Corrections for the State of Oklahoma in 1907, and reelected in 1910, making her the first woman ever elected to a statewide office. A champion of pension, prison, and labor reform, she retired in 1914.

A BLACK WOMAN PIONEER

Crystal Bird Fauset (1894–1965), Pennsylvania Democrat, was elected to that state's legislature in 1938, making her the first black to sit in any state house.

MY MOTHER THE MAYOR

A wife and mother of four, with a master's degree in social work, Janet Gray Hayes beat out six male opponents to become the mayor of San Jose, California, in January, 1974, the first woman to head a large city.

THE LIBERAL LABOR SECRETARY

Franklin D. Roosevelt appointed Frances "Ma" Perkins (1880–1965), a native of Boston, as secretary of labor (she was sworn in March 4, 1933), making her the first woman Cabinet member in history. She remained secretary of labor until Roosevelt's death in 1945, when she resigned. Among legislation she shepherded into law: unemployment, child labor, maximum hour and minimum wage controls, workmen's compensation, Social Security.

GAY AND PROUD

In 1974, twenty-eight-year-old Elaine Noble, the daughter of a miner who worked her way through college and Harvard graduate school to become an ardent community activist, became the first publicly declared homosexual to win election to any state office. Describing herself as "a candidate who was gay, not a gay candidate," Ms. Noble had strong support from the elderly in her district, whose interests had been of special concern to her.

OVERSEAS DUTY

On December 5, 1922, Lucile Atcherson Curtis (b. 1894) became the first woman in the Foreign Service when she passed the Service examinations and was assigned to the State Department's Latin Affairs division.

FOREIGN AFFAIRS

On April 13, 1933, Franklin Roosevelt appointed Ruth Bryan Owen as minister to Denmark, making her the first woman foreign minister. Mrs. Owen (1885–1977) was also the first congresswoman from the Deep South and the daughter of William Jennings Bryan.

MADAME AMBASSADOR

President Truman appointed Eugenie Moore Anderson (b. 1909, Iowa) as first woman ambassador in U.S. history; she was ambassador to Denmark from 1949 to 1953.

LUCIDITY

Playwright, author, war correspondent, congresswoman, and political activist, Claire Boothe Luce was appointed U. S. ambassador to Italy by President Dwight Eisenhower; she served from March, 1953 to December, 1956.

AT THE COURT OF ST. JAMES'S

Anne L. Armstrong (b. 1927, New Orleans), Republican party worker and former counselor to President Nixon, was named by Gerald Ford as ambassador to Great Britain and Northern Ireland, and sworn in February 19, 1976, the first woman to receive the prestigious diplomatic post.

MIND YOUR MANNERS

After a highly successful career as a child film star (she was the first child to amass a million dollars from professional earnings), an unsuccessful bid for Congress (1967), and a term as U.S. ambassador to Ghana (under Nixon), Shirley Temple Black was the first woman named chief of protocol, by President Ford in 1975, while still assigned to Ghana. During her tenure as chief, she was responsible for entertaining heads of state visiting Washington.

A SPECIAL CASE: *The First (Known) Former Bordello Madam Elected Mayor of a U. S. City.*

Sally Stanford (née Marcia Busby, in Oregon), pursued a varied career as a bootlegger and speakeasy operator in Ventura County, California, during the 1920's before becoming legendary as Madam Sally Stanford (she picked up the name from the university, which undoubtedly supplied a good part of her clientele), owner of a famous San Francisco bordello. Sally retired in 1949 (San Francisco was "too full of squares") to nearby Sausalito, where she opened the Valhalla restaurant—a very "legit" establishment. Sally began getting involved in local politics, sponsored the Little League team, gave instruments to the school marching band, ran for city council seven times, and finally, was elected mayor in 1972 at age seventy-two.

Said Sally when elected, "I should have run for President of the United States. At least there's some dough in it."

Madame Mayor has a heart of gold: Sally Stanford, the first former bordello madam to be elected mayor of a town. Here, Miss Stanford is shown with a prize steer, Mr. Pettijohn, that she bought for her customers in 1953. Mr. Pettijohn was destined not for the bordello, which had already been closed at this point in Miss Stanford's career, but for her restaurant in Sausalito, California, the town that elected her mayor in 1972.   WIDE WORLD PHOTOS

FIRST WOMEN IN A MAN'S WORLD

ELIZABETH BLACKWELL, PHYSICIAN

When Elizabeth Blackwell (1821–1910) decided that she was bored with schoolteaching and wanted to become a doctor, she was able to gain the knowledge to qualify for medical school only by becoming governess for various doctors' families and reading in their medical libraries in her spare time. One doctor gave her encouragement and, after eleven rejections, she was finally accepted by Geneva Medical College in New York in 1848. The faculty, who had admitted her only because of her former employer's reputation as a doctor, let the student body vote on Elizabeth's acceptance. They apparently did so as a joke.

Ms. Blackwell was a capable student and received her degree in 1849, though only after considerable debate by the faculty. Unfortunately, she was rejected by all American hospitals and was forced to go to Paris and England for work and study.

In 1851 she returned to New York to open a practice, but even had difficulty in finding someone to rent her office space. She was finally forced to buy her own house and set up a small practice, which expanded in 1857 to become the New York Infirmary for Women and Children. The infirmary was the first hospital in the world with an all-female staff and which allowed women medical students to take internships.

The *Boston Medical Journal* wrote in 1849, when Blackwell received her degree, "It is to be regretted that she had been induced to depart from the appropriate sphere of her sex and led to aspire to honors and duties which, by the order of nature and the common consent of the world, devolves alone upon men."

ARABELLA MANSFIELD, ATTORNEY

Born in 1846 in Iowa, Belle Mansfield graduated from Iowa Wesleyan in 1866, then apprenticed along with her brother; she passed the bar exam in 1869 with high honors, but would not have been admitted to the bar because of a clause stating that "any white male person" was eligible to practice law. Fortunately, a liberal judge ruled the wording invalid, and Belle was admitted to the Iowa bar. She never practiced law, however, and confined her work to legal scholarship until her death in 1911.

MARGARET HICKS, ARCHITECT

Ms. Hicks (1858–83) received her degree in architecture in 1880 from Cornell University, though she had already had one of her designs, a "Workman's Cottage," published in a professional journal. Her career was cut short by death at age twenty-five. (In 1975 the Task Force on Women in Architecture reported that only 1.2 percent of registered architects and 3.7 percent of all practicing architects are women.)

MAGGIE LENA WALKER, BANK PRESIDENT

In Richmond, Virginia, in 1903 Maggie Lena Walker became the first woman—and first black woman—president of a bank, the St. Luke Penny Savings Bank. Ms. Walker had been the secretary-treasurer of the Grand United Order of St. Luke, a fraternal organization founded in 1867 by an ex-slave to provide proper health care and funeral services for blacks; when the United Order formed a bank in 1903, she became its head, and remained so until 1929, when it was absorbed by Consolidated Bank and Trust Company, of which she became chairwoman of the board.

ANNA MAE HAYS AND ELIZABETH P. HOISINGTON, U.S. ARMED FORCES GENERALS

On June 11, 1970, two women acheived star rank for the first time in the 196 years the U. S. Army had been in existence. Anna Hayes, who started out as an operating-room nurse during World War II, and who served as Eisenhower's nurse during his 1956 heart attack, was named Brigadier General in the Army Nurse Corps. The same day, Elizabeth Hoisington received the same rank in the Women's Army Corps, where she had served since 1942 as an enlisted woman.

ANTOINETTE L. BROWN, ORDAINED MINISTER

On September 15, 1853, Antoinette Brown was ordained in the Butler, New York First Congregational Church, after graduating from Oberlin College in 1850. Related by marriage to the first woman doctor Elizabeth Blackwell, Reverend Brown mothered six children; wrote ten books; traveled to the Holy Land in her seventies to get water from the River Jordan to baptize her grandchildren; went to Alaska on a missionary trip, also while in her seventies; and lived to a ripe ninety-six, when there were an estimated three thousand women ministers in the United States.

KATHERINE SWITZER, MARATHON RUNNER

In 1967 Ms. Switzer was the first woman to run the famous Boston Marathon, though she was able to do so only by registering as K. Switzer because officials wouldn't allow women to register. During the race officials attempted to tear the number from her back, and she was so hindered by them that she was forced to run alongside the track for most of the route. The result of her run was a ruling by the Amateur Athletic Union—which had previously allowed women to compete in distance races among themselves—threatening women who ran in races with men with disqualification from *all* running events. It was a five-year battle for Ms. Switzer to become the first woman to run officially in the 1972 marathon: Today literally thousands of women routinely enter—and complete—the grueling marathon races.

MARION BERMUDEZ, GOLDEN GLOVES BOXER

If male resistance to competing with women has been strong in sports in general, it's been nowhere as strong as in contact sports. Yet in the 1975 Golden Gloves boxing tournament in Mexico City, Marion Bermudez, age twenty-three, won her first match against a male opponent. Ms. Bermudez is also a U. S. national karate champion, and has won against male opponents in that sport as well.

FIRST FAMILIES:
The Road to Riches

THE ASTORS

John Jacob Astor (1763–1848) was born in Heidelberg, Germany, the son of a butcher. When he was sixteen (the family butcher business not holding much promise) he went to London to work with his older brother who manufactured flutes. After four years there, the youth moved to New York, where he was going to peddle his brother's English-made flutes. Instead, he decided, at the age of twenty-two, to get into the fur business, and began traveling up the Hudson, then the major trade route for the rich American fur trade. John Jacob spent the next forty years establishing for himself a virtual monopoly on the fur trade in the American Northwest. He not only cornered the fur market, but cultivated lucrative and powerful friendships with presidents and politicians—Thomas Jefferson, for example, allowed an Astor ship laden with furs to trade with China during the embargo of 1807—and Astor brought back a neat profit of $200,000. By 1834 Astor switched interests, and bought up huge chunks of undeveloped real estate on the outskirts of New York City. As a result, he found himself the largest single owner of property in what is now midtown Manhattan.

J. J., described by a contemporary as "a self-invented money making machine," left at his death what was a vast fortune in 1848 dollars: 20 million worth, making him the richest man in America.

THE VANDERBILTS

Cornelius Vanderbilt was born in 1794, the son of a Staten Island farmer. Young Vanderbilt received only a rudimentary education before "dropping out" at age sixteen to ferry passengers from Staten Island to Manhattan with a boat he had purchased. Within two years he had three boats; by the age of thirty he had ferries, steamships, and freight boats plying waters in the New York area. By the time he was fifty-six, he had a fast passenger service from New York to California, via Nicaragua—a service that is reputed to have made him 10 million dollars alone. During and after the Civil War he expanded into railroads—with great success, of course, due to lucrative passenger and government business. By his death in 1877, the farmer's son was worth a staggering 100 million dollars and the Vanderbilt name was synonymous with wealth and social prestige.

THE MORGANS

Junius Spencer Morgan, born in 1813 in West Springfield, Massachusetts, started his career as a dry-goods clerk in Boston while still a boy. Within a few years he had become a partner in a mercantile firm in Hartford, Connecticut. He became so successful in the dry-goods business that George Peabody, a successful Yankee merchant, asked Junius to join his private banking firm in London. This marked the turning point in the Morgan fortunes: By the time of the Franco-Prussian War in 1870, the Peabody bank had become J. S. Morgan and Company, and the former dry-goods clerk was in a position to lend 50 million dollars to the French Government, the largest bank transaction up to that time.

But old Junius's accomplishments paled in comparison to his son J. P.'s, who joined the firm after his education: J. P. turned the Morgan bank into the most powerful banking interest in the world. In 1895, he acquired 65 million dollars in gold for the U. S. Government so that the hard-pressed Treasury wouldn't have to stop redeeming paper money in bullion. Even more spectacular, in 1901 he masterminded the creation of U. S. Steel, the first billion-dollar corporation in the world.

THE MELLONS

Thomas Mellon was born in 1813 into a Scottish-Presbyterian family of modest means on a twenty-three-acre farm in County Tyrone, Northern Ireland. When young Thomas was five his father moved the family to America to join relatives who had emigrated earlier, and they settled in the ironically named town of Poverty Point, Pennsylvania.

Thomas had a slow road to travel to wealth. He worked his way through college at Western University, then taught school while still helping in the fields on the family farm. He worked awhile in a lawyer's office while studying for his own law degree, and became an attorney in 1839. By 1849 he had managed, by being extremely frugal, to amass fifteen hundred dollars, which he invested in real estate. His careful investments paid off, and by the 1860's he'd made a small fortune in coal. By 1870, he was able to found a private banking house, T. Mellon and Sons, which prospered under his son, Andrew W. Mellon. Old Thomas died in 1908 at the age of ninety-five; today his fifteen-hundred-dollar nest egg has become a family fortune estimated (as of 1978) to be in excess of 5 billion dollars.

THE CARNEGIES

Andrew Carnegie was born in 1835 in Dumfermline, Scotland, the son of a poor linen weaver. When mechanized weaving brought hard times to the cottage industries of Scotland, the Carnegie family emigrated to Allegheny, Pennsylvania, where Andrew's father continued in the weaving business. Young Andrew got his first job as a bobbin boy in a textile mill. He earned $1.20 a week. When he was fourteen, Carnegie went to night school to learn to be a bookkeeper —while still working as a bobbin boy. He got his first taste of the business world as a telegraph boy, delivering messages to businesses; by 1851 he got a raise from $2.50 to $3.00 a week when he became a telegraph operator. (He incidentally became one of the first telegraph operators in the world who could understand Morse code by ear, rather than taking it down in dots and dashes and then translating.) By 1852 Carnegie had become a secretary and telegrapher for the Pennsylvania Railroad for $35.00 a month. By 1859, when he was twenty-four, he was a railroad superintendent and was in a position to make some investments in iron manufacturing by 1864.

A year later he was able to resign from the railroad and devote full time to investments Eight years later, In 1878, he was already acquiring steel firms, having recognized the country's growing need for steel. By 1900, when Carnegie was sixty-five, Carnegie Steel Company was producing one-fourth of all steel in the United States—not to mention controlling interest in related areas: iron mines, coke ovens, railroads, and ore ships. In 1901 Carnegie sold out to Morgan's U.S. Steel merger—for a neat 250 million dollars—and retired to devote himself to his favorite philanthropies: libraries and concerts.

THE FORDS

Henry Ford, the man who was to revolutionize world industry, was born on a farm near Dearborn, Michigan, in 1863, the son of Irish immigrants. Henry attended school until he was fifteen, when he dropped out to work as a machinist's apprentice in Detroit. In his spare time he disassembled and reassembled watches, fascinated by their mechanics. By the time he was twenty-five, the mechanically minded Ford was an engineer for the Edison Company in Detroit. By 1899, Ford had gotten interested in the automobile and joined in with several partners to form a custom-car manufacturing company, the Detroit Automobile Company. By 1903 Ford was ready to start his own firm, and got backers to launch the Ford Motor Company, capitalized at $100,000. The first Model T was introduced in 1908, and made automotive history. By 1927 Ford had built 15 million Model T's, and the company had a cash surplus of 700 million dollars. By the time Ford died in 1947, the Ford empire was worth billions.

THE ROCKEFELLERS

John Davison Rockefeller was the son of a peddler, born in Richford, Tioga County, New York, in 1839. In 1853 the family moved to Cleveland, where young J. D. attended high school before getting his first job as a clerk and bookkeeper. When Rockefeller was twenty, the first oil well was drilled in Titusville, Pennsylvania, and by the age of twenty-four, he had joined with two partners in forming an oil refining company. By 1870, the company was operating the larg-

The beautiful rich: John D. Rockefeller, Sr., the first billionaire, celebrating his 90th birthday. If each candle on the cake were worth 10 million dollars, they still wouldn't equal a billion bucks.   THE BETTMANN ARCHIVE, INC.

est refinery in Cleveland, and in the same year was capitalized as the Standard Oil Company. By 1879, Standard Oil, through aggressive and ruthless expansion, controlled 90 to 95 percent of all the oil refined in the United States. During the last decade of the century, Rockefeller was fighting antitrust battles, and in 1899 formed Standard Oil of New Jersey, capitalized at 110 million dollars, but that too was subject to antitrust suits and dissolved in 1911. Nevertheless, by 1911, J. D. Rockefeller had amassed the largest personal fortune in the United States, valued at 1 billion dollars, making him the first billionaire.

After his retirement in 1911, J. D. gave an estimated 600 million dollars to charities and philanthropies, a process which the family has continued to this day—by 1955 it was estimated that the Rockefeller family had given away endowments and charities worth an estimated 3 billion dollars.

AWARD-WINNING FIRSTS

THE NOBEL PRIZE

It is not recorded if any recipient has ever described this, the most famous and prestigious award in the world, as "Dynamite!", but that would not be an unapt description, for it was the vast fortune amassed by Alfred Nobel (1833–96), the Swedish chemist who invented dynamite in 1866, which endowed the Nobel Prize Fund.

The first Nobel prizes were given in 1901 in five areas (the amount of the prize varies from year to year). The first winners were: *Peace,* Jean H. Dunant, the Swiss founder of the International Red Cross, and Frederic Passy, founder of the first French peace organization; *Chemistry,* Jacobus van't Hoff, the Dutch chemist who discovered the laws of chemical dynamics and osmotic pressure; *Physics,* Wilhelm Roentgen, the German discoverer of X rays; *Physiology and Medicine,* Emil A. von Behring, the discoverer of antitoxin treatments for diphtheria and other diseases; *Literature,* René F. A. Sully-Prudhomme, French poet, for his *Stanzas and Poems.*

The first woman to win the Nobel prize, and the first person to win it twice, was the great Marie Curie of France, who shared the 1903 prize in Physics with her husband, Pierre, and colleague A. H. Becquerel for their discovery of radioactivity (a term she coined). She also became the first person to win two Nobel prizes in 1911 when she received the Chemistry prize for the isolation of pure radium.

The first American to win the prize was Albert A. Michelson, who received the Physics award in 1907 for his work in optical measure-

166

ments and spectroscopic phenomena. Michelson, however, was German born, and it wasn't until 1914 that Theodore W. Richards became the first native-born American to be honored. He received the Chemistry prize for his work on atomic weights.

The first American woman winner was Gerty T. Cori, who shared the 1947 prize in Physiology and Medicine with her husband, Carl. Mrs. Cori was born in Czechoslovakia. The first native-born American woman to be honored was Rosalyn S. Yalow, who received the 1977 prize in Physiology and Medicine (along with two male associates) for the discovery of the radioimmunoassay.

THE PULITZER PRIZE

Joseph Pulitzer (1847–1911), publisher of *The New York World,* endowed the prizes bearing his name beginning in 1917. The prizes are made by Columbia University in New York based on recommendations by a prize committee. The first prizes were awarded in 1917 for reporting, editorial writing, American history writing, and biography, but over the years numerous categories have been added.

The first years' (1917) winners were:
Reporting: Herbert Bayard Swope of *The New York World*
Editorial Writing: New York Tribune
History: J. J. Jusserand, *With Americans of Past and Present Days*
Biography: Laura E. Richards and Maude Howe Elliott assisted by Florence Howe Hall for *The Life of Julia Ward Howe.*

The most familiar awards to the public are those given for Fiction and Drama (the committee gives preference to those dealing with American themes), though the familiarity is in part because the award is used by publishers and producers to stimulate book and ticket sales.

The first winners in these categories (1918) were:
Fiction: Ernest Poole for the novel *His Family.*
Drama: Jesse Lynch Williams for *Why Marry?*

THE MISS AMERICA CONTEST

The most famous beauty pageant was dreamed up in 1921 by the city fathers of Atlantic City as a gimmick for prolonging the tourist season past Labor Day, and to that end they staged a modest contest

There she is: Margaret Gorman, the 16-year-old, 108-pound bathing beauty who took the first Miss America title in 1921.   THE BETTMANN ARCHIVE, INC.

with only eight contestants who represented cities instead of today's states. The first Miss America was Margaret Gorman, Miss Washington, D.C. Miss Gorman, who stood five feet one inch tall and weighed 108 pounds, measured 30-25-32 and had blond hair and blue eyes. She was sixteen years old.

Though she was supposed to be star of the affair, most of the attention in the press went to King Neptune, the first version of Bert Parks. The king, complete with sea-god costume and flowing beard, was Hudson Maxim, heir to the armaments fortune, who no doubt aroused fantasies of fame, fortune, and advantageous marriage in the minds of the young hopefuls.

And now for the evening gown competition: Contestants in the 1923 Miss America contest strut their stuff. At the far right, looking a bit left out, is the first winner, Margaret Gorman, who took the title in 1921.

THE BETTMANN ARCHIVE, INC.

The first contest of any size was the 1924 extravaganza, when eighty-three misses competed in swimsuit and evening gown events (talent above and beyond looking pretty wasn't a requirement in those simpler times), and the *Atlantic City Press* was moved to write, "The girls are exposed to grave dangers from unscrupulous persons, and the shocking costumes which such contests encourage certainly call for protests from organizations interested in girls' welfare."

FIRST VICTIMS:
Kind and Usual Punishment

THE GUILLOTINE

The "terrible swift sword" of the French Revolution was, contrary to popular belief, merely *proposed* by Dr. Joseph Ignace Guillotin. The actual mechanism was designed by an officer of the Academy of Surgery, Dr. Antoine Louis, and was built by Tobias Schmidt, a German harpsichord maker. Schmidt tested the invention on cadavers at the Hôpital Bicêtre, and then on live sheep in the alley outside his shop. Once the preliminary tests gave positive results, it fell to a highwayman named Pelletier to be the first live, human victim of the guillotine, on April, 1792, in the Place Greve in front of the Hotel de Ville, Paris.

During the revolution, 2,498 souls fell before the swishing steel of the guillotine; the doctor whose name was given to the machine died in 1814 (of natural causes), complaining that his name had been given unjustly to "Schmidt's machine."

THE ELECTRIC CHAIR

The electric chair was invented by Harold P. Brown, working with Dr. A. E. Kennelly, the chief electrician on Thomas Edison's Menlo Park (New Jersey) research staff. "The chair" was tested extensively on animals prior to the first human execution. According to eyewitnesses, animals who failed to succumb to the electric current were

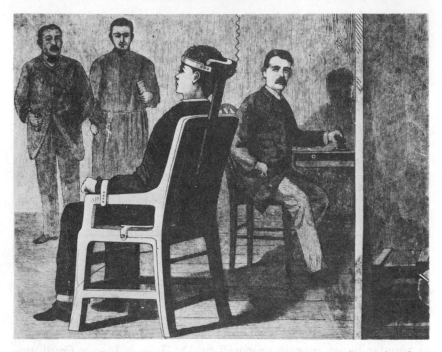

Future shock: Though the first electric chair execution wasn't to take place until 1890, tabloid readers were being shown the wonders of modern penology several years in advance, as this 1888 illustration demonstrates.

THE BETTMANN ARCHIVE, INC.

eventually killed with a brick blow to the head. On August 6, 1890, at Auburn Prison, Auburn, New York, William Kemmler, a convicted murderer, may have wished for a brick to be smashed over his head: Once he was strapped in the chair, the first burst of current failed to kill him, and he was still breathing after the current had been turned off for several minutes; a second dose of electricity finally did Kemmler in, but not until after Kemmler had thrashed about, convulsed, and had had the flesh on his head and extremities burned off where the electrodes came in contact. The whole process took eight minutes.

The animals electrocuted by Brown in 1890 were not the first to be killed by electricity, however. In 1773 Benjamin Franklin wrote in a letter that he had used six Leyden jars for the successful electrocution of a ten-pound turkey, a lamb, and a quantity of chickens.

THE GAS CHAMBER

Major D. A. Turner of the U.S. Army Medical Corps was responsible for developing the "gas chamber" wherein a poisonous gas could be introduced into a sealed compartment containing a doomed prisoner. In comparison with the electric chair, the gas chamber fulfilled its humanitarian intentions. The first guinea pig, Gee Jon, a Chinese convicted of a Tong gang killing, only took *six* minutes to expire due to hydrocyanic (cyanide) gas poisoning on February 8, 1924.

VICTIMS AND VOLUNTEERS:
Deaths Which Were the First of Their Kind

THE FIRST CHRISTIAN MARTYR

The disciple James, who led the early Christians in Jerusalem after Christ's death, became the first martyr in A.D. 62 when he was stoned to death at the instigation of the anti-Christian priests.

THE FIRST DEATH OF THE AMERICAN REVOLUTION

On February 22, 1770, an anti-British mob attacked the Boston home of Ebenezer Richardson because of Richardson's support of a merchant friend who had been importing British-made goods despite a merchant's boycott. One of the mob was eleven-year-old Christopher Snyder, who was shot and killed by Richardson when the besieged man fired on the crowd. Richardson served two years in jail. The famous Boston Massacre took place a few days later, when three members of a patriot mob were killed by British sentries; one of the dead was Crispus Attucks, the first black to die in the Revolution.

THE FIRST DEATH OF THE CIVIL WAR

On April 12, 1861, the first shots were fired on Fort Sumter, South Carolina, by Confederates, and thirty-four hours later Union commander Major Anderson surrendered without a single casualty on either side. During the Confederate celebration ceremonies a fifty-gun salute was fired, and on the fiftieth round a spark caused an explosion, killing gunner Daniel Hough.

WORLD WAR I

On June 28, 1914, fifty-one-year-old Archduke Francis Ferdinand of Austria and his wife were assassinated by Gavrilo Prinzip, a tubercular high school student, as they rode through Saravejo, Serbia. Serbian terrorists hired Prinzip, and war officially began one month later, when Austria declared war on Serbia.

THE FIRST AMERICAN DEATHS IN WORLD WAR II

The first U. S. deaths weren't at Pearl Harbor—but more than a month before, on October 31, 1941, when a German U-boat torpedoed the U. S. destroyer *Reuben James* in the North Atlantic, with the loss of 100 lives.

THE FIRST DEATH OF THE COLD WAR

On August 25, 1945, Captain John M. Birch, a Baptist missionary and Army intelligence expert, was killed by Communists in Anwei Province, China. The first victim of the cold war had his name perpetuated by Robert Welch, founder of the right-wing John Birch Society.

LAND OF THE FREE, HOME OF THE BRAVE:
A Quiz

1. Which of the following countries was the first to abolish slavery?
   Great Britain
   Argentina
   Mexico
   Brazil
   United States
   Colombia

2. Which of the following countries was the first to give women the right to vote in national elections?
   Finland
   New Zealand
   Russia
   Canada
   Australia
   United States
   Great Britain

3. Which of the following countries was the first to abolish the death penalty?
   United States
   Great Britain
   Russia
   New Zealand
   Finland

4. Which of the following countries was the first to legalize compulsory sterilization—castration of criminals and undesirables?
Germany
United States
Russia

ANSWERS: If you answered United States to any of the questions except the last, you were wrong. The countries are as follows:

(1) Argentina, 1813; Colombia, 1821; Mexico, 1829; Great Britain, 1833; United States, 1863; Brazil, 1889.

(2) New Zealand, 1893; Australia, 1902; Finland, 1906; Canada, 1917; Russia, 1917; United States, 1920 (Wyoming gave women the right to vote in state elections in 1896. They could vote for governor, but not for President.); Great Britain, 1928.

(3) Russia, 1826 (Czar Nicholas I proclaimed capital punishment illegal, but it was reinstated in 1936 for "crimes against the state"); New Zealand, 1936; Finland, 1949 (though there hadn't been an execution since 1824); Great Britain, 1965; United States, 1972. On June 29, 1972, the Supreme Court ruled that capital punishment was illegal because it was, in practice, being imposed both arbitrarily and inconsistently on the state and federal levels. This voided all death penalties on the books, but left the way open for states to write new death penalties into their law books. There have been several much-publicized executions since 1972, notably that of Gary Gilmore in Utah in 1979.

(4) Indiana was the first state to have an effective judicial castration law, from 1904 until ruled unconstitutional in 1921; Kansas Territory as early as 1855 provided a punishment of castration for a black or mulatto male who raped, attempted to rape, or attempted to marry (!) a white woman. Germany didn't pass their eugenics law until 1933; and Russia has had no sterilization laws.

FARAWAY
FIRSTS

Where have I been?: Plennie Wingo, "Mr. Backwards," the first man to walk across America in reverse, is seen here, in his seventies, during his backward walk down U.S. 1 from San Francisco to Santa Maria, California.

FAR CORNERS, AND WHO SAW THEM FIRST

It's perhaps a good indication of the western European chauvinist mind that literally hundreds of places—in fact, the bulk of the earth —were "discovered" and "claimed" (usually for financial gain) by explorers when in fact there had been men living there for thousands of years. But the Columbuses and Da Gamas get all the credit, and not the nameless aborigines who really were there first. Here's a list of some remote places that Europeans "found"—and the Europeans who found them.

NORTH AMERICA

Visited ca. A.D. 1000 by Norse Vikings who sailed from their outposts in Iceland and Greenland to places they called Helluland, Markland, and Vinland—probably Labrador, Nova Scotia, Newfoundland, and (perhaps) New England. During 1960–63 Norwegian archaeologists discovered a settlement in northern Newfoundland which indicated a Norse culture, and which was carbon-dated to ca. A.D. 900.

THE WEST INDIES

The first voyage of Christopher Columbus (with about eighty-eight men) arrived at San Salvador, Bahamas, October 12, 1492, then sailed to Hispaniola and Cuba.

SOUTH AMERICA

On his third voyage, in 1498, Columbus arrived in Trinidad, then saw the South American mainland for the first time on August 1, 1498. Columbus thought it was an island, but changed his mind on reaching the mouth of the Orinoco River (Venezuela), on August 14. He made the first landing on the continent at the Gulf of Paria (between Trinidad and South America) on Sunday, August 5, 1498, though he still thought he was on an island.

DAYTONA BEACH AND KEY BISCAYNE, FLORIDA

Juan Ponce de León, who had voyaged years before with Columbus, set out in 1513 from the colonial outpost at Puerto Rico to search for the fabled fountain of youth, which, as rumor had it, was most effective in restoring the vigor of Indian chiefs who visited it. As historian Samuel Eliot Morison points out, Ponce wanted "a cure for *el enflaquecimiento del sexo,* and hoped to find it in the land to the north. Ponce's first landing was on April 3, 1513, at an inlet near modern Daytona Beach; after the disillusionment of not discovering the fount, he sailed with his men south past the Gold Coast and stopped at what is probably Key Biscayne, where they tried the spring water once again, and found it good only for quenching thirst."

MEMPHIS, TENNESSEE

Hernando de Soto, who had dreams of building a Spanish vice-royal empire for himself comparable to those of Mexico and Peru, decided, in 1538, that his fame and fortune lay in the interior of the land known after Ponce de Leon's journey as Florida. De Soto, who, like many Spanish conquistadores, considered Indians to be less than human, and who, according to one companion, killed them for sport, arrived in Florida on May 25, 1539, and spent three years hacking and killing his way across the southern United States, aided by 570 men and 223 horses. He arrived at the Chickasaw Bluffs below Memphis, where his expedition built barges and crossed the Mississippi, and made it as far as the junction of the Arkansas and Canadian rivers in present-day Oklahoma. De Soto's empire was to come to naught, for he died of a fever at the mouth of the Red River in 1542, and his name would be remembered not so much for his exploration of the Mississippi as for the automobile namesake of another era.

NEW YORK HARBOR

The site of the greatest city of the twentieth century was first discovered on April 17, 1524, by Italian explorer Giovanni da Verrazano, sailing up the coast from his exploration of Cape Hatteras and the Carolina coast. Anchoring in the narrows now spanned by the bridge bearing his name, Verrazano described "a very pleasant place, situated among certain little steep hills; from amidst which hills there ran down into the sea a great stream of water, which within the mouth was very deep. . . ." After being greeted by natives who rowed out "making great shouts of admiration" and sailing farther up, he saw what is now upper New York Harbor (minus the skyline that would dominate the setting four hundred years later). He was forced by an unfavorable wind to depart without setting foot on land.

CALIFORNIA

Juan Rodriguez de Cabrillo sailed up the coast of California for Spain in 1542, and crossed the present-day international boundary between Mexico and the United States on September 27. On his sail north he stopped at the harbor of what was to become San Diego, went past the Santa Catalina islands, missed the Golden Gate, and stopped at the modern Drake's Bay, and possibly as far north as Bodega Bay. Cabrillo and his men were the first to see the famous Big Sur coast, which he described as "bold, and the mountains very high."

EASTER ISLAND

The remote and mysterious island, 2,200 miles off the coast of Chile, was discovered on Easter Sunday, 1722, by Dutch navigator Jakob Roggeven. The grassy, windswept island was inhabited by about 4,000 natives of Polynesian stock; their ancestors had erected the famous monolithic statues carved from volcanic rock, weighing up to fifty tons, many of which had been carried over long distances to their sites. The Europeans introduced smallpox, which, by 1887 (with a little help from the Spanish slave trade), had reduced the island's population to 100 people.

LHASA, THE FORBIDDEN CITY

According to John Macgregor in *Tibet: A Chronicle of Exploration,* the first Westerner to see the fabled "forbidden city" high in the Himalayas was one Friar Oderic, who was sent by Rome in 1327 to look for the legendary kingdom of Prester John, a Crusader who conquered the Infidels and set up a Christian colony in the East. Though Prester John was a tall tale, Oderic's journey to find him did lead him through India and through the Himalayas to "the chief and royal city, Lhasa . . . built with walls of black and white, and all its streets are well paved. In this city no one shall dare to shed the blood of any, whether man or beast." Oderic was the last to see Lhasa for three hundred years.

THE GRAND CANYON

First seen in 1540 by a Spanish overland expedition led by García López de Cardenas. The first man to navigate the length of the canyon by boat was the American John W. Powell and his party in 1869. Powell had lost one arm at the battle of Shiloh, and weighed a scant 110 pounds.

THE NORTH POLE

Robert Edwin Peary, a naval engineer who made a name for himself with his pioneering exploration of Greenland and the Arctic during the 1890's, made his first attempt to reach the Pole by sled team during 1898–1902, but he only reached a latitude of 84° 17′ N. His second attempt was in 1905–6, when he got within 175 miles of his objective before being forced back. Peary finally made it on his third try, on April 6, 1909, when he, his black assistant Matthew A. Henson, and four Eskimos reached the top of the world. On his

On top of the world: Matthew A. Henson, little known Arctic explorer who was with Admiral Peary and two Eskimos on the first expedition to reach the North Pole, April 6, 1909. Henson, shown here at age 88 with his wife and President Eisenhower, explored the Arctic for two decades.   WIDE WORLD PHOTOS

return, Peary found that Frederick A. Cook, a physician and fellow explorer who had been with him on an 1891–2 expedition, claimed to have reached the Pole in April, 1908. Peary immediately accused Cook of fraud, and the controversy got sensational coverage. Cook, who also claimed to have scaled Mount McKinley in 1906 after several attempts, was generally discredited, and his McKinley claim was proven false. He later went to jail for an oil-field swindle in Texas, but swore to his dying day that he got to the Pole before Peary.

THE SOUTH POLE

Like the North Pole, the Antarctic pole became a headlong race between rival explorers. Norwegian explorer Captain Roald Amundsen, who had lost out to Peary for the North Pole honors, was being challenged in the Southern Hemisphere by British Captain R. F. Scott. After establishing a base at the Bay of Whales on the Ross Ice Shelf, Amundsen left with four companions on October 19, 1911. The Amundsen group crossed the Ross Shelf on dog sleds, then crossed the Transantarctic Mountains via the Axel Heiberg Glacier. Amundsen was the first to see this portion of the range (now named after Queen Maud) with peaks ranging from thirteen thousand to fifteen thousand feet. Amundsen then crossed the South Polar Plateau and reached the South Pole for the first time on December 14, 1911. The Norwegian flag was planted at the Pole.

While Amundsen was crossing the ice shelf on sleds in his all-out race for the Pole, another team was crossing the frozen waste, heading for the same barren spot: the expedition of Captain Scott, destined to be the second man at the South Pole, but the first of the tragic polar heroes.

Scott's third, and last, expedition, departed from the British base on Ross Island in October. The five men in the group had all the makings of media heroes: young, handsome, adventurous, setting out to conquer one of nature's last virgin places. Adding fuel to the fire was the competition from the Norwegian group.

Scott made one very proper decision for his journey—and one that may have cost him his life: As on his earlier trips, Scott was concerned with gathering scientific data along the way. Amundsen, on the other hand, streamlined his team to cover as much territory in as little time as possible. Scott unwisely chose to take ponies instead of dog teams to pull his sleds. The ponies, though capable of withstanding the extreme temperatures, had to carry their own food with them. Pack dogs, on the other hand, *are* their own food, since Eskimos—or explorers—on long winter trips gradually butcher the teams to feed the remaining animals and themselves.

Scott, with Dr. E. A. Wilson, Lieutenant Bowers, Captain Oates, and Petty Officer Edgar Evans reached the Pole on January 17, 1912, almost a month after Amundsen. They found the Norwegian tent still intact. The disheartened team, already exhausted from a difficult journey, began the long trek back to Ross Island. En route, they were overtaken by a blizzard. Oates and Evans died first, followed by Wilson, and Bowers around March 29. The bodies were found on November 12, 1912—a mere eleven miles from a supply base. With them Scott's diary was found, which recorded the tragic journey up to the last entry, when Scott knew that all was lost.

BOUVET

The remotest island in the world is the Norwegian Dependency of Bouvet, an uninhabited speck in the South Atlantic (54° 26′ S., 3° 24′ E.) which was sighted on January 1, 1739, by Pierre Bouvet and first landed on by Captain George Norris of Britain on December 16, 1825.

LAKE VICTORIA AND THE SOURCE OF THE NILE

The Victorian British had a mania for finding African sources, and no quest was more assiduously pursued than finding the beginning of the world's longest river. The source of the Blue Nile was identified as Lake Tana as early as 1770 by Scottish explorer James Bruce, but the source of the longer White Nile eluded explorers until 1858 when Britisher John Speke became the first European to see Lake Victoria, the largest lake in Africa, located in the highlands of east-central Africa. Speke predicted that Victoria was the principal source of the Nile, but it wasn't until a second expedition that he found the outlet from the lake (July 28, 1862) which he named Ripon Falls, which proved to be the beginning of the Nile itself. (The farthest headwater of rivers feeding the lake, and therefore the remotest source of Nile water, is the Luvirondi River of Burundi.)

TIMBUKTU

For centuries Timbuktu was to Europeans a kind of African El Dorado, synonymous with mystery, wealth, magnificence, and remoteness. The actual city began as a Tuareg seasonal camp in the eleventh century, and the site became an important trading center for the Mali-Saharan area. Something of the legendary magnificence of Timbuktu was dissipated in 1827 when Frenchman René Caillié (1799–1838) became the first European to reach the city and return alive.

FOOTLOOSE:
Remarkable First Walks

PREHISTORIC MAN

Without doubt the first, and greatest marathon walk was made by prehistoric man. About 5 million years ago, *Australopithecus,* the apelike ancestor of man, began living on the ground and using tools in Africa. By a million years ago *Australopithecus* had walked from Africa to Europe and even Asia; in the meantime he had evolved to *Homo erectus,* developed a brain of 1,000 cc. (twice what he'd previously had), and learned to use more sophisticated tools, fire, and probably even language. By 75,000 years ago *Homo erectus* had evolved into early *Homo sapiens* and had walked into and settled vast areas of Africa, Asia, and Europe. By 50,000 to 25,000 years ago, when he had evolved into fully modern man, *Homo sapiens* had already walked across the Bering Strait land bridge into North America and all the way south to Tierra del Fuego. Though it took a million years to get from East Africa to the tip of South America, man's first great walk around the globe in search of food and shelter is an impressive feat: literally millions of miles covered on foot, with no highways, maps, or motels.

CABEZA DE VACA, PART I

In 1528 a Spanish exploration expedition under Pánfilo de Narvaéz arrived on the west coast of Florida, probably at Tampa Bay, where hostile conditions and Indians quickly put an end to most of the Spaniards. Among the survivors was the expedition's treasurer, Alvar Núñez Cabeza de Vaca (ca.1480–1557), who, with a group of 246 surviving companions, sailed across the Gulf of Mexico in barges they made, hoping to get to the safety of Mexico City. Along the way the men's barges were shipwrecked on what is probably Galveston Island, where the unfortunate Cabeza and the only three survivors were enslaved by the local Indians. In 1533, after four and a half years of slavery, Cabeza and his three companions, including Estevanico, a black, made good their escape and walked over one thousand miles across the totally uncharted American Southwest desert, through present-day Texas, New Mexico, and Arizona. The mammoth walk took three years, most of it made totally without clothing. It's little wonder that the three whites (Cabeza was a brawny redhead) and one black gained a reputation among the Indians along their route as gods. By the time the walkers had reached New Mexico, word of their almost messianic powers traveled ahead of them, and they were often followed for great distances by hundreds of curious and faithful Indians, who put great stock in the power of these strangers' prayers.

Cabeza and crew were the first Europeans to see the interior of North America, the first to see buffalo, and the first to see the pueblos of the Southwest Indians.

They finally reached the northern Spanish outpost of Culiacan, Mexico, in 1536. Cabeza, his years as a wandering Indian shaman over, wrote his account of the journey in 1542, and contributed to the myth of the Seven Cities of Cibola that spurred much of the Spanish settlement of the American West.

CABEZA DE VACA, PART II

In 1540 Charles V of Spain appointed hardy old Cabeza de Vaca, now past sixty, as governor of La Plata, the region of modern Paraguay and Argentina he was colonizing. With three ships, four hundred men, and forty-six horses, he arrived on the coast of Brazil at Santa Catarina Island. Cabeza realized that the roundabout route to Asunción, his new capital on the Paraguay River in modern Paraguay, by way of the Paraná River and Buenos Aires, was difficult and time-consuming. So he decided that he and his men should walk across southern Brazil. The six-hundred-mile trip took four months and nine days. The men had to walk the route since horses were needed to carry supplies; they had to build rafts to cross many of the major and minor rivers, including the Iguacu and Parána; in one day alone the men had to build eighteen bridges to cross streams and valleys. Only one man drowned during the journey, when he fell overboard, and no horses were lost. One of the most remarkable sights was the enormous Iguacu Falls, larger than any in Europe. What is remarkable about Cabeza de Vaca's second journey—besides his age at the time—is his success in crossing for the first time unknown territory. Part of the reason for his success was that unlike most of his conquistador countrymen, de Vaca had the ability to deal tactfully with the local inhabitants—a talent that had saved his life in Texas and his expedition in Brazil.

THE FIRST MAN TO WALK 100,000 KILOMETERS

In 1910 the Touring Club de France sponsored a 100,000-kilometer (62,137 miles) walking race. Of the two hundred entrants, only one completed the race: Dimitru Dan (born July 13, 1890, in Rumania). Beginning April 10, 1910, he walked an average of 27 miles a day to complete the race in 1916.

THE FIRST TO WALK AROUND THE WORLD

On June 10, 1970, two brothers, David and John Kunst, set out from Wanseca, Minnesota, to circumnavigate the globe on foot. In 1972, John was killed by bandits in Afghanistan; his brother continued the journey and arrived back in Wanseca after a walk of 14,500 miles on October 5, 1974.

An American, George M. Schilling, was reported to have walked around the world in the 1890's, but the trip has not been verified.

THE FIRST WOMAN TO WALK ACROSS AMERICA

In 1960 Dr. Barbara Moore (née Anya Cherkasova, USSR), a health enthusiast who publicized her ideas through walking marathons, walked across the United States at age fifty-six, the first woman

These heels are killing me! In the 1920's, Jacob Wissman left Berlin in an attempt to walk around the world in women's high heels. Though his sign proclaims hopefully "In women's shoes around the world," Wissman didn't complete his epic journey.   THE BETTMANN ARCHIVE, INC.

known to have done so. Along the way, Dr. Moore encountered bad weather, police harassment, and being hit by a car.

Dr. Moore had been an engineer in Russia after the revolution, and the former USSR women's long-distance motorcycling champion. She emigrated to England in 1939 and became a British citizen.

THE FIRST MAN TO WALK ACROSS AMERICA AND EUROPE BACKWARD

Plennie Wingo (b. 1895, Abilene, Texas), the most famous exponent of walking backward, reached the height of his fame as "Mr. Backwards" during the flagpole-sitting and marathon-dancing years of the twenties and thirties. On April 15, 1931, he began his backward walk from Santa Monica, California, across the United States, then across Europe to Istanbul, Turkey—a total distance of more than 8,000 miles—arriving on October 24, 1932. Mr. Backwards used special rear-view mirrored glass to see where he's going.

MOUNTAIN HIGH:
The First Footsteps
on Some of the Tallest Peaks in the World

MOUNT EVEREST (Himalayas, Northeast Nepal)
29,028 FEET, HIGHEST POINT ON EARTH

On May 29, 1953, a British expedition led by Colonel (later Honorable Brigadier) Henry Cecil John Hunt became the first to reach the highest point on the earth's surface when Sir Edmund Hillary, a New Zealander, and the Nepalese Sherpa Tenzing Norgay reached the summit of Everest at 11:30 A.M. The eighty-day ascent required 362 porters and 10,000 pounds of baggage. News of the success reached Queen Elizabeth II on the eve of her coronation.

Ten earlier expeditions had failed, including a Swiss one in 1952 which got within only 150 feet of the summit before being forced back by bad weather.

On June 28, 1924, George Leigh Mallory, a veteran of earlier attempts, and Andrew Irvine, an Oxford student, were the first to die attempting Everest when they disappeared in a swirl of snow at the 28,230-foot level.

The first woman to climb Everest was Junko Tabei, member and deputy leader of an all-woman Japanese expedition, who reached the summit on May 16, 1975. Mrs. Tabei, who stands four feet eleven inches and weighs ninety-four pounds, describes herself as "just a housewife."

Ninety-seven-pound weakling: Mrs. Junko Tabei, ninety-four-pound house-wife and the first woman to climb Mount Everest. WIDE WORLD PHOTOS

K-2, CHOGORI, OR GODWIN AUSTEN MOUNTAIN
(Karakoram Range, Northern Kashmir)
28,250 FEET, SECOND HIGHEST PEAK

The first attempt was made in 1902 by a party of Swiss, British, and Austrian climbers who were forced back at the 21,000-foot level.

In 1954 an Italian team under Ardito Desio, a professor of geology at the University of Milan, reached the summit. The well-equipped team, with eleven climbers, six scientists, and five hundred porters (many of whom deserted) reached camp 8 at 25,000 feet. The summit team, Achille Compagnoni and Lino Lacodelli, reached the peak on July 31, in spite of running out of oxygen on the final leg.

KANCHENJUNGA I (Himalayas, Eastern Nepal)
28,208 FEET, THIRD HIGHEST PEAK

In 1905 a Swiss-French-British expedition made the first attempt to climb "the Five Treasures of the Snow." At their 20,000-foot camp an avalanche killed four climbers, forcing the expedition to turn back.

On May 25, 1955, a small British party led by Charles Evans got within seven feet of the summit—considered to be a successful conquest of the mountain. The summit team of Joe Brown and George Band could have reached the top, but the Sikkimese Government had objected to the climb because they consider the peak sacred. By mutual agreement, the Sikkimese allowed the climb as long as the expedition did not actually touch the topmost point of the mountain. The two men considered their climb a mountaineering—and diplomatic—success seven feet from the top, when it was obvious that the peak could easily have been reached.

LHOTSE I (Himalayas, on Tibet-Nepal Border)
27,923 FEET, FOURTH HIGHEST PEAK

On May 18, 1956, an expedition under Albert Eggler of Switzerland, sponsored by the Swiss Foundation for Alpine Research, reached the peak; the summit team members were Ernst Reiss and Fritz Luchsinger.

195

MAKALU I (Himalayas, Northeast Nepal)
27,824 FEET, FIFTH HIGHEST PEAK

The first attempt on Makalu (known as the armchair peak because of its cleft summit), was made in 1954 by a Sierra Club expedition under William Siri. They reached the 23,000-foot level. On May 15, 1955, Jean Couzy and Lionel Terray of the French expedition under Jean Franco reached the summit; the other members of the group climbed to the summit the following day.

DHAULAGIRI I (Himalayas, Northern-Central Nepal)
26,795 FEET, SIXTH HIGHEST PEAK

In 1802 Robert Colebrook, surveyor-general of Bengal, determined that Dhaulagiri, or "White Mountain," was over 25,000 feet in height—the first mountain known to be higher than those in the Andes. On May 13, 1960, a team of twelve led by Max Eiselin, a sportswriter, reached the summit. They were the first Himalayan expedition to use a plane in the assault. The plane, after a series of mishaps which nearly aborted the expedition, finally succeeded in dropping supplies at 16,000 feet.

MANASLU, OR KUTANG I (Himalayas, Western Nepal)
26,768 FEET, SEVENTH HIGHEST PEAK

On May 9, 1956, a Japanese expedition led by sixty-two-year-old Yuko Maki reached the summit. The group of twelve climbers and four hundred porters encountered resistance from villagers at the mountain's foot, who feared the climb would anger the mountain god.

CHO OYU I (Himalayas, Northeast Nepal)
26,750 FEET, EIGHTH HIGHEST PEAK

The first attempt was in 1952, by Eric Shipton and party, who reached 22,500 feet. On October 14, 1954, an Austrian group—Dr. Herbert Tichy, Joseph Joechler, H. Heuberger, and Sherpa Pasang Dawa—were successful, and without the use of oxygen equipment. Only Heuberger didn't reach the summit.

NANGA PARBAT, OR DIAMIR (Western Massif of Himalayas)
26,660 FEET, NINTH HIGHEST PEAK

British pioneer mountaineer A. F. Mummery tried to climb Nanga Parbat as early as 1895, but turned back on the final assault when his Gurka companion became ill.

The first successful climb is one of the great feats of mountaineering endurance. In 1953, a German expedition—two earlier ones had failed in 1934 and 1937—was in the final stages, with a two man "summit team" nearing the top. When Herman Buhl found that his companion was suffering from severe lethargy due to oxygen deprivation, he left his tent alone as 2:30 A.M. and made the final seventeen-and-a-half-hour ascent alone. By the time he reached the summit (July 3), he had discarded his rucksack with food and supplies, taken off his warm outer clothing to lessen his load, and crawled to the top on his hands and knees along the 14,000-foot precipice of the south face of the mountain.

ANNAPURNA I (Himalayas, Central Nepal)
26,546 FEET, TENTH HIGHEST PEAK

The conquest of Annapurna remains one of the great feats of mountaineering. It was the first "eight-thousander" to be conquered—that is, the first peak over eight-thousand meters—and it was conquered on the first attempt, though not without tremendous risk. In 1950 a French expedition under Maurice Herzog took on the giant, and the summit team of Herzog and Louis Lachenal, a professional guide, set up their final camp at 24,300 feet. They reached the summit June 3, but on the descent the two were caught in a sudden snowstorm. Herzog lost his gloves, and Lachenal at one point slipped and fell 300 feet down the sheer mountain face. Lachenal was rescued by Lionel Terray, from camp 5, but the full force of the storm had not abated, even after the two were rescued by the rest of the team: On the final descent, the party was both lost and caught in an avalanche. By the time they had reached safety, Lachenal had lost his toes to frostbite, and Herzog all his fingers and toes.

Annapurna's treachery was not confined to the first expedition, however. In 1978 an American team of thirteen women—the first American all-woman team to conquer an eight-thousander—

197

reached the summit on October 15. On the descent, two climbers, Vera Watson and Alison Chadwick-Onyszkiewicz, who were roped together, fell down a 1,500 slope to their deaths.

CERRO ACONCAQUA (Cordillera de Los Andes, Argentina)
22,835 FEET, HIGHEST IN SOUTH AMERICA

The first attempt on Aconcaqua, the highest peak in the Western Hemisphere, in the Andes near the Chilean border, was made in 1883 under German Alpinist Paul Güssfeldt. His party was forced back by storms only 1,300 feet from the summit. The first to reach the top was Matthias Zurbriggen of Switzerland in 1897.

MOUNT McKINLEY (Alaska Range, Alaska)
20,320 FEET, HIGHEST IN NORTH AMERICA

The first Westerner to see Mount McKinley was British explorer George Vancouver in 1794; the natives called it *Denali,* Home of the Sun. In 1896 W. A. Dickey of the United States reached the edge of the ice fields on the mountain, naming the peak for then-presidential candidate William McKinley. The first scaling attempt was in 1903 under Judge Wickesham of Fairbanks, but the first successful climb came in 1913 under Archdeacon Hudson Stuck, along with Harry Karstens, Robert Tatum, Walter Harper, and two Indians from the missionary school, Johnny and Esaias.

MOUNT KILIMANJARO (Tanzania)
19,565 FEET, HIGHEST IN AFRICA

Located in what was formerly Tanganyika, near the Kenya border, "The Mountain of Cold Devils" was "discovered" by missionaries Johannes Rebmann and Ludwig Krapf in 1848. The higher peak, Kibo, was climbed first in 1889 by Dr. Hans Meyer of Germany.

ELBRUS WEST PEAK (Caucasus Range, Northwest Georgia, USSR)
18,481 FEET, HIGHEST IN EUROPE

The lower peak of volcanic Elbrus (18,356 feet) was first climbed in 1868 by Douglas Freshfield, A. W. Moore, and C. C. Tucker of Britain. The higher peak was conquered in 1874 by F. Crawford Grove, F. Gardiner, Horace Walker, and Peter Krubel.

VINSON MASSIF (Ellsworth Mountains, Antarctica)
16,860 FEET, HIGHEST IN ANTARCTICA

On December 20, 1966, a team of ten men led by Nicholas Clinch, a thirty-six-year-old lawyer from Los Angeles, climbed the last remaining unconquered continental high point. The expedition, sponsored by the National Geographic Society and the American Alpine Club, was made up of three scientists and seven mountain climbers. All ten reached the peak: Clinch, Peter K. Schening, Elichi Fukushima, Brian Marts, Richard Wahlstrom, James Corbet, Dr. Samuel Silverstein, William E. Long, John P. Evans, and Charles Hollister, all of the United States.

A SPECIAL CASE: THERE'S MONEY IN MONT BLANC

On July 14, 1808, Maria Paradis of Chamonix, Switzerland, became the first woman to climb France's 15,771-foot Mont Blanc, the second highest peak in Europe. Maria made the climb on the suggestion of mountaineer Jacques Balmat, who said, "Climb the mountain with us and then visitors will come and see you and give you money." She took his advice, and later set up a stall at the foot of the mountain where the curious could come and visit the woman mountain climber —for a fee. Said Maria many years after, "Thanks to the curiosity of the public I have made a nice profit out of it, which is what I intended to do."

FAR OUT:
Astronomical Firsts

WHICH WAY TO POLARIS, JACK?

Hipparchus, a Greek astronomer, is credited with making the first star map in 134 B.C. after seeing a new star appear in the constellation Scorpio. He hoped his map would make it easier for future stargazers to spot new sky happenings.

LIGHTS OUT

The first recorded total solar eclipse occurred in China, October 22, 2137 B.C.: The two royal astronomers Hi and Ho were drunk and neglected to frighten away the dragon that had eaten the sun, for which negligence they were beheaded by Emperor Chung K'ang.

NOT WITHIN WALKING DISTANCE

Ancient astronomers had attempted to measure the distance of stars by using the trigonometric method of parallax, which had given them decent values for the distance of the sun, and for the diameter of the Earth. However, they had no concept of the immense vastness of space, and the minute measurements required for measuring the parallax of stars was wa-a-ay beyond their instruments.

In 1838, three astronomers, working independently, each mea-

200

sured with reasonable accuracy the distance of a star. They were Friedrich Bessel of Königsberg Observatory, Germany, who gave a distance of less than 11 light-years for 61 Cygni. Thomas Henderson, Astronomer Royal of Scotland, gave a figure of 4.3 light-years for Alpha Centauri; in Russia, F.G.W. von Struve announced a figure of 27 light-years for Vega.

For the first time, man knew that space was very big, indeed.

SO BIG YET SO SMALL

In 1845 the third Earl of Rosse, an amateur astronomer of some means, built the world's largest telescope on his estate in Ireland. The earl's reflecting telescope had a seventy-two-inch metal mirror, and was suspended between two ivy-covered stone walls. The telescope revealed that what had appeared to be stars in other telescopes were actually glowing spiral objects. Ross did not realize, however, that these tiny spiral objects were galaxies, each as large as or larger than our own, each with hundreds of millions of stars.

FASTER THAN A SPEEDING BULLET

In 1675, Ole Roemer of Denmark noticed that satellites of Jupiter were eclipsed by the giant planet at irregular intervals—when Jupiter was closest to Earth the eclipses came too soon, and vice versa when Jupiter was at its farthest point. Roemer understood, of course, that the light was taking longer or shorter times to reach Earth, and by careful measurement and calculation he was able to estimate the actual speed of light. His answer was 186,000 miles per second—an amazingly accurate figure for 1675: The modern value is 186,282.397 m.p.s. The figure was so astonishingly high that Roemer didn't believe his own calculations.

FIRE IN THE SKY

In A.D. 1054 Chinese and Japanese astronomers recorded the sudden appearance of a new, remarkably bright star in the sky. We know today that it was a supernova—a star that, in a one-day explosion, can increase in brightness up to one million times. The remnants of the 1054 explosion are today's Crab Nebula.

GALILEO'S MANY FIRST SIGHTINGS

When Galileo turned his newly built telescope on the Italian sky in 1609 (see: "Better Mousetraps"), he saw more things for the first time than almost any astronomer since. To wit: the mountains of the moon; the rings of Saturn (which puzzled him); the "invisible" Pleiades (six stars of the constellation are visible to the naked eye, but Galileo saw forty in his telescope). In 1610 Galileo spotted three satellites of Jupiter, and in 1611 he observed for the first time sunspots and stars in the Milky Way.

COME AGAIN

In 1705, English astronomer Edmund Halley realized that the comets which were recorded in 1531, 1607, and 1682 were one and the same, and predicted that it would appear again in 1758. Halley died in 1742, but his prediction came true on Christmas Day of 1758, and the heavenly wanderer was duly named after him. Halley's comet last appeared in 1910, and it's due again in 1986.

VENICE ON MARS

In 1659 the Dutch astronomer-physicist Christian Huygens noticed that the planet Mars had markings on its surface. In 1877 Italian astronomer Giovanni Schiaparelli discovered narrow, regular lines crossing the Martian desert, and named the markings *canali*. The public—and some astronomers—soon came up with all sorts of fanciful ideas about the origins of these "structures," though Schiaparelli himself never suggested that they were anything other than natural features. We now know there are no canals on the red planet, and the "canals" are structural features of the planet's crust.

SPACE ROCKS

The first sighting of an asteroid came when Sicilian astronomer Giuseppe Pazzi discovered a 623-mile-diameter asteroid, which was named Ceres, on January 1, 1801. There are now estimated to be forty thousand asteroids in the great belt between Mars and Jupiter.

THE FIRST PLANET TO BE "DISCOVERED"

Until 1781 the solar system consisted of six planets: Mercury, Venus, Earth, Mars, Saturn, and Jupiter. In that year William Herschel, a young musician who studied the heavens through a telescope in his spare time, was enjoying his nightly "review of the heavens" when he noticed a strange disc. Herschel thought it was a comet, but when he showed the disc to other astronomers, they realized the amateur had discovered the first new planet in man's history. The planet, 1.7 billion miles from Earth, was named Uranus. George III gave Herschel a pension as a reward, and he settled down to a lifetime of stargazing. Among other things, Herschel was also the first to show the arrangement of stars in the Milky Way.

IT'S GOT TO BE THERE SOMEWHERE

Once Uranus was discovered, it was studied closely, and astronomers noticed certain irregularities in its orbit. In 1834, the Reverend T. J. Hussey, an astronomer and the rector of Hayes, Kent, theorized that the presence of yet another planet was causing the irregularities. Astronomers then worked out theoretically where the distant, "invisible" planet should be, and on August 4, 1846, Professor James Challis picked up the planet through a telescope. The new planet was named Neptune.

WHITE DWARF—THE DARK COMPANION

In 1834 Bessel, one of the first to measure star distances with accuracy, noticed that Sirius, the Dog Star, had irregular motion which could only be accounted for by an unseen body. In the case of Sirius, a large star, the "dark companion" (as it became known) would have to be at least as massive as our own sun to exert such a strong gravitational force on Sirius.

In 1862 Alvan Clark, an American astronomer testing a new telescope, became the first to see Sirius's dim companion star. The new star, Sirius B, nicknamed the Pup, turned out to be the first in a series of unusual kinds of stars that astronomers were to discover in the next century. Sirius B is a very small, dim, but massive star. Only 24,000 miles in diameter (smaller than Jupiter, Saturn, or Uranus), it has as much mass as our sun—867,000 miles in diameter. A matchbox full of Sirius matter would weigh fifty tons on earth. This type of star, known as a white dwarf, results when a medium-size star, like our sun, evolves through a red giant stage, burning up its fuel, leaving a cold, dense, dying core.

FAST AND HEAVY

In 1939 J. Robert Oppenheimer (who also did important work on the first atom bomb) demonstrated mathematically how a star somewhat larger than our sun could, under certain conditions, implode, that is, suddenly collapse into a superdense body, smaller and denser than a white dwarf. Such a body would be only about ten miles across, and a cubic inch would weigh *10 billion tons.* The atoms in the body would be so compressed that most of the atomic matter would have been thrown off, leaving only neutrons tightly packed together.

In 1967 the first of these neutron stars was discovered at Cambridge University when Jocelyn Bell, a graduate student, detected weak but very precise radio signals coming from a spot in space. The signals were flicking on and off at intervals of 1.33730113 seconds. When Bell presented her discovery to Anthony Hewish, head of the team, it was at first thought that an intelligence might be sending the signals. However, the signals continued at the same precise intervals for months, and the astronomers realized that they had discovered a neutron star. The small, dense body, with an intense magnetic field, was rotating extremely fast (imagine a sphere ten miles in diameter rotating once every 1.3 seconds!), and with each rotation a radio signal created by the magnetic field was being thrown our way. These pulsing radio sources were dubbed pulsars, and others were soon found. The fastest known is the pulsar in the Crab Nebula, which signals thirty-three times a second. It is also the first (and so far, only) visible pulsar, discovered by astronomers at Seward Observatory in Arizona in 1969. The object, named NP0532, is the remnant of the star which exploded creating the Crab Nebula, which was visible on Earth as the supernova of A.D. 1054.

BLACK HOLES

In 1939, when Oppenheimer did his mathematical work on neutron stars, he theorized an even more bizarre object, which would be created if a very large star—one fifty times the size of the sun—imploded. The mass of the star would be so great in an implosion that its gravitational pull would collapse it, not into a neutron star, but into a black hole. The black hole, which would be no more than forty miles across, would exert such tremendous gravitational pull that not even light could escape—hence its invisibility. Even more provocative, a black hole would literally pull matter into nothingness—a concept new to astronomers—and it has been theorized that black holes are actually holes in our universe where matter leaks into other universes, which possibly run in reverse to ours.

The first black hole was detected in 1972 in the binary star X-ray source, Cygnus X-1. The source is a massive, radiating star with a black hole companion which has a mass about ten times that of the sun, but a diameter of only 3.67 miles.

FARTHEST OUT: QUASARS

In 1963 Maarten Schmidt, a Dutch astronomer working at Mount Palomar in California, was looking for a star in the Milky Way which was believed to be a source of unusual radio signals. He found an object in the sky, but it turned out not to be a star at all, but something quite different. First of all, it was very far away—about 1 billion light-years, the most distant thing seen up to that time. Second, it was very bright—as bright as two hundred Milky Way galaxies put together (there are 100 billion stars in the Milky Way). Third, it was moving away from us very fast—almost at the speed of light.

Dubbed quasi-stellar radio source, or quasar 3C273, Schmidt's finding was only the first of many. Astronomers have now found more than two hundred quasars, and they are the most distant (and therefore, the oldest observable) objects in space. The most distant quasar was discovered in 1974, and is receding from the center of the universe at 95.5 percent of the speed of light.

GIANT LEAPS:
Firsts from Blastoff to Man on the Moon

One of the most astonishing feats in man's history is the landing of man on the moon sixty-six years after the Wright brothers' first flight, and just forty-three years after the first fuel-propelled rocket flight. Here are some milestone firsts along the way.

BLASTOFF

Dr. Robert H. Goddard (1882–1945) of the United States developed and tested the first liquid fueled rocket. Goddard's work was done primarily without outside help, and with limited funding. (The Smithsonian Institution gave him a five-thousand dollar grant.) The first test of Goddard's rocket was made in November, 1923, when a liquid fuel missile was given a static test—that is, fired while attached to a holding platform. Though the static test was successful, Goddard spent three years modifying his apparatus before conducting the first rocket free-flight, on March 16, 1926, in a field near Auburn, Massachusetts. The three-foot rocket was ignited by Goddard himself, using a blowtorch attached to a long pole. The rocket attained a height of 184 feet and a speed of 60 m.p.h. Goddard, who was accompanied only by his wife Estha and two assistants at this historic moment, decided not to publish or announce his success since his earlier work on rockets had been ridiculed severely in many newspapers.

In less than half a century, Goddard's modest rocket had given birth to the giant Saturn V, over 100 times as high as the first model, and the five thousand dollar Smithsonian grant had grown to a 50-billion-dollar United States Government space program investment.

SOVIET SURPRISE

On September 4, 1957, the world was stunned by the announcement that Russia had launched *Sputnik 1,* the first artificial satellite to orbit the earth. *Sputnik,* weighing a modest 184.3 pounds and measuring only 22.8 inches in diameter, gave the USSR the world lead in space and rocketry technology until the mid-sixties.

A lagging United States managed to get its first satellite, *Explorer 1,* into orbit on January 31, 1958. *Explorer,* a featherweight 18.2 pounds, carried instruments designed by Dr. James Van Allen. The instruments detected for the first time the intense belts of radiation which surround the earth. They were named the Van Allen belts in the good doctor's honor.

BUT IS THERE LIFE ON MARS?

The precocious Russians chalked up another first on November 3, 1957, when they launched *Sputnik 2,* carrying a female dog named Laika. Laika was the first living thing from earth to be shot into space —except for a possible germ or two on *Sputnik 1.* Laika also became the first space-race victim when she died in her 1,100-pound capsule on the sixth day, due to a faulty temperature control mechanism. *Sputnik 2* continued to orbit the earth for 162 days; it burned up on reentering the Earth's atmosphere.

FREE AT LAST

A major first in the journey to the moon came on January 2, 1959, when Russia launched *Lunik 1,* the first object to break away from the gravitational pull of the Earth. *Lunik* passed within 4,000 miles of the moon before moving on to fall into orbit around the sun— making it the first artificial planet.

THE MAN IN THE MOON GETS A PIE IN THE FACE

Humankind's first contact with the moon was less than dignified. The Soviet's *Lunik 2,* the first man-made earthly object to touch another heavenly body, smashed into the moon's surface on September 13, 1959. Since the satellite's instruments were destroyed in the crash, no data were relayed back to Earth to record man's first physical contact with the moon.

THE DARK SIDE OF THE MOON

The first satellite to orbit the moon was *Luna 3,* launched by Russia on October 4, 1959. The satellite carried a single photographic camera (with self-contained film processing equipment), which transmitted photos back to Earth. A gyroscopic system kept the camera lens oriented continuously toward the moon. After a year of orbiting, *Luna* had sent enough pictures back to Earth to enable Russian scientists to publish an atlas of the heretofore unseen dark side of the moon.

STRELKA AND BELKA, COME HOME

A major step in the space race was taken with Russia's *Sputnik 5,* launched August 19, 1960: For the first time, a live payload—in this case consisting of two dogs named Strelka and Belka—was recovered after orbiting the Earth for twenty-four hours. The animals returned safely to Earth via an ejection mechanism which pulled them from the capsule as it reentered the atmosphere and lowered them by parachute to a soft landing on the ground. The Russians continued to pioneer dry-ground landings, while the United States concentrated on ocean landings.

SPACED OUT

On April 12, 1960, the Soviets launched *Vostok 1,* a 7½-foot, 10,416-pound spherical capsule which contained Yuri Gagarin, a twenty-seven-year-old cosmonaut, the first human being to enter space and to orbit the earth. The capsule orbited the earth one time, in 89.34

seconds, and the total flight lasted only 108 minutes from takeoff at 9:07 A.M. in Tyura Tam, Kazakhstan, to touchdown at 10:55 A.M. near Smelkova, Saratov, USSR.

Gagarin became an overnight celebrity, but his fame was over-shadowed by persistent rumors penetrating the cloud of secrecy around the Russian space program. The rumors were to the effect that Gagarin had not in fact been first man in space and that fellow cosmonaut Serge Ilyushin had made a three-orbit space flight three days earlier than Gagarin, but had been hospitalized immediately after landing. The rumors were never proven or disproven.

Gagarin died seven years later in a plane crash, at age thirty-four.

OUR BOYS IN SPACE

In 1958 NASA, or the National Space and Aeronautics Administration, selected seven men to be the United States' first space travelers. The chosen few—all married men—were picked from 508 volunteers and candidates from military and civilian test pilots. They were: M. Scott Carpenter; Leroy Gordon Cooper, Jr.; John H. Glenn, Jr.; Virgil I. "Gus" Grissom; Walter M. Schirra, Jr.; Alan B. Shepard, Jr.; and Donald K. Slayton.

UNCLE SAM KEEPS UP

The first American in space—a year after Gagarin—was Alan B. Shepard, Jr., who was launched from Cape Canaveral on May 5, 1961. Shepard's flight, which arched into space and back again without achieving orbit, reached an altitude of 114 miles and a speed of 5,181 mph.

THE QUEEN OF OUTER SPACE

On June 16, 1963, the Soviets launched their *Vostok 6* carrying Valentina Tereshkova, a former textile worker, in a forty-eight-orbit flight. The first woman in space later married fellow cosmonaut Andrian Nicolavev, making them the first spacemates.

THREE'S A CROWD, COMRADE

The Russians also took honors for being the first to put more than one man at a time into space. On October 12, 1964, they launched *Voskhod 1,* carrying three men: Vladimir Komarov; Boris Yegorov (an Air Force doctor); and Konstantin Feoktiskov, a civilian scientist. The last two were the first doctor and the first civilian in space, respectively. Their flight was also the first with a pressurized cabin, enabling the three men to forego pressurized space suits and helmets.

ON RYE WITH EXTRA MUSTARD

American astronaut John Young, who made the first multimanned U. S. flight with Gus Grissom starting March 23, 1965, was the first man to eat a corned beef sandwich in space. Young smuggled the sandwich on board to supplement the usual fare of dehydrated foods. However, stray crumbs posed a threat to the capsule's complex machinery, and Young was reprimanded by NASA officials for his celestial cravings.

SHOOTING THE MOON

On January 31, 1966, Russia launched *Lunik 9,* weighing 3,490 pounds, which approached within fifty miles of the lunar surface and released a spherical landing capsule. The capsule then made the first soft-landing on the moon.

On touchdown in the Ocean of Storms (February 9), the *Lunik 9* landing capsule opened four petal-like panels to expose a camera lens, which then took three panoramic photo views of the lunar surface and transmitted them back to Earth—man's first close look at his nearest neighbor in space.

RIVER OF NO RETURN

The first man to die in space was Russian cosmonaut Vladimir Komarov. His *Soyuz 2* satellite was launched from Tyura Tam, USSR, on April 23, 1967, on a scheduled twenty-five-hour, eighteen-orbit flight. Komarov died when the parachute straps lowering the capsule to earth "became twisted and the craft descended at a great speed." Western scientists have questioned the story, however, because Russian capsules have a device which ejects cosmonauts from their capsules as they reenter the atmosphere. Komarov did not eject possibly because of equipment failure, or because the capsule overheated on entering the atmosphere.

The first official statement after Komarov's flight was "Komarov . . . is in good health and feeling well." The death was not announced until twelve hours after the crash-landing.

The first American astronauts to die were Virgil Grissom, Roger Chaffee, and Ed White—on January 27, 1967, when their capsule was swept by fire during a routine on-the-ground test. The fire, thought to have originated from a faulty electrical cable, swept through the sealed capsule so quickly that the astronauts couldn't activate escape mechanisms. A subsequent investigation cited "113 significant engineering orders" that had been improperly carried out in the building of the capsule. The tragedy resulted in considerable redesign and reengineering work on the *Apollo* capsule.

GREEN CHEESE IT AIN'T

The first firsthand look at the moon came on the *Apollo 8* expedition, launched by the United States in December, 1968, with Frank Borman, James Lovell, Jr., and Bill Anders on board. Among the highlights of man's first orbit of the moon were the crew's reading of the opening verses of Genesis, "In the beginning, God created the Heavens and the Earth. . . . ," and Borman's description of the moon's surface: "Looks just like plaster of Paris."

SO NEAR YET SO FAR

On the *Apollo 10* expedition Tom Stafford, John Young, and Eugene Cernan came within miles of immortality: It was their job to give the lunar landing module a dry run for the later moon landing. With the command module in orbit, Young and Cernan took the lunar lander to within eight miles of the lunar surface—the first close pass for the landing vehicle—and then returned to the command module for docking and flight back to Earth.

EAT YOUR HEART OUT, JULES VERNE

Apollo 11, the U. S. mission destined to land on the moon, blasted off from Cape Kennedy at 9:32 A.M. Eastern Daylight Time, July 16, 1969. The Saturn V rocket stood 363 feet tall, weighed 6,000,000 pounds, and developed a 7,600,000-pound thrust. On board were Neil Armstrong, thirty-eight, commander of the expedition, Edwin E. "Buzz" Aldrin, the lunar module pilot, and Colonel Michael Collins of the U. S. Air Force. The expedition went without a hitch, and the lunar module with Armstrong and Aldrin touched down on the moon at 20.17 hours 42 seconds, G.M.T., July 20, 1969. Aldrin's first words after touchdown—the first by man from another body in the solar system—were, "Tranquility Base: the Eagle has landed."

NO PIE IN THE SKY

The first meal eaten on the moon—consumed by Armstrong and Aldrin before their historic moonwalk—consisted of four bacon squares, three sugar cookies, peaches, pineapple-grapefruit drink, and coffee.

PUT YOUR LITTLE FOOT

At 2:56 hours, 15 seconds, G.M.T., July 21, 1969, Neil Armstrong became the first human to set foot on another world when he descended from the lunar landing module. His words were "I'm at the foot of the ladder. The LM [lunar module] footpads are only depressed in the surface about two inches, though the surface appears to be very, very fine grained as you get close to it, like powder. Okay. I'm going to step off the LM now. *(Pause)* That's one small step for [a] man, one giant leap for mankind. The surface is fine and powdery. I can kick it loosely with my toe."

DO YOU MIND IF I TAKE THIS CALL?

President Richard M. Nixon placed the first phone call to the moon, on July 21, when he spoke to Armstrong and Aldrin in their lunar module parked on the moon's surface. Said Nixon, "Neil and Buzz,

Do you mind if I tape this call? President Richard M. Nixon places the first phone call to the moon, July 21, 1969, when he spoke to Neil Armstrong and Buzz Aldrin, 240,000 miles away. THE BETTMANN ARCHIVE, INC.

I'm talking to you from the Oval Room of the White House, and this certainly has to be the most historic telephone call ever made."

Like most of Nixon's phone calls, this one was both tape recorded and widely disseminated among the public. However, it was one taped call he wasn't later to regret. Nixon summed up his feelings about the moon landing by saying, "This is the greatest work in the history of the world since its creation."

SPORTING
FIRSTS

Waiting for Howard Cosell to happen: The first television coverage of a sports event—NBC at the Princeton-Columbia baseball game, Baker Field, New York, May 17, 1939.   THE BETTMANN ARCHIVE, INC.

KICKOFFS:
How Famous Games Got Started

PUT 'EM UP!

The sport of fighting with fists—as opposed to the unorganized, street kind of fistfighting—is very ancient. Stone carvings found at Khafaje, Iraq, in ancient Mesopotamia dating from ca. 3000 B.C. show wrestlers and fistfighters with hands wrapped in leather—the first known evidence of fisticuffs. The sport enjoyed a long and bloody history in ancient Greece and Rome, where fighters usually wore the cestus, a metal spike-studded leather hand wrapping, to better enable them to kill their opponents—the object of the match. Thus Theagenes of Thasos is credited with killing 1,425 opponents during his reign as the Muhammad Ali of ancient Greece.

The first boxing champ of the modern era was James Figg (b. ca. 1696), who was so proficient with his fists that he could flatten any opponent without resorting to the usual barroom tactics of kicking, gouging, or holding. Thus Figg is credited with inventing the sport of pure hand fighting. "Figg's fighting," as it was called, became so popular in England that Figg opened the modern world's first fistfighting school, Figg's Academy for Boxing, in 1719, on Tottenham Court Road, London. Figg retired, undefeated, at age thirty-four.

The first systematic rules for bare-knuckle fighting were put forth by Jack Broughton (1704–89), who called for a chalked "ring" in which the fight would take place, referees and umpires to maintain decorum and to decide disputes in the fight, and no hitting below the belt. Broughton was the undefeated English champ for sixteen years, until beaten on April 11, 1750, by Jack Slack. Slack's winning backhand punch blinded Broughton in both eyes.

The first fights with gloves and three-minute rounds took place at a tournament in London in 1872. The idea of "humanizing" the barbaric sport of bare-knuckle fighting came from John Sholto Douglas, eighth Marquess of Queensbury (1844–1900), working with Arthur Chambers, a British boxer. They formulated a set of rules calling for gloved fists, breaks in the fighting ("rounds") every three minutes, a standard-size ring, the ten-second count for a fallen fighter, and other rules that constitute the basis of modern boxing. The first heavyweight championship fight under the Queensbury rules took place in Cincinnati, Ohio, on August 19, 1885, when John L. Sullivan defeated Dominick McCaffery.

THE FIRST HOLE

The Scots were the first people to play golf, and the game had become so popular by 1457 that King James II outlawed "golfe" because it took up leisure time of his subjects that could better be spent in learning archery or some other sport that would come in handy in time of war.

Golf continued to be popular in Scotland, however, especially among the royal family. Mary, Queen of Scots (1542–87), like her grandfather, James IV, played often and well, and to her goes the title of first known woman golfer. When she became Queen in 1542 she openly advocated the game. During her reign, in 1542, the first major golf course, and the oldest still in use—St. Andrews—was founded.

The first golf balls were made of small leather bags stuffed with feathers.

LA PREMIÈRE TOUCHÉ

The art of swordsmanship has been around since the invention of bladed weapons, but it wasn't until the fourteenth century that German swordsmen began practicing their art for something other than dueling or warring. The first known fencing guild, the Marxbruder Guild of Lowenburg, was established as early as 1383. The first fencer to use handguards was Gonzalvo di Cordova, an Army captain (d. 1515).

TENNIS, ANYONE?

The vastly popular game of tennis (or, more properly, lawn tennis), is just over a century old. It was played for the first time at a lawn party in Wales in 1873. The game was conceived by Major Walter C. Wingfield, a British Army officer, as a diversion appropriate for women and young ladies to play at parties, and he based this new sport on the older indoor game of court, or royal tennis, now rarely played outside England.

Lawn tennis was first called "Spharistike," a term meaning "to play" that Wingfield borrowed from the Greeks.

The game caught on with the upper-class social circles the major moved in, and within two weeks, one of the men who played in the first game had taken balls and rackets with him to Bermuda. Tennis-on-the-lawn, as it was sometimes called, caught on there, too. A young American, Mary Ewing Outerbridge, played tennis while on vacation in Bermuda, and decided to take the game back with her to New York. In March, 1874, Miss Outerbridge took the first tennis rackets and balls to the United States, and the first tennis games in America were played that year at the Staten Island Cricket and Racquet Club.

ALL HANDS

Handball was originated by the Irish in the tenth century A.D., and remained almost exclusively the Emerald Isle's sport until the nineteenth century. The game was first called "Fives"—from the five fingers. Handball came to the United States in 1882 with Phil Casey, an Irish handball champ, who was amazed to find that there were no handball courts in America. Along with a few other Irish immigrants, who passed the time batting balls against brick walls in Brooklyn, Casey raised enough cash to build the first handball court in America, in Brooklyn, in 1882–3.

AND THE PHARAOH ROLLS A GUTTER BALL

The first evidence of a bowlinglike game comes from an Egyptian child's tomb, ca. 5200 B.C. In it were found nine stone "pins" which were to be knocked down by a rolled stone ball. In the Egyptian game the "bowling alley" also had three arches of marble through which the bowling stone had to pass, giving the game a bit of croquet as well.

Our modern game was first played in the third and fourth centuries A.D. as a religious ceremony, when a pious German would place a *Kegel*—a wood club used mainly for self defense—at the end of a stone passageway in the cloister of the local church. He would then roll a stone at the *Kegel,* and if he knocked it down, he was cleansed of sin! Over the centuries, the Germans made it more difficult to absolve themselves, for the number of pins to be knocked down increased, and by the early fourteenth century, anywhere from three to seventeen pins were used in the rite. According to German bowling historian William Pehle, it was no less an authority than Martin Luther who determined that nine was the ideal number of pins to be bowled over. Luther no doubt derived his number from religious numerology, since threes and multiples thereof have always played an important part in Christian symbolism.

The first indoor, wood bowling lane was built in London about 1450.

The first bowling in America came in the early nineteenth century, perhaps earlier, though the origins are obscure. And, for reasons not known to sports historians, in America a tenth pin was added. The first reference to bowling at tenpins was made by Washington Irving in "Rip Van Winkle" in 1818.

THE DANES LOST BY A HEAD

Soccer, the most popular and widespread sport in the world, originated in England. Two towns claim to have played the first soccer game: Derby claims to have played the game on Shrove Tuesday, sometime in the eleventh century, as part of a celebration of the victory of English warriors over Roman invaders in A.D. 217; the other first soccer game took place in the eleventh century when the men of Chester—also on Shrove Tuesday—began kicking around the head of an executed Danish soldier.

Soccer remained a traditional Shrove Tuesday game until April 13, 1314, when Edward II issued the first ban on soccer playing, "forasmuch as there is great noise in the city caused by hustling over large balls from which many evils might arise which God forbid." The ban didn't work, and centuries later Henry VIII, James II, and Queen Elizabeth I were still trying to get their subjects to stop playing soccer, on pain of imprisonment. They're still playing.

FIRST DOWN

The first intercollegiate football game took place at New Brunswick, New Jersey, when Rutgers played Princeton on November 6, 1869. This traditional "first" football game was not American college football, but soccer, with twenty-five men to a team, and with no moving of the ball except by kicking or head and shoulder contact.

True American football grew out of what was called the Boston Game, a kicking game in which the round inflated rubber ball could be picked up and carried by the players. Harvard University declined to adopt the Rutgers-Princeton type of soccer game as their official "football" game, and instead adopted the Boston Game. The first intercollegiate football game with players carrying the ball—the immediate ancestor of American football—took place at Cambridge, Massachusetts, when Harvard played McGill University of Montreal, on May 14, 1874. By agreement, the first game on that day was played by Harvard rules, derived from the Boston Game. The score was 3-0, Harvard. The second game was played by Rugby rules, and resulted in a scoreless tie. In both games, eleven men played on a team—but only because four of McGill's scheduled fifteen players had to cancel the trip.

The Harvard-McGill games were momentous in football history, because they led to the marriage of the Boston Game and Rugby that became our familiar football. The quarterback was first introduced in 1880, and the scrimmage line appeared the same year. The first use of "downs" and of play signals came in 1882.

The first school to use yelling—the forerunner of cheering—as a psychological weapon against opponents was Princeton, at the early soccer-rules game against Rutgers, November 6, 1869. The "scarer," as the yell was then called, was called out by the players themselves at crucial points during each play. Apparently the exertion of yelling was too much on the team, and they lost 6-4 (Rutgers's first and only win against Princeton until 1938). At their second game, on November 13, 1869, the Princeton team got smart, and instead of screaming out the scarer themselves, they persuaded their sidelined teammates and the few fans at the game to do the yelling for them. Grandstand cheering was born.

ON THE REBOUND

Basketball is one of the few sports that was invented without origin or borrowings from earlier games. In 1891 Dr. James Naismith, an instructor at the International Y.M.C.A. College at Springfield, Massachusetts, nailed two peach baskets to the balcony of the school's gymnasium. Naismith had "decided that there should be a game that could be played indoors in the evening and during the winter seasons. (I was) assigned the task of inventing a game to fill this particular part of our work." The teams at first had seven players, and played three twenty-minute periods.

The first professional games were played in 1898 by the National Basketball League, which had teams in New York, Philadelphia, Brooklyn, and New Jersey. The league folded in 1900.

ABNER DOUBLEDAY, YOU'RE OUT!

For many years, Abner Doubleday was credited with inventing the game of baseball in 1839 in Cooperstown, New York, and because Cooperstown was chosen as the site of the Baseball Hall of Fame (mainly because of the erroneous Doubleday legend), the myth still persists. During the 1930's, a report written in 1907 by A. G. Mills credited Doubleday as the father of baseball. In *The Encyclopedia of Sports,* Frank Menke discusses the Doubleday affair in detail, and concludes that Doubleday probably never even played the game, let alone invented it.

Baseball originated prior to 1800, when boys began playing with balls and sticks a game similar to cricket, but not using wickets. This simple "sandlot" game was combined with the English game of rounders, and by the 1840's the game closely resembled today's sport.

The first adult baseball organization was the Knickerbocker club, founded in New York in 1845. The club was instrumental in stand-

Diamonds are a girl's best friend: Just as Abner Doubleday was not the man who first thought up the game of baseball, the liberated women of the twentieth century were not the first to organize all-female teams. This 1883 woodcut was originally captioned "The Daisies of the Diamond Field—How the girls shake their petticoats and go in for vigorous and athletic exercises which develop the muscle, expand the chest, and keep the blood from stagnating."
THE BETTMANN ARCHIVE, INC.

ardizing the game. In 1845 Alexander Cartwright, a club member, designed the modern baseball diamond, which soon replaced the square and five-sided fields that had been used by teams according to their preference, without standard base line lengths. The first game between organized clubs on the Cartwright diamond took place between the New York Nine and the Knickerbockers on June 19, 1846, in Hoboken, New Jersey. The Nine defeated the Knicks 23–1.

The first professional team—to get paid, that is—was the Cincinnati Red Stockings in 1869. Captain and shortstop George Wright got the most—$1,500—while Asa Brainard, the pitcher, got $1,100. Low man was utility player Richard Hurley, salary $600. Their season lasted from March 15 to November 15, and they won 65 of their 66 games, tying the single game with the Troy, New York, Haymakers.

SUPERSPORTS:
The First Great Events

THE WORLD SERIES

The first attempt to have a postseason playoff between rival baseball leagues was in 1882, when the Cincinnati team of the American Association (formed the same year) challenged Chicago of the National League. Two games of the projected series were played before league executives decided to call a halt to the playoffs. The teams won one game each.

The first modern World Series, in 1903, was between the Pittsburgh Pirates of the National League and the Boston Red Sox of the American League. Boston took five games to Pittsburgh's three. The most notable name on the Boston team was thirty-six-year-old Cy Young. Total attendance for the series was 100,420 spectators, and a winning player received $1,182, while a losing team member got $1,316. The losers received more for their failure because Pittsburgh club owner Barney Dreyfuss divided the club's share of the receipts among the team members.

THE KENTUCKY DERBY AND THE TRIPLE CROWN

The first horse to win the Kentucky Derby, a mile and one-quarter race at Churchill Downs, was Aristides in 1875. The Triple Crown —the Derby, the Preakness Stakes at Pimlico, and the Belmont

Stakes at Belmont Park—has been won by only nine horses The first was Sir Barton in 1919.

WIMBLEDON

The historic and prestigious Wimbledon Tennis Championships were first held for men's singles in 1877—only four years after lawn tennis had been introduced by Major Wingfield—and was won by Spencer Gore of England. The first American to win in men's singles at Wimbledon was Bill Tilden in 1920 and 1921. Women's singles were introduced in 1884, and Maud Watson of England won. In 1905 May Sutton of the United States became the first American to win at Wimbledon.

THE AMERICA'S CUP

In 1851 members of the New York Yacht Club built a 101-foot schooner christened the *America*. On August 22 of that year, the first international yacht race was held in England, when the *America* challenged British yachtsmen in a race around the Isle of Wight under the auspices of the Royal Yacht Squadron. The trophy, then known as the Hundred Guinea Cup, was won by J. C. Stevens in the *America*. The trophy became known as the America's Cup, and the race has been won by United States yachts since the first race.

THE U.S. OPEN

In 1894 a group of American golf enthusiasts decided that the game —popular in America for less than a decade—should have a tournament to determine a champion. So, that year they held the first United States Open—the tournament was open to anyone who wanted to take a stab at it—at the St. Andrew's Golf Club in Yonkers, founded in 1888. Willie Dunn beat Willie Campbell by two strokes in four rounds of match play.

THE SUPERBOWL

The end-of-season battle of giants, the football Superbowl was held for the first time on January 12, 1967, at Los Angeles, when the National Football League champion Green Bay Packers defeated the American League champs, the Kansas City Chiefs, 35–10.

ANCIENT OLYMPIC FIRSTS:
Games People Used to Play

GODS AND GAMES

The earliest ancient Olympics—the most famous sporting event ever
—is shrouded in myth. Though the Olympics are remembered
mainly for their athletic competitions, for most of their thousand-
year history they were closely connected with religious observances.

The ancient Greeks measured time in four-year periods, which
eventually became known as olympiads, and at the end of each
period it was the custom for Greek cities and tribes, which weren't
united into one nation at that time, to hold religious observances and
memorial ceremonies in their area for men who had died during that
four-year period. During the early days of these ceremonies—before
they became known as Olympian games—it was thought that the
spirits of the departed watched over the ceremonies, so the Greeks
began staging events that had been of special interest to the departed:
orations, poetry recitals, music recitals, and, of course, sports events.

The date for the beginning of these tribal memorial services is
generally held to be 1453 B.C., though there is no definite historical
record.

GOODWILL GAMES

Tradition has it that the idea for holding joint ceremonies, with
participants from all Greek cities, came from one Heracles of Ida,

who was interested in promoting goodwill between the often-warring towns. The idea caught on among the Greek chieftains, and all-Greece observances were held at Olympus sometime in the eighth century B.C. Olympus was chosen as the site for the meet for several reasons: Olympus, the 9,570-foot mountain on the border of Macedonia and Thessaly, was revered as the residing place of the gods. On the more practical side, its remote location insured there wouldn't be too much political conflict between attending cities, since no single tribe could claim to be "home team." And finally, the Olympic plain at the foot of the mountain was an ideal natural gathering place for large crowds.

FAST COOKIE

The first historically verified Olympics were held in 776 B.C., and it was at this meet that the term "Olympic Games" was used for the first time. From this meet written records were kept until the Olympics were disbanded in A.D. 392 by order of the Roman Emperor Theodosius—1,168 years after the first games. The traditional sponsors of this meeting were Iphitus, King of Elis, Lycurgus, King of Sparta, and Cleosthenes, King of Pisa.

The first Olympics consisted of one physical competition (in addition to the usual religious and artistic ceremonies). This was a 200-yard footrace, which was won by Coroibus, a citizen of Elis. The tradition of amateur athletes competing in the Olympics, still the rule today, got its start here. Coroibus was a cook, and an amateur runner. What other competitions there were in 776 B.C. are lost in history, though we do know that in the early days, the Olympian games included wrestling and jumping events.

MORE GAMES PELOPONNESIANS PLAYED

We do have exact dates for several popular contests added to later Olympics. The original footrace, which Coroibus won, was a race from one end of the Olympic stadium and back again. In 724 B.C. at the fourteenth Olympics, the double race was added, which had an extra lap or stadium length added. In 708 at the eighteenth events, the pentathlon was added, and consisted of five events—leaping, footracing, wrestling, discus throwing, and javelin throwing. Boxing joined the Olympic roster in 688 at the twenty-third Olympics. In Greece and Rome, boxing was a brutal sport, with opponents using leather-bound fists, often studded with metal spikes. The fight was usually to the death, and therefore losing fighters were considered the greatest of sports heroes. In 680, chariot races were held for the first time at the Olympics. The chariots were small, lightweight, two-wheeled affairs, and were pulled by two small horses. In 580 the armored footrace joined the Olympic roster, probably one of the less graceful running events ever devised.

YOU CAN'T EVEN WATCH

The earliest Olympics, with their strong religious overtones, were strictly forbidden to women (as well as slaves, foreigners, and "disreputable men"). Women were known, however, to sneak a look at the Olympics from nearby hillsides and bushes. If caught, however, they were put to death—a high price to pay for gate-crashing a footrace! According to tradition, the first woman to witness the Olympics and survive was Phrenice, in the eighth century B.C. A widow, Phrenice wanted so badly to witness her son Peisidorus in the pugilism competition that she sneaked into the stadium disguised as her son's "trainer." When the young man won, his mom was so excited that she hugged and kissed him (something a good Greek trainer would apparently not do—at least not in public). Her deception revealed, Phrenice was put on trial, with death sentence the likely outcome. But she was freed by the judges, apparently conducting her own defense on "motherly love." However, to prevent this kind of thing happening again, at future Olympics all "trainers" were required to appear naked—a kind of ancient version of the chromosome test used at modern athletic competitions.

The Phrenice incident apparently inspired the Olympic rule-makers to reconsider their stand on women, and within a few olympiads of Phrenice's trial, women were openly allowed to attend as spectators, though they were never allowed to compete.

The first women's Olympic-type meets were begun as an alternative to the male-ruled Olympics. The meets were called Herae, and were organized along similar lines to the Olympics. Herae were held in four-year cycles as well, but the cycle overlapped the Olympics. The traditional founder was Hippodaemia, who organized the first

Hera to celebrate her marriage to Pelops, sometime before 600 B.C. Herae were held until the Roman conquest of Greece, 456 B.C.

STRIPPED FOR ACTION

At the fifteenth Olympics, in 720 B.C., an embarrassing accident led to the first nude Olympics. Orsippus of Megara, one of the entrants in the footrace, happened to lose his loincloth while running. Apparently he wasn't considered a front runner, but in spite of losing his garb (fortunately he didn't trip on it as it fell off) he won the race. His unexpected victory was attributed to his unexpected nudity, and in future events, athletes chose to run in the nude to better their chances and cut their running times. So the Olympics became a nude athletic event for centuries to come. One of the naughtiest competitions was certainly the armored footrace—with shield-carrying men racing one another, wearing only helmets and arm and leg shields, and nothing else.

GOLD MEDAL FIRSTS:
The Modern Olympics

GREEK REVIVAL

The beginning of the modern Olympics, much like the first ancient Olympics in 776 B.C., was the brainchild of one man who saw an international amateur sports competition of the highest standards as a means of promoting peace and understanding between nations. The modern version of Heracles of Ida was one Pierre de Fredy, Baron de Coubertin (1863–1937), who first presented his proposal for a revival of the Olympics on an international scale to the Athletic Sports Union in Paris in 1892. His idea received little support from the French athletic union, but at an international athletic conference in 1896, de Coubertin was able to get approval of his idea, and the Olympics were born—or reborn. Launching the mammoth sports meet was not easy though, and physical and financial arrangements proved difficult. Fortunately, an "angel" in the form of the Egyptian merchant George Averoff appeared. Averoff gave a million drachmas to underwrite the cost of the first meet.

The first modern Olympics were held in Athens in April, 1896. Eight countries were represented, though the United States team was not an official, Government-sponsored group. The countries were: Denmark, England, France, Germany, Greece, Hungary, Switzerland, and the United States. There were twelve track and field events in the 1896 games, which attracted the most attention since they were the closest in spirit to the ancient competitions. But events were also held in swimming, cycling, fencing, gymnastics, tennis, and shooting.

THE AMERICAN CONQUEST

The first United States team to compete in the Olympics was not an official team, since the United States Olympic Committee had yet to be formed. Yet the ten men won nine of the ten events they entered, and nine of the events on the program—a record still unequaled in the track and field category. Even more remarkable is how the athletes came to participate at all. A Princeton student named Robert Garrett had heard about the Olympics, and wanted to participate, but since there was no official body to send him, he had to do it himself. Fortunately, Garrett was of means enough to take not only himself, but three schoolmates, Francis A. Lane, Herbert A. Jamison, and Albert C. Tyler. Along the way, a Harvard student named James B. Connolly joined the group, also paying his own way. The third contingency which joined the Princeton boys and Connolly were five men—Arthur Blake, Ellery H. Clark, William W. Hoyt, Thomas E. Burke, and Thomas Curtis—who managed to get themselves sponsored by the Boston Athletic Association. One of the Athletic Association coaches, John B. Graham, joined up to act as trainer, coach, and manager.

The group of eleven arrived in Naples by tramp steamer on April 1, 1896. The joke was on them, so it seemed, since they discovered upon arrival that the Olympics were scheduled to start on April 6, not April 18, as they'd thought. It seems they had neglected to take into account the difference between the Greek and Western calendars. They managed to get to the port town of Patras by boat, four days later, on the fifth of April, only ten hours before the events were scheduled to begin in Athens. The men had not trained or exercised, due to the cramped sailing quarters, since they had left New York on March 20. The team arrived at the stadium literally as the trial heats for the 100-meter dash were beginning. The first final was the hop, step, jump event, which was entered by James Connolly. He won the event with a leap of 45 feet, and became the first Olympic winner since 392 A.D.—1,504 years before.

WINNING RECORDS

The winning times and distances of the twelve track and field events of the first Olympics, and the current records, for comparison:

	1896	**RECORD**
100-meter dash *(Burke, U.S.)*	12 sec	1968: 9.9 sec (Hines, U.S.)
400-meter run *(Burke, U.S.)*	54.2 sec	1968: 43.8 sec (Evans, U.S.)
800-meter run *(Flack, Britain)*	2 min 11 sec	1976: 1 min 43.5 sec (Juantorena, Cuba)
1500-meter run *(Flack, Britain)*	4 min 33.2 sec	1968: 3 min 34.9 sec (Keino, Kenya)
Marathon *(Loues, Greece)*	2 hr 55 min 20 sec	1976: 2 hr 9 min 55 sec (Cierpinski, E. Ger)
High jump *(Clark, U.S.)*	5 ft 11¼ in	1968: 7 ft 4¼ in (Fosbury, U.S.)
110-meter hurdles *(Curtis, U.S.)*	17.6 sec	1972: 13.2 sec (Milburn, U.S.)
Pole Vault *(Hoyt, U.S.)*	10 ft 9¾ in	1972: 18 ft 5¼ in (Nordwig, E. Ger)
Broad jump *(Clark, U.S.)*	20 ft 9¾ in	1968: 29 ft 2½ in (Beamon, U.S.)
Hop, step, jump *(Connolly, U.S.)*	45 ft	1968: 57 ft ¾ in (Saneyev, USSR)
Shot put *(Garrett, U.S.)*	36 ft 2 in	1972: 69 ft 6 in (Komar, Poland)
Discus *(Garrett, U.S.)*	95 ft 7½ in	1976: 221 ft 5.4 in (Wilkins, U.S.)

GOLD IN THE COLD

The first winter Olympics were held in Chamonix, France, in 1924 under the patronage of the Olympic International Committee. Though the meet was not then considered an official Olympic Games, two years later it was given the title "First Winter Games" by the committee. The events included speed skating, cross-country skiing, ski jumping for the first time; events for figure skating had been introduced in the regular Olympics in 1908, and ice hockey in 1920.

FIRST LADIES

The first women's events in the Olympics were at the 1912 Stockholm games, and were limited to three swimming and diving competitions. Fanny Durack of Australia won the 100-meter race in 1 minute 22.2 seconds (current record, 55.65 seconds); Greta Johanson of Sweden won the plain high dive (with 39.9 points; later winners scored under a different system); and the British women's team won the 400-meter freestyle relay in 5 minutes 52.8 seconds (current record, 3 minutes 44.82 seconds). The first women's events in track and field were added to the 1928 games. Elizabeth Robinson became the first United States contestant to win a women's event, the 100-meter dash in 12.2 seconds, (current record, 11.01 seconds).

WORTH THEIR WEIGHT IN GOLD

The first and only athlete to win seven gold medals at a single games is Mark Spitz of the United States, at the 1972 Munich meet. Spitz's famous feat, which received wide press coverage and established him for a period as something of a media star, included medals for four individual events and three team events. The individuals were: 100-meter freestyle (51.2 seconds, then a record, now broken); 200-meter freestyle (1 minute 52.8 seconds, then a record, now broken); 100-meter butterfly (still the record at 54.3 seconds); 200-meter butterfly (then the record at 2 minutes 7 seconds, now broken). The team events were the 400-meter freestyle relay (3 minutes 26.4 seconds, still the record); the 400-meter medley relay (3 minutes 48.2 seconds, then the record, now bested); the 800-meter freestyle relay (then a record at 7 minutes 38.8 seconds, now bettered). Spitz also won two relay (team) medals at the 1968 Mexico Olympics.

The first and only woman to win seven gold medals (the all-time record) was Vera Caslavska of Czechoslovakia, who won the beam, side-horse vault, and all-around events at the 1964 Tokyo games, and the floor exercises, side-horse vault, uneven bars, and all-around champion at the 1968 Mexico City games.

The first athlete to win five individual gold medals at one Olympic competition was Eric Heiden of the United States, who won all five men's speed skating events at the 1980 winter games at Lake Placid. Though Mark Spitz won seven golds in the 1972 Munich games, he won four individuals and three team medals. Heiden won the 500-, 1,000-, 1,500-, 5,000-, and 10,000-meter races.

HITLER WAS UNHAPPY

The first black to win a gold medal in the Olympics was Jesse Owens of the United States in the 1936 games in Berlin. The now-famous German games, staged at the height of the Nazi regime under Hitler, were designed by the Germans to be the most elaborate and impressive of all time, while displaying to full advantage the racial and athletic superiority of the Aryan race. The Germans built what was for those days an immense stadium with a 100,000 seating capacity, the Reich Sports Grounds. The number of athletes who entered the games—3,959—was more than twice the number who had attended the Los Angeles games in 1932 (though only 54 more than attended Amsterdam in 1928).

The German athletes performed remarkably, and won the "unofficial" (but widely followed) team score, which awards points to a country for every medal won by its entrants. It would have been a clean propaganda sweep for the Nazi regime had not Jesse Owens put on his remarkable performance in track and field, and put a fly in the ointment of racial superiority theories. Owens won four gold medals, three individual, and one team. He ran the 100-meter dash in 10.3 seconds, tying the record; the 200-meter dash in 20.7 seconds, setting a new Olympic record; and leaped 26 feet, 5 21/64 inches in the running broad jump, also a new record. He also won a medal for the 400-meter relay, which the U. S. team ran in 40 seconds flat, also a new record. Owens's records held for twenty-five years.

The first black woman to win an Olympic gold medal was Wilma Rudolph of the United States, who won the 100-meter dash in 11 seconds, a new Olympic record, and the 200-meter dash in 24 seconds at the 1960 Rome Olympics.

KIDDIE KOMPETITION

The first child (that is, an individual under the age of thirteen) to win a gold medal in the Olympics was the coxswain of the Netherlands pair-oared shell at the 1900 games in Paris. The coxswain's age was

The Führer was furious: Jesse Owens displeased Hitler and destroyed the Germans' racial superiority theories when he became the first black to win an Olympic gold medal in the 1936 Berlin Olympics. Here, he sets a new world record in the broad jump at the games.   WIDE WORLD PHOTOS

given as ten years, though some Olympics historians say he may have been younger. The Dutch rowers were R. Klein and F. A. Brandt, and the original coxswain was to have been an adult, Hermanus Brockman, who was scuttled from the crew because of weight. The team's winning time was 7 minutes 34.2 seconds, a record that held until 1960. It is perhaps an indication of the role the press plays in making athletes famous, and it is certainly an indication of what big press Olympic athletes have become today, that in 1900 the first child to win a gold medal remained nameless, unknown to this day. Today he would be an instant media star, "The kid who came from nowhere to coax the Dutch to victory." Numerous teen-agers have been involved in Olympics competition, beginning in 1896, and in fact have made brilliant shows in several fields, especially swimming and gymnastics.

"10"

The first individual to receive a perfect ten score in a gymnastics competition was fourteen-year-old Rumanian gymnast Nadia Comaneci, who competed at her first Olympic games in Montreal in 1972. The four-foot-eleven, eighty-six-pound gymnast's perfect scores (which have not been equaled by any male gymnast) were in the uneven bars, balance bar, and beam events; the outstanding performance, if one can be chosen from her three, was in the uneven bars, where she received an overall score of 20.00. Nadia received gold medals for Uneven bars, Beam, and Best All-Around.

INDIAN GIVERS

The first American Indian to compete in the Olympics was the famous Jim Thorpe (1888–1953), who was named in 1950 the Greatest United States Athlete of the first half of the twentieth century by the Associated Press Poll of American sportswriters. Thorpe, who was born near Prague, Oklahoma, and attended the Indian School at Carlisle, Pennsylvania, was a remarkably talented athlete. At the 1912 Stockholm games he won both the pentathlon and the grueling decathlon, a feat that has never been equaled. However, in 1913 Thorpe was asked by the Amateur Athletic Union to return his medals to the International Committee, which he did. The reason: Thorpe had played semiprofessional baseball in 1909–10 with a Rocky Mount, North Carolina, team. Almost from the time Thorpe returned his awards, there was agitation to reinstate him as champion in the two events, but it was not until after his death that the Amateur Athletic Union voted to reinstate Thorpe. The International Olympic Committee has not followed suit, however, and Thorpe still does not appear on the Olympic gold medals roster.

NEXT OLYMPIAD WE GOTTA GET ORGANIZED

The first Olympics held in the United States were the 1904 games in St. Louis, Missouri. The St. Louis games, and the earlier Paris games of 1900, were criticized for their lack of organization and wide international representation. The 1904 meet especially came under fire because of strong American domination of the event in all fields of competition. This situation led to the first—and so far, only—modern Olympics held outside the four-year Olympiad period: the 1906 Athens games, under Greek auspices. While the 1906 games were something of a maverick (it is only recently that the scores there have been added to the Olympic roster of winners), they pointed up the need for tighter controls, better organization, and consistent official policies. The 1908 London games are considered to be the first successfully organized, large-scale games, due in great part to the formation of the International and National Olympic committees to oversee the vast, multinational project.

SPORTS + POLITICS = STRANGE BEDFELLOWS

The Olympics, though the product of great international cooperation (chiefly by the various national Olympic committees), have never been totally free from political overtones, and the competition between major nations and political ideologies is fierce, notably the Communist-American rivalry. The first Olympics with major political rumblings were the famous Berlin games of 1936, when a black American athlete "stole the show" as it were, and upset the Führer (see "Hitler was Unhappy"). Politics of a dire nature were responsible for the first and second interruption of the games, when the 1916 games were canceled due to World War I, and the 1940 and 1944 games because of World War II. The 1940 games had been scheduled for Tokyo but were canceled, and the next Olympics were held in London, 1948.

The most famous and tragic political "statement" at any games was at Munich in 1972, when Arab terrorists kidnaped and killed nine members of the Israeli Olympic team. The tragedy almost caused the cancellation of the games, but the Israeli Government, with great nobility, urged the International Committee to continue the contests. The Israeli team members were the first—and hopefully, the last—athletes to be murdered at an event.

HELL NO, WE WON'T GO!

At the 1980 Moscow Olympics, for the first time since the modern games began in 1896, the United States was not represented by a team. The United States boycott, proposed by President Jimmy Carter and backed by Congress, in response to the December 27, 1979, Soviet invasion of Afghanistan, caused what is perhaps the biggest political rift in Olympic history, with the U. S.-sponsored boycott receiving support from some allies, such as West Germany —and none from others, such as Great Britain.

Though Moscow 1980 were the first Olympics boycotted by the United States, they were not the first Olympic Games to be boycotted: When Queen Elizabeth II opened the 1976 Montreal games on July 17, thirty-two Asian and African countries were not in attendance. The boycott began July 9, when Tanzania announced that it was not attending the Olympics because New Zealand, who was attending, had sent its national Rugby team on a tour of apartheid South Africa. The "third world" boycott caught on, and among the thirty-one other nations that joined Tanzania were Algeria, Egypt, Chad, Morocco, Tunisia, Sri Lanka, and Zambia.

At the same games, Taiwan staged a "mini-boycott." The Taiwanese Government withdrew its team on July 16 in a dispute over the status under which it was to compete: Taiwan, or Republic of China, a title claimed by mainland China and backed by the Canadian hosts of the games.

SINK OR SWIM:
Marathon Firsts

Since swimming as a sport originated in England, it's no surprise that the twenty-mile Dover Strait in the English Channel became the first arena for man versus time and tide. Since the first channel crossing, men and women have looked for even greater long-distance and endurance swims to conquer.

FROM THE WHITE CLIFFS OF DOVER

Captain Matthew Webb of England swam from Dover to Cape Gris-Nez, France, a distance of about twenty miles, in 21 hours 45 minutes on August 24–25, 1875. Captain Webb used the breaststroke rather than the newfangled overhand stroke that had been introduced only recently to Europe from South America.

J. W. Forney, in his book *The Centennial Commissioner in Europe,* claimed that an American, Captain Paul Boynton, was the first to swim the channel, on April 10, 1875, several months before Webb. Later research revealed that Boynton did cross, on May 29, 1875, in a time of 23 hours 30 minutes. However, he wore a lifesaving suit (much like a life preserver), which kept him afloat while he paddled across.

The unkindest cut of all: When Gertrude Ederle, daughter of a New York City butcher, became the first woman to swim the English Channel in 1926, she found herself an overnight celebrity. And, like most celebrities, she found herself posing for less than dignified publicity photographs, devised to make the man on the street aware of her very real and dignified achievement.

THE BETTMANN ARCHIVE, INC.

ESTHER WILLIAMS SHE AIN'T

On August 6, 1926, Gertrude Ederle of New York became the first woman to conquer the channel, from Cape Gris-Nez, France, to Kingsdown, England, in the fast time of 14 hours and 31 minutes— a good two hours better than the previous men's record.

IF YOU DON'T LIKE IT HERE, JUST SWIM BACK

In 1927 Edward H. Temme of England swam from France to England in 14 hours 29 minutes. Then in 1934 he swam from England to France in 15 hours 34 minutes. Though his rest period was a bit long, he still was the first man to swim both ways.

Florence Chadwick, a Californian, was the first woman to swim both ways, England to France in 16 hours 19 minutes on September 11, 1951. She swam the other way on September 4, 1953.

FROM POINT A TO POINT A

Antonio Abertondo, a forty-two-year-old Argentinian, swam from England to France in 18 hours 50 minutes on September 20–21, 1961. When he got to France he rested for about four minutes, then swam back to England, arriving at St. Margaret's Bay 24 hours and 16 minutes later, for a total time of 43 hours 10 minutes.

TANKED

Fred Baldasare, thirty-eight, of the United States, swam from France to England, using scuba equipment, in 18 hours 1 minute on July 11, 1962. He remained submerged the entire time.

CASHING IN ON THE CATALINA CHANNEL

In 1927 the Wrigley Company sponsored the Catalina channel swim, a twenty-one-mile route from Catalina Island to Los Angeles, with a $25,000 prize. George Young of Toronto, Canada, took the prize with a time of 15 hours 48 minutes.

Florence Chadwick was the first woman to conquer the Catalina Channel in 1952 in 13 hours 47 minutes—breaking the record held by George Young since 1927.

AND I'LL GET TO SCOTLAND AFORE YE

Thomas Blower of Nottingham, England, in 1947 was the first to swim the twenty-five miles across the Irish Sea from Donaghadee, Northern Ireland, to near Portpatrick, Scotland, in a time of 15 hours 25 minutes. Blower also has three channel crossings to his credit.

THE WET ROAD TO MOROCCO

Daniel Carpio of Peru was the first to swim from Spain to Spanish Morocco across the Gibraltar Strait in July 22, 1948—a distance of eight miles in 9 hours 20 minutes.

OLD MAN RIVER

Though no distance swimmer has ever conquered the 2,350 miles of the Mississippi, John V. Sigmund of St. Louis did manage to swim 12.5 percent of the river's length in July, 1940, when he swam 292 miles downstream from St. Louis in a time of 89 hours 42 minutes. His feat is still the world's record for distance and time in the water —89 hours 42 minutes.

IN GREAT STRAITS

In 1966 the Indian marathon swimmer, Mihir Sen of Calcutta, completed an astonishing five long-distance swims: the Palk Strait (April), Gibraltar Strait (August), the Dardanelles (September), the Bosporus (August), and the Panama Canal (October). Two of the swims were firsts: the Palk Strait from India to Ceylon (about 40 miles in 25 hours 35 minutes, April 5–6), and the Dardanelles (about 40 miles in 13 hours 55 minutes, Gallipoli, Europe, to Seddülbahir, Asia Minor, on September 12). Sen also qualifies as the first swimmer to successfully complete five major swims in one year.

WHICH WAY TO THE BERMUDA TRIANGLE?

American long-distance swimmer Diana Nyad, who tried unsuccessfully to swim the 105 miles of shark-infested, swift currents of the straits of Florida from Cuba to Key West in August, 1978, became the first person to swim from the Bahamas to Florida in August, 1979. Her first attempt, on August 4, 1979, failed when she was badly stung by a Portuguese man-of-war 12½ hours out. Only two weeks later, August 19–20, she swam the eighty-nine miles from North Bimini Island, Bahamas, to Juno Beach, Florida, in 27 hours 38 minutes.

HARDLY A HANDICAP

In 1938, Charles Zimmy, a legless long-distance swimmer, swam from Albany, New York, down the Hudson River to New York City. No time was recorded for the 147-mile course, though it is still the distance record for a handicapped swim.

A SPECIAL FIRST: LEANDER AND THE HELLESPONT

Modern marathon swimmers should give due credit to Leander, the dedicated long-distance swimmer of Greek mythology, who swam across the Hellespont (the modern Dardanelles), a distance of one to four miles every night to meet his girl friend, Hero, a priestess of Aphrodite at Sestos. Though Leander's swim is a short distance by modern standards, it must be taken into account that he swam the route daily, in darkness, and both directions. His assignations were no doubt strenuous in themselves, and the return swim late at night must have sometimes been rough going indeed. Leander's luck didn't hold out, though, for one night, in a storm, the light that Hero held up to guide her lover blew out, and he was drowned and washed up on the rocks at her feet. In despair, Hero threw herself into the sea.

ENTERTAINING
FIRSTS

Claws: Max Schreck portrayed the bloodsucking *Nosferatu,* the 1922 German film that introduced Dracula to film audiences. Here, the vampire appears to be more in need of Madge the Manicurist than fresh human blood.

FLICK FIRSTS

MOVIOLA

The first man to capture motion with a single camera was Jules-Étienne Marey of France, in 1882, who developed a lens which rotated a single, glass photographic plate in front of the lens aperture of his camera. The plate rotated one-twelfth of its diameter in one-twelfth of a second, resulting in a multiple exposure plate of continuous action.

Curiously, Thomas Eakins, the great American painter, used a similar rotating lens to capture images for his figure studies. Edweard Muybridge, the photographer and inventor usually credited with "inventing" motion pictures in 1877, used multiple cameras for his motion studies.

The motion picture industry can be said to have begun in 1888 with Thomas Edison, who took out a patent application for an "optical phonograph." In January, 1889, Edison staff member William Kennedy Dickson was assigned to develop Edison's idea. Dickson made quick progress, and by May 22, 1891, he had filmstrips of good enough quality to show to 147 members of the National Federation of Women's Clubs, who were lunching with Mrs. Edison. These early strips used roll film, but apparently did not have sprockets, which Dickson introduced the following year to insure a uniform feeding of the film through a viewer.

The Dickson process (for which Edison took all the credit—Dickson left Edison labs in 1895 after quarreling with the Wizard of

Menlo Park) and its subsequent commercial development by Edison, was not conceived as a *projection* process. The films which Edison & Co. produced were designed to be viewed, one person at a time, in a peep-show type apparatus that Edison dubbed the Kinetoscope.

A SPECIAL CASE: THE GREAT FILM DISAPPEARANCE

A Bermuda-Triangle type mystery surrounds the earliest days of motion pictures. A French fellow by the name of Louis A. A. Le Prince, who was living and working in the United States at the Institute for the Deaf, New York, apparently developed a workable motion picture camera in 1885, and he applied for a U. S. patent in 1886, three years before Edison began serious work on his motion pictures.

In 1887 Le Prince and *famille* moved to Leeds, England, where the inventor continued work and applied for a British patent for his motion picture camera. Several fragments of film from the years 1888–89 survive (including one of his mother-in-law, who died in 1888, giving an indisputable date for the film). By 1889 Le Prince had started using the celluloid roll film developed by George Eastman, and his camera and projector had been developed to a point that Le Prince was ready to go into production with what was not only a workable invention, but one that was, in concept and design, a decade ahead of its time.

On September 16, 1890, the hopeful inventor took his newest model camera, film, and a projector and boarded the train at Dijon for Paris, where he had an appointment to demonstrate his remarkable invention to the secretary of the Paris Opera, noted for its progressive attitude toward innovations in staging.

M. Le Prince, in an incident worthy of Hitchcock, Christie, or *The Twilight Zone,* disappeared from the train. No trace was ever found of him, or of his equipment.

There is one curious coincidence in all this. Le Prince vanished in September, 1890, after a year of intensive work on his remarkably advanced motion picture process. Thomas Edison, a great genius who was never kindly disposed to rival inventors working in fields too close to his, was in Paris for the exposition of October, 1889, eleven months before the Le Prince disappearance. Is there possibly some connection between the two?

BLACK MARIA

On February 1, 1893, Thomas Edison completed construction of the world's first motion picture studio at the Edison laboratories in West Orange, New Jersey. The studio was built for shooting filmstrips for the infant Edison Kinetoscope business, and consisted of a frame structure, covered in black tar paper, with a glass roof to let in sunlight. The entire structure revolved on a platform to follow the sun and thereby increase the number of filming hours per day.

The studio was soon dubbed "the Black Maria" because of its resemblance to a gigantic paddy wagon which bore the same nickname in those days.

AUDIENCE REACTION

As we mentioned, the Edison films were designed for viewing through a Kinetoscope, and to that end the first Kinetoscope Parlor opened on April 14, 1894, at 1155 Broadway, New York City. Customers paid a nickel to watch brief filmstrips of Buffalo Bill and his six-guns; Eugene Sandow, the first great bodybuilder, doing exercises and gymnastics; and a closeup of Fred Ott, an Edison employee, sneezing on camera. The parlors were popular with teen-age boys and Victorian ladies.

It was in France that film projection got its start. Two brothers, Auguste and Louis Jean Lumière (1862–1954 and 1864–1948), sons of a photographer, patented their *Cinématographe* in 1895. The *Cinématographe* was the first machine to photograph, print, and project motion pictures onto a screen. The first film made by the Lumières was *Workers Leaving the Lumière Factory,* shot before March, 1895. Besides being the first outdoor film ever made, it was the first projected film shown to an audience, in a series of private screenings from March to December, 1895.

The Lumières were also the first to use the word *cinema.* On December 28, 1895, the Lumières projected several of their films in the "Indian Salon" in the basement of the Grand Café, Boulevard des Capucines, Paris. The Indian Salon thus qualifies as the first public theater. One of the films shown was *L'arrivée d'un train en gare (The Arrival of a Train at the Station).* As the steaming locomotive rushed toward the audience on the screen, the viewers screamed and ducked, and the Lumières had demonstrated for the first time the ability of motion pictures to cause audiences to cease to disbelieve.

The first showing of a projected film for a paying audience in the United States took place on April 23, 1896, at Koster and Biall's Music Hall, 34th Street and Broadway, New York (the present site of Macy's). The screening was of several Edison filmstrips which had been adapted for projection under the trademark "Vitascope." The films were shown as part of the live vaudeville acts at the hall. As early film historian Tery Ramsaye recorded, "The program included . . . several dancing girls who displayed their versatility . . . and one of Robert W. Paul's pictures of the surf at Dover, England. The Dover picture was accepted by the audience as something from down the New Jersey coast. . . ."

GLITZ AND GLITTER

In August, 1895, Le Roy Latham, an early film inventor whose inventions somehow never got into the mainstream of motion picture history—primarily because Latham was a wealthy dilettante—hired a black youth named Henry Southall for fifty cents a day to pass out handbills in Norfolk, Virginia, advertising Latham's film productions. Though Latham's career soon faded, Southall stayed in the business for some time, handling advertising and promotion for film companies, making him the first film publicist and, from what is known, the first black in the film business.

THE FIRST WOMAN DIRECTOR

A remarkable and little-known first: In 1895 León Gaumont, one of the pioneers of the European film industry, hired a twenty-one-year-old woman named Alice Guy as his secretary. Gaumont, who was mainly concerned with manufacturing film and photographic equipment, decided early in 1896 to let Alice write, photograph, and direct a film. With the help of her friend Yvonne Mugnier-Serran, Alice directed her first film, *La fée aux choux—The Cabbage Fairy.* (Keep in mind that all this is happening at the same time as the very first film screening in New York City!) From 1896 until 1905 Alice directed every film produced by Gaumont. From 1906 to 1907 Alice also directed more than 100 sound films, using a wax cylinder synchronized with the film. In 1910, having married an Englishman named Bolton-Blaché, she became the first woman head of a studio —one she founded—known as the Solax Company, which produced more than three hundred films in four years. Solax, incidentally, was located in Flushing, New York (she and hubby had emigrated), making Alice the first woman director in American film. Her career in the United States continued until the sound era.

KISS AND CONTROVERSY

The first screen osculation—which precipitated the first screen censorship controversy—was *The Kiss* made in 1896 by Edison Studios, and featuring Broadway stars John C. Rice and May Irwin, who recreated on celluloid their smacker that was currently the talk of the Broadway stage. As film historian Ramsaye describes it, "It was a high-vacuum kiss, attended at its conclusions by sounds reminiscent of a steer pulling a foot out of the gumbo at the edge of a water hole. It was, in brief—and in length—the world's greatest kiss, as of that date, 1896, A.D. Here was a jewelled dramatic moment which this motion picture could perpetrate and disseminate for the delectation of the multitudes in the hinterlands. . . . It was perhaps the world's first educational motion picture; the kiss had come to the screen and the future of the art was from that day assured."

A less perspicacious critic commented, "Such things call for Police Interference. The Irwin kiss is nothing more than a lyric of the stockyards."

DOUBLE TROUBLE

The first use of a screen double occurred in March, 1896 (probably March 24), when the famous dancer Loie Fuller refused to risk her health and well-being by doing her well-known dance routine, scantily clad, in the unheated Edison Studio's Black Maria in West Orange, New Jersey. Loie's lesser-known sister *could* be persuaded, however, and performed before the Edison cameras in her sister's stead—and the filmstrip went around the world under the name Loie Fuller.

FILMS FATALES

On May 4, 1897, at the annual charity bazaar sponsored by the Societé Charité Maternelle in Paris, the projectionist running the machinery in the film section of the bazaar struck a match while repairing the projector bulb; the ether he was filling the bulb with ignited, starting a fire which spread quickly through the flammable film stock and then to the wood and paper decorations and partitions of the bazaar. Result: the first film fatalities. One hundred and eighty persons died—more than 130 of which came from titled and noble European families. For decades, fire remained a major hazard in theaters, until the introduction of celluloid film during the late silent era.

LIGHTS! ACTION!

On the night of November 3, 1899, American Mutoscope and Biograph Company set up four hundred arc lamps over the boxing ring of the Coney Island Athletic Club in order to film the Tom Sharkey-Jim Jeffries fight (by arrangement with fight promoter William Brady), shooting the first artificially lit film. During the fight the arc lights became so hot that the trainers held umbrellas over Jeffries and Sharkey. When the wiring overheated and threatened to burn out, ice was brought from a local saloon and packed around the overhead lines and fuse boxes. As the ice melted from the intense electric heat, hot water rained down on the fighters, who still managed to go twenty-five rounds.

In a devious stunt typical of the rowdy early days of film, Edison's Vitagraph Company cameramen set themselves up in the back row of the auditorium and filmed the whole fight, taking advantage of rival company Biograph's hard work in setting up the lighting. To add insult to injury, Edison heavies stole Biograph's own film of the fight later that night. The mess wound up in court, and Biograph finally got a settlement against Vitagraph.

ON THE CUTTING ROOM FLOOR

The first film shot and edited with intercutting for a complex narrative—rather than telling a story as if it were a filmed stage play—

was Edwin S. Porter's *The Life of an American Fireman* in 1902. It was the first film to use editing to tell a story from two points of view, and to intercut between two places and courses of action. It depicts a fireman dreaming, then cuts to the fireman rushing to a fire; later, a rescue scene is shown both from the fireman's point of view, and from that of the woman and child being rescued. Filmgoers take this kind of editing for granted today. It was revolutionary in 1902.

THROUGH THE RAINBOW

For those of us who associate color films with 1939 and *Gone With the Wind,* it's amazing to learn that the first color films were made in 1906 in England by George A. Smith, who developed a process called Kinemacolor. Smith's first films were taken in his front yard, and showed his children playing; by 1909 the first public demos of color were made by the Charles Urban Company (for which Smith worked), and in March of the same year Urban went into commercial production. The first full-length color film in Kinemacolor was *The World, the Flesh, and the Devil* in 1914.

Though color films enjoyed a brief vogue in Britain, the expense of installing the special projection equipment needed for Kinemacolor kept the process from becoming a commercial success.

The first practical, commercial color process was three-color Technicolor, which was introduced in 1932 in Walt Disney's *Flowers and Trees* (also called *Silly Symphony*). The first feature film in Technicolor was *Becky Sharp,* directed by Rouben Mamoulian in 1935.

TALKING ANIMALS

James Stuart Blackton made *Humorous Phases of Funny Faces,* a primitive precursor of later animation, for Edison's Vitagraph in 1906. The first sound cartoon was *Steamboat Willie,* a Walt Disney-Mickey Mouse collaboration of 1928. *Willie* is a landmark in animation—combining the freedom of invention that animation art allowed with the potential of sounds and music: to wit, Mickey playing music on a cat's tail and a washboard, and using a cow's teeth like a xylophone. The first full-length color animated film was Disney's great *Snow White and the Seven Dwarfs* of 1937.

CALIFORNIA, HERE WE COME

Filmmakers moved to sunny California in 1907, in part for the good weather, in part to escape the ruthless and violent patent wars that were being waged in the East by rival film studios. The first filmmakers to arrive in the future film capital of the world were Francis Boggs and Thomas Persons of the Selig Company. Their assignment in Los Angeles (Hollywood had yet to be discovered) was to complete *The Count of Monte Cristo,* an epic film, the interior scenes of which had been shot in Chicago. The completing exterior scenes were shot by Boggs and Persons in California, and who was to know (least of all the audience) that the cast had been completely changed between Chicago and L.A. The man hired to complete the role of the count, begun by another actor in Chicago, was an out-of-work hypnotist. He was the first film actor "discovered" in California.

The first major films produced in California were Cecil B. De Mille's *Squaw Man* of 1913 and D. W. Griffith's *Birth of a Nation,* 1914.

FANZINE FOLLIES

Photoplay originated in 1912 as a film theater program. By 1914 audience interest in that new phenomenon, the film star, had become so great that *Photoplay* became an independent publication—the first fan mag. The first editor was James R. Quirk, and the magazine featured articles on the likes of D. W. Griffith, Mack Sennett, and Mary Pickford.

IS IT OVER YET?

The first "long" flick, and the first "art" film successfully distributed in America was the French production of *Queen Elizabeth,* directed by Louis Mercanton and starring Sarah Bernhardt, in 1912. Though the film was nothing more than a stationary camera pointed at the stage while the Divine Miss S. did her thing, *Queen Elizabeth* did prove to American filmmakers that audiences would pay to see a feature-length movie, and that stars had drawing power. Before *Elizabeth,* producers had been content to give their audiences one- and two-reel short subjects.

THE SPICE OF VARIETY

D. W. Griffith (1874–1948), great film innovator and often cited as the first producer-director in the modern sense, was the first filmmaker to make extensive use of long, medium, and close shots in film editing, as well as to use tracking and panning shots. The first medium shot (waist up) is *Fred Ott's Sneeze* from Edison Studios, 1889; the first extreme close up is *A Big Swallow* by G. A. Smith in 1900 (both a bit reminiscent of Andy Warhol's early films in the 1960's), but these kinds of shots were considered special effects and rarely used until Griffith came along. He first made films for Biograph in 1908.

BIG BUCKS

D. W. Griffith's *Intolerance,* which premiered at the Liberty Theatre, New York City, September 6, 1916, is reputed to have cost $1,900,000—a staggering sum for early film, and the first to hit seven figures. The most famous section of the film is the gigantic Babylon set which loomed over the studios on Sunset Boulevard. Griffith shot 300,000 feet of negative, and the first rough cut of seventy-five hours was finally edited down to thirteen reels. As historian Ramsaye wrote in 1929, "Stupendous expenditures were incurred; setting new precedents in grandiose gesture for the motion picture. The influence of the glorification of dimensions in *Intolerance* have been discernible in screen spectacle down to *The Ten Commandments* and *Ben-Hur* [the silent versions]."

WIDE-EYED

Seventy-millimeter, wide-screen films were introduced as early as 1897, when the Jim Corbett–Robert L. Fitzsimmons heavyweight championship boxing match was filmed in Reno. The film had a ratio of 2:1, or a projected image twice as wide as high.

Wide screen was pretty much ignored until 1929 when 20th Century-Fox introduced the 70-mm Fox Grandeur process. Their first wide-screen film was *The Fox Movietone Follies of 1929,* which premiered at the Gaiety Theatre, New York, in September. Other studios soon followed Fox's lead, and wide-screen films would have come to Hollywood on the heels of sound but for one thing: the Depression. The public loved and demanded sound, and fortunately it was fairly inexpensive to install in any former silent theater. Wide-screen, however, was costly—not only were new large projectors required, but in many cases entire theaters would have had to be rebuilt for the big screens.

It wasn't until the fifties, when television was killing film, that a desperate Hollywood found it financially worthwhile to reintroduce wide-screen flicks to try to lure audiences away from their home tubes. The first of these features, in the CinemaScope process, was *The Robe,* by Fox in 1953. CinemaScope was invented by Henri Crétien, and had an advantage over other wide-screen methods because it used 35-mm cameras and projectors—theaters only had to put a new lens on their projector to show wide, wide pictures.

Cinerama, the three-screen, three-camera process with its ability to make audiences feel like they really were in the roller coaster, was introduced in 1952 with *This Is Cinerama.* The first narrative feature film was *How the West Was Won* in 1962. Abel Gance (b. 1889), a pioneer French film director, was the first to use synchronized three-screen projection—which he called Polyvision—in his epic *Napoleon,* which premiered in Paris at the Théâtre National de l'Ôpéra, April 7, 1927.

REACH OUT AND TOUCH . . .

The 3-D process gets its uncanny sensation of depth from two projectors run simultaneously with the image "reconciled" by polarized glasses. Like many other film gimmicks, it's been around for a long time. The first 3-D film, *The Power of Love,* was made in 1922, and MGM made a few experimental films in 1935. But again, it wasn't until the financial crisis of the fifties that studios revived the gimmick to lure audiences back to theaters. The first 3-D film of the "great era" was *Bwana Devil* (MGM, 1953), a deservedly forgotten film.

YOU AIN'T HEARD NOTHIN' YET!

Sound film was pioneered by Thomas Edison, who experimented with synchronizing his wax cylinder phonograph recordings with his early filmstrips in 1889–90. In 1895 Edison manufactured about fifty

Kinetophones, which were sound versions of his Kinetoscope. The machines had a film reel and a wax cylinder, and the viewer, after plugging his nickel into the machine, held an earpiece to listen to the sound track while watching the show through the viewing window. The Kinetophones were a brief novelty, and didn't take off, possibly because they cost $350, instead of the $200 for silent Kinetophones.

The first projected films with sound were shown from April to October, 1900, at the Paris Exposition by two rival French companies. They played a phonograph disc, which was synchronized with the film. One film featured Sarah Bernhardt acting a scene from *Hamlet,* making her the first name actress to speak from the screen, and the first to speak Shakespeare.

The first process for recording sound directly on the film (which is the method used today) was developed by French-Anglo inventor Eugène Lauste in 1906. The Lauste process was workable, but World War I interfered with its commercial development. The sound-on-film process which led to the revolution in Hollywood in 1928 was that developed by radio pioneer Lee De Forest, who developed his Phonofilm process ca. 1922–23. De Forest made a number of short talkies with such big names as Gloria Swanson, Eddie Cantor, and George Jessel, between 1923 and 1927. The first demonstration of Phonofilm was at the Rialto Theatre, New York, on April 15, 1923. De Forest eventually sold his patents to Fox, who made it a commercial and technical success.

The rage for sound films began on August 6, 1926, when Warner Bros. premiered *Don Juan,* starring John Barrymore, the first film to use their Vitaphone process. The sound track was an orchestral accompaniment to the otherwise conventional silent, performed by the New York Philharmonic conducted by Henry Hadley. The film opened with a speech by Will Hays, later to become Hollywood's official arbiter of film morals.

Ironically, the Vitaphone system was merely a sound-on-disc system, like the French system of 1900. *Don Juan* with sound was a qualified success; most theaters showed the silent version. The real turning point came in October, 1927, when Warner Bros. released *The Jazz Singer* starring Al Jolson. Usually called the "first" talking picture, *The Jazz Singer* had a Vitaphone disc synchronized with the film, and had Jolson utter the famous line, "You ain't heard nothin' yet." The sound track had a few lines of dialogue and a few songs, but the bulk of the film was silent. It was a tremendous public success, however.

The so-called first "all talking" film was Warner's *Lights of New York,* released July 15, 1928.

THE ENVELOPE, PLEASE

The original Academy Awards, first given by the Academy of Motion Picture Arts and Sciences on May 16, 1929, were a far cry from today's world-famous media "event." While today there are 100 million television viewers in North America alone for the annual springtime awards ceremony in Los Angeles, the original ceremony was held quietly at the Hollywood Roosevelt Hotel at a banquet attended by about two hundred members of the film industry. The famous gold statuette was there, though it hadn't acquired its famous nickname yet; Douglas Fairbanks, then president of the academy, handed out the dozen awards in less than five minutes. There was no national newspaper or radio coverage, and no great excitement over the winners, since their names had been announced three months earlier, and the whole evening was like thousands of other business awards banquets that have been held since someone thought up giving awards to business and creative associates. But the academy's little affair was to be the beginning of a spectacular career for the statuette (actually gold-plated bronze) that was soon to be known as "Oscar." Awards were given for films made in the 1927–28 season.

The first Academy Award-winners include some of the most famous names in Hollywood history, and all nominated films were silent for the first and only time. Winner of Best Film was the Paramount production of *Wings,* a World War I combat film directed by William A. Wellman and starring Clara Bow, Richard Arlen, and Buddy Rogers.

The first winner of the Best Actor award was Emil Jannings, the Brooklyn-born, European-raised actor who became a major German silent film star and was brought to Hollywood where his first films won him the Academy Award. The winning performances, which could be for more than one film under the original academy rule, were in *The Last Command* and *The Way of All Flesh.*

The first actress to win was Janet Gaynor for her performances in *Sunrise, Street Angel,* and *Seventh Heaven.*

Award for Best Director went to Frank Borzage for *Seventh Heaven.* For the first and only time there was an award for best comedy directing; the winner was Lewis Milestone for *Two Arabian Knights.*

Best Writing award for Adaptation went to Benjamin Glazer for *Seventh Heaven,* and Best Original Story award was given to Ben Hecht for *Underworld.*

The Cinematography award went to Charles Rosher and Karl Strauss for their work on *Sunrise;* Interior Decoration awards went to William Cameron Menzies for *The Dove* and for *The Tempest.*

Two important special awards were given at the first ceremony: the first one to Charles Chaplin "for versatility and genius in writing, acting, directing, and producing *The Circus.* " The second, indicative of the parallel lives of "Oscar" and sound films, was to Warner Bros. for producing *The Jazz Singer,* "the pioneer outstanding talking picture, which has revolutionized the industry." By the time the next awards were given out, for the 1928–29 season, sound films dominated the awards just as they had swept the film industry since the release of *The Jazz Singer* in 1927.

YOU CAN CALL ME MR. ACADEMY AWARD

The first use of the nickname "Oscar" for the gold-plated bronze statuette that has become, like the Coca-Cola bottle, a universally known silhouette, is clouded in academy history.

Several people claim to have first used the moniker to describe the award. The earliest claimant, and often considered the one with the strongest case, is Margaret Herrick, former executive director of the academy, who claims to have named the svelte Art Deco statue after her uncle, Oscar Pierce, in 1931.

The second claimant, chronologically, is Sidney Skolsky, the Hollywood columnist, who claims he used the punch line of a vaudeville joke ("Will you have a cigar, Oscar?") as the source of the nickname.

The final, and most illustrious, contender is Bette Davis, whose first husband, Harmon Oscar Nelson, Jr., is reputed to have been the inspiration for the statue's new name.

The great mystery of who first named Oscar "Oscar" will, like the identity of Jack the Ripper, probably be forever lost in the mists of time. The only thing that is known is that by the mid-1930's the statue had been christened, however unofficially, as Oscar, and would ever after bear the name.

A NIGHT TO REMEMBER

The first film to sweep all major awards—and only one other film has done it again since—was *It Happened One Night,* which took the 1934 awards for Best Film, Best Director, Best Actor, Best Actress, and Best Screenplay (Adaptation).

It Happened One Night is a classic example of the Hollywood "sleeper"—a low-profile, low-budget film project that surprised everyone, director, producers, and stars, by turning out much better than they expected. The voting academy and the filmgoing public were taken by storm—all with the simple story of a runaway heiress who teams up with an unemployed newspaper reporter.

The top-notch team included Frank Capra (director), Robert Riskin (writer), and the famous pairing of Claudette Colbert and Clark Gable as the heiress and the reporter.

The major Oscar sweep was not duplicated until *One Flew Over the Cuckoo's Nest* in 1975.

AMATEUR NIGHT

The first nonprofessional actor to win an Oscar was Harold Russell, an ex-GI who had both hands amputated following a World War II battle injury. Russell portrayed a battle-injured vet in William Wyler's *The Best Years of Our Lives,* which was named Best Picture in 1946. Russell was voted a special honorary Oscar for his courage and example, but it was the award of the Best Supporting Actor to Russell, over the likes of Claude Rains, James Coburn, and Clifton Webb, that showed the academy's admiration of a handicapped nonprofessional's unprecedented acting achievement.

LIVE! FROM HOLLYWOOD

The first televised Academy Awards ceremonies were for the 1952 awards, on March 19, 1953. NBC-TV paid $100,000 for the broadcast rights, and the program was dual-telecast from the Pantages on the West Coast and the International Theatre in New York. The show drew the largest television audience on record up to that time. The evening's hosts were Bob Hope and Conrad Nagel.

A TRUMBO BY ANY NAME

The first person to win an Academy Award under a "false" name (that is, a name used to cover true identity, rather than a professional or stage name) was Dalton Trumbo. Screenwriter Trumbo was one of the Hollywood figures blacklisted during the Communist witch-hunts of the McCarthy era; like many actors, directors, and writers, Trumbo was unable to work on Hollywood films. In 1956, a fellow by the name of Robert Rich was nominated for—and won—the Oscar for Best Original Story for *The Brave Ones.* On presentation night, when Robert Rich was announced as winner, Jesse Lasky, Jr. accepted the award for Rich. Then people began to ask just who Rich was, and word leaked out that he was none other than Dalton Trumbo. Trumbo and associates had cleverly outwitted Hollywood politics, and pointed out the ugly foolishness of the blacklisting. That same year another writer, Michael Wilson, had been nominated for his screenplay *Friendly Persuasion,* but the academy was "persuaded" to remove Wilson's name from the nominees because he had been blacklisted. Fortunately Trumbo was clever enough to get around the McCarthy politics simply by pretending to be someone else—someone who didn't exist at all.

TEN PLUS

The first film to win more than ten Oscars was *Ben-Hur,* which received twelve nominations in 1959, winning eleven. The only loser: Best Screenplay, which went to *Room at the Top.*

IN LIVING SCARLETT

The first color film to win the Best Picture Oscar was *Gone With the Wind* in 1939. *GWTW* was the first major Hollywood production filmed in color, and became an instant film classic and one of the biggest-grossing and longest-running films in history. The film, based on Margaret Mitchell's equally famous book, was produced by David O. Selznick, directed by Victor Fleming, and photographed in Technicolor by Ernest Haller.

The sweet smell of success: Gardenia-bedecked Hattie McDaniel, the first black to win an Oscar, for her 1939 performance as Mammy in *Gone With the Wind*. Miss McDaniel is shown here with actress Fay Bainter, who presented the award. WIDE WORLD PHOTOS

MAMMY!

The first black to win an Oscar was Hattie McDaniel, who won the Best Supporting Actress award in 1939 for her popular and memorable role as Mammy in *Gone With the Wind*.

THANKS FOR THE MEMORIES

Bob Hope, the emcee most associated with the Academy Awards ceremonies during the 1940's and 1950's, made his first appearance as host for the 1939 awards, in ceremonies held February 29, 1940, at the Ambassador Hotel.

GONE BUT NOT FORGOTTEN

The first actor to be nominated for an Oscar posthumously was James Dean. Dean, who was killed in an auto accident in 1954, shortly after completing the film, was a Best Actor candidate in 1955 for his swan-song performance in *East of Eden.* Winner of the award in '55 was Ernest Borgnine in *Marty.*

The first actor to be nominated for and to win an Oscar posthumously was Peter Finch, who was named Best Actor for his performance as Howard Beale, the messianic TV personality, in *Network,* 1976. The announcement of the award to Finch provided one of the more emotional moments in recent Academy Award history. No actress has ever received a posthumous Oscar nomination.

WHO NEEDS IT?

George C. Scott, who has for many years made his dislike of film awards quite public, was nominated for Best Supporting Actor in 1959 for *Anatomy of a Murder.* Scott didn't protest a bit about the nomination, and he didn't win either. In 1961 he received the Best Supporting nomination again, for *The Hustler.* This time, Scott requested that the academy remove his name from the list of nominees. The academy board refused, and notified Scott, "Nominations and awards are voted for achievements as they appear on screen, therefore a person responsible for the achievement cannot decline the nomination after it is voted." The named stayed on the ballot, and Scott didn't win that year either. Round three came in 1970, when Scott was nominated as Best Actor for *Patton.* This time Scott didn't try to refuse the nomination, though his position was well-known in the film community. To the astonishment of many, Scott won the award, though he refused to accept it or have anyone accept it for him.

LITTLEFEATHER, BIG FUSS

The first actor to send an emissary to *refuse* an Oscar was Marlon Brando, who won Best Actor for *The Godfather,* 1972. Brando had said nothing at nomination time, but on the night of the awards, a woman named "Satcheen Littlefeather" went to the rostrum to refuse Brando's award because of "the treatment of the Indians by the film industry, TV, and in movie reruns." Miss Littlefeather, in Indian regalia, was later revealed to be a starlet named Maria Cruz. No doubt, with the enormous television audience at Academy Awards time, the future will see more rejections for political or personal reasons.

Actors, however, don't have a monopoly on refusing Oscar.

BY GEORGE, HE'S GOT IT AND DOESN'T WANT IT

The first person to raise a fuss about being awarded an Oscar—in effect, refusing the honor—was none other than George Bernard Shaw. Shaw was given the Oscar in 1938 for *Pygmalion,* which had been adapted from his play by Ian Dalrymple, Cecil Lewis, and W. P. Lipscomb (who received an award for Best Adaptation). In typical Shavian manner, the playwright announced, "It's an insult. My position as a playwright is known throughout the world. To offer me an award of this sort is an insult, as if they had never heard of me before."

To date, no actresses have refused an Academy Award.

STARSTRUCK FIRSTS

SO YOU WANT TO BE A STAR?

The pioneers of film had no intention of creating film stars, much less a star system. In the early days, film was a commercial product, and the people appearing on the screen were like so many props—kids off the street, lab technicians, office secretaries, friends of the cameramen. "Actors" (they were hardly considered that!) were never credited. But after a few months of cranking out one-reelers and Kinetoscope film loops, the Edisons and Lumières and Seligs began to notice that a few people were better than others in front of the camera, so these folks, who never intended to be actors, somehow fell into it.

The first hint of things to come came in 1912, when a French group called *Film d'art* released one of its films of a stage play in America. The film was *Queen Elizabeth* and it starred Sarah Bernhardt and members of the Comédie Française. The film was the first full-length feature film to be successfully shown in the United States, and it showed that established stage stars could draw crowds. However, the studio bosses of that era—Biograph, for example—resisted the idea, reasoning that if their film stars became as established in the public eye as a Bernhardt, they would want as much money as a Bernhardt.

Precisely. But what the producers didn't realize was that the creation of film stars would not only cost them more money, but it would make them vast sums as well. The public would come in droves to see their favorites.

As early as the first Edison film loops in the late 1890's, known individuals had appeared with title credit—famed strongman Eugene Sandow, for example, and Broadway stars John Rice and May Erwin reenacting their famous 1896 stage kiss on camera. These popular stage and vaudeville stars never appeared more than a time or two before the voracious filmgoing public. But the uncredited kids at studios like Biograph did appear in film after film, the Little Marys and Biograph girls, playing the same role in film after film. The audiences followed their heroes and heroines closely, and often thought they were playing themselves on the screen. They had become, in fact, uncredited stars.

The next logical step was for an actor to demand screen credit, and a higher salary.

This happened in Germany in 1907, when an actress named Henny Porten, who had become famous as The Messter Girl, demanded her name "in lights," so to speak. Messter studio officials gave in, and she became the first screen actress in the world to be credited by name.

A STAR IS BORN

The first American performer to receive screen credit (other than a stage star reenacting a stage role) was Florence Lawrence, who had become famous as The Biograph Girl. Florence, who apparently had been agitating at Biograph for screen credit, was wooed away from Biograph by a newly formed rival group: Carl Laemmle's Independent Motion Picture Company, known as IMP. IMP fully realized the potential of creating stars, and they launched Florence in true Hollywood fashion—by creating the first film publicity stunt. When Flo went over to the new studio, she arranged to mysteriously disappear. Planted stories appeared in the newspapers that The Biograph Girl was missing, whereabouts unknown; then the story broke that she had been killed in St. Louis; finally, an announcement was placed in the papers by the IMP studios saying that the whole thing was a silly lie—and that their first film starring Florence Lawrence, the new IMP girl, would be released shortly. The first American film star died a suicide, all but forgotten, in 1939.

The first male film star was "Bronco Billy" Anderson, who appeared as Bronco Billy in numerous Westerns made by Essanay Studios from 1908 to 1915. Born Max Aronson, later changed to William Aronson, he, like The Biograph Girl, was known to fans as just plain Bronco Billy.

KID STUFF

Children have been popular in films since the Lumières' *L'Arroseur arrosée* in 1895. Numerous child actors had substantial careers thoughout the teens and twenties, but the first major silent child star was Jackie Coogan (b. 1914), who appeared in Chaplin's *The Kid* in 1920 and remained the top child star through the decade.

The first male child star of the talkie era was the talented Jackie Cooper (b. 1921), who began at age six in the silent *Our Gang* shorts, then began his rapid rise to child stardom with his first sound film, *Movietone Follies,* in 1928. Jackie became the first child actor to be nominated for a full Academy Award (Best Supporting Actor), for *Skippy* in 1931.

The first female child star of talkies—and arguably the most talented child star ever (no one doubts she's the most famous)—is Shirley Temple (b. 1928), who appeared in *The Red-Haired Alibi,* a short, at the remarkable age of three. Even more remarkable were the films to come: By 1934 she was the star of her own film, *Little Miss Marker,* and the prodigiously talented child had sung, danced, joked, cried, and flirted her way into the hearts of America. She is also the youngest person to have earned a million dollars, and probably the first child ever to have done so.

WHAT A VAMP!

The first sex goddess—a type that became a staple of Hollywood with the advent of the star system—was Theda Bara, a total product of filmland hype. The original Vamp, the classic twenties seductress (her name an anagram of ARAB DEATH) was transformed by studio publicity from Theodosia Goodman, the daughter of a Jewish tailor from Chillicothe, Ohio, into the symbol of exotic, foreign, sexual decadence.

MILLION DOLLAR BABIES

The star system was so successful, and lucrative for the producers, that a mere six years after Flo Lawrence got the first screen billing, her coworkers Mary Pickford and Charles Chaplin were able to demand, and get, seven-figure contracts. Chaplin reached a $670,000 deal with Mutual in 1916. When word of Chaplin's record-setting contract reached Mary Pickford (one of the most astute business-women in Hollywood history), she wouldn't settle for less than a million. On June 24, 1916, she signed with Adolph Zukor at Para-mount for $1,040,000, for two years of film work, plus bonuses; the money was technically paid to the Mary Pickford Company. After Chaplin's 1916 contract expired, he signed an eight-film contract with First National Pictures (April, 1917) for $1,075,000, including certain production controls. Pickford signed her second million-dollar contract that year, also with First National. Little Mary got $1,050,000.

OVER AND OUT

The first film star to commit suicide mid-career was Olive Thomas, who had risen from popular Ziegfeld showgirl at sixteen to Selznick studios' main star at age twenty. Olive, the popular star of *Prudence on Broadway* and *The Follies Girl,* the recent bride of Jack Pickford (the actor-brother of Little Mary), was found dead in a Paris hotel room on September 10, 1920, from an overdose of mercuric chloride. The film world was shocked by the first star suicide, but what fol-lowed was even more shocking, and launched Hollywood on its first drug scandal. Just before her death, Olive had been seen with a number of French underworld figures. The reason: She was trying to score heroin to feed her habit.

TROUBLE IN PARADISE

The first film star to lose his career through scandal was the famous silent comedian Roscoe "Fatty" Arbuckle. Arbuckle, one of the great pioneers of silent comedy, had started out with Mack Sennett, later worked with Keaton on some of the best short comedies of the era, and finally become a major comedy star on his own. Fatty's private life was even more exuberant than his screen comedies. Fond of drink, pretty young girls (the more the better), and wild, wild booze-and-sex parties, Arbuckle's carousing had more than once caused the Paramount studio bosses to grease a few palms to quiet things down. On Labor Day weekend, 1921, Arbuckle threw a big party at the St. Francis Hotel in San Francisco to celebrate his 3-million-dollar contract with Paramount. Among the carloads of starlets present at the three-day bash was young Virginia Rappe, a starlet who had been hanging around the Arbuckle entourage for some time. Pretty, dark-eyed Virginia, who had posed for the cover of the sheet music for "Let Me Call You Sweetheart," caught Fatty's eye. At some point, after the couple had slipped into one of the hotel suite bedrooms, other guests heard a ruckus in the closed room. Arbuckle finally emerged, and Virginia was found writhing in pain on the bed. She was taken to Pine Street Hospital, where she died five days later from peritonitis—exactly one year after Olive Thomas's suicide.

Arbuckle was subsequently charged with first-degree murder, and acquitted at three lurid, banner-headline trials. The great scandal, and one the press played upon with only the most thinly disguised euphemisms, was that Virginia had been fatally injured by a "foreign object"—rumored to be a champagne or soda bottle—being forcibly used by Arbuckle on the young starlet during their drunken sex bout.

The Arbuckle case aroused the anti-Hollywood, antidecadence troops around the country. Arbuckle was dropped from Paramount, and spent the rest of the twenties, when his contemporaries Chaplin and Keaton were establishing themselves as immortals of the silent screen, as a mere ghost of his former self. He was box office poison (several audiences had rioted when Arbuckle films were shown after the scandal broke), and he got by on a handful of directing jobs. Fatty turned more and more to drink, and died a destitute alcoholic in 1933.

NOTORIOUS

The first married film star to have an open affair with a man not her husband was Ingrid Bergman. The Swedish actress had taken Hollywood by storm with such films as *Intermezzo* (1939), her first American film, and *Gaslight* in 1944, which won her the Oscar that year. She scandalized Hollywood and the filmgoing public when, in 1949, she began an open affair with Italian director Roberto Rossellini, while still married to Peter Lindstrom. Bergman's "Ivory Soap" image was further wrecked when she bore Rossellini a child, February 13, 1950, while still Lindstrom's wife. Once again, the ministerial and moral groups raised an outcry; Bergman remained in Europe, her American career destroyed—until her stunning comeback in *Anastasia* in 1956, which won her a second Academy Award.

SMOKE GETS IN YOUR EYES

The first film star to be arrested, tried, convicted, and serve a jail term while a star—and to emerge from jail still a star—was Robert

Mitchum. On August 31, 1948, Mitchum, then a popular young actor under contract to Selznick Studios, was arrested in a raid on the home of Hollywood starlet Lila Leeds, a friend of Bob's. Mitchum, who *had* been scheduled to address a rally on the steps of Los Angeles City Hall the next day as a part of National Youth Week (the speech was canceled, not surprisingly), hired famed attorney Jerry Geisler to defend him. The result was a two-month jail sentence for possession of marijuana, which Mitchum served in full. On his release, Mitchum's career went into anything but a tailspin: Howard Hughes bought out Bob's contract from Selznick for $200,000, and the sleepy-eyed leading man went on to make some of his best-known films, including those with Jane Russell, the knockout Hughes discovery.

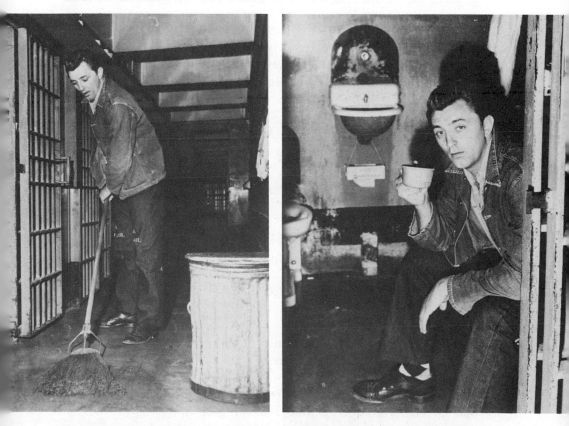

A Hollywood set it isn't: Robert Mitchum, the first film star to serve a jail term while still a star—sits out part of his 60-day sentence for "conspiracy to possess marijuana" in 1949. WIDE WORLD PHOTOS

WE ALL HAVE TO START SOMEWHERE:
Stars Whose First Films Are Totally Forgettable

1. CLINT EASTWOOD in *Revenge of the Creature* (1955)
The thing no doubt made an *Escape from Alcatraz* looking for *A Fistful of Dollars*.

2. ELVIS PRESLEY in *Love Me Tender* (1956)
The King should have abdicated rather than be seen in this one.

3. ROBERT REDFORD in *Warhunt* (1962)
Biding his time until Butch Cassidy came along.

4. PAUL NEWMAN in *The Silver Chalice* (1954)
Biding his time until the Sundance Kid came along.

5. BURT REYNOLDS in *Angel Baby* (1961)
It paid the rent.

6. BETTE DAVIS in *Bad Sister* (1931)
No relation to Margo Channing.

7. SUSAN HAYWARD in *Girls on Probation* (1938)
She should have gotten *20,000 Years in Sing Sing*.

8. SOPHIA LOREN in *Quo Vadis* (1950)
The future star was an extra in the cast of thousands.

9. JENNIFER JONES in *Dick Tracy's G-Men* (1939)
She was four years away from singing *The Song of Bernadette*.

10. MARIA MONTEZ in *The Invisible Woman* (1941)
Her fans complain they didn't see enough of her; her critics lament she wasn't The Inaudible Woman as well.

CATEGORICALLY SPEAKING:
First Films in Major Genres

SHOOT 'EM UP

Westerns, more than any other genre, are linked with Hollywood and films, and they became popular settings for movies from the earliest days. The first Westerns made were two short films out of the American Mutoscope and Biograph Company, titled *Kit Carson* and *The Pioneers.* Both were released in August, 1903. The two films introduced some plot staples that were to be seen thousands of times over the next decades: Indian raids, cowboy heroes, and Western settlers.

The film usually called the first Western, Edwin S. Porter's *The Great Train Robbery,* was actually released four months after the Biograph films, in December, 1903. The Porter film is justly famous for another first: Porter's use of ellipsis (moving back and forth in time and place in telling the story). It was one of the first steps taken by Porter toward shaping a more complicated narrative style, and had a great influence on other early filmmakers, notably D. W. Griffith.

The first Western talkie was *In Old Arizona,* produced by Fox Movietone and directed by Raoul Walsh and Irving Cummings. Billed as "the First All-Talking Outdoor Picture," *In Old Arizona* was the first talking picture to be shot primarily on location outdoors.

SCI-FIDELITY

The great-granddaddy of *Star Wars* and *Close Encounters of the Third Kind* was pioneer French filmmaker George Méliès's *A Trip to the Moon,* 1902. A whimsical fantasy, full of humorous trick photography (disappearing moon creatures, faces that become stars), *A Trip to the Moon* showed early on that sci-fi would go hand in hand with the development of special effects.

BE A CLOWN

The first comedy film credit goes to the Lumière brothers, whose *L'Arroseur arrosé* (literally, the Hoser Hosed) shows a prankish little boy causing the family gardener to douse himself with the hose by sneaking up behind the gardener and stepping on the coil. When the gardener looks into the hose to see what happened to the water, the boy lets go and, *voilà,* the silent comedy gag is born. *L'Arroseur* was one of the first films the Lumières made in their breakthrough year of 1895, and was included on the bill at the first public film screening in Paris on December 28, 1895.

SCARED SILLY

The first horror film was a 1908 one-reel version of *Dr. Jekyll and Mr. Hyde* starring Richard Mansfield, filmed by the Selig Polyscope Company of Chicago. The film was a direct recreation of the stage version, with no attempt at cinematic technique.

The first sound horror film was the famous *Dracula,* made by Universal Studios in 1931, starring Bela Lugosi as the bloodsucking count, and directed by Tod Browning.

The first psychological horror film, and one which still captivates audiences, was the influential German film, *The Cabinet of Dr. Caligari* (1919, 1920 U.S.), directed by Robert Wiene and written by Carl Mayer and Han Janowitz, and starring Conrad Veidt. The first expressionist film, *Caligari* was shot entirely in the studio (the preferred method in Germany after World War I), with stark, distorted sets. In its course it deals with hypnosis, madness, zombiism, and dreams—some of the favorite fodder of films to come.

A CAST OF THOUSANDS

The first epic film—one of Hollywood's favorite genres until rising costs turned casts of thousands into rare birds—was D. W. Griffith's *Birth of a Nation*. Based on *The Clansman,* a novel by Thomas Dixon, *Birth of a Nation* was pioneer director Griffith's first independently made film, produced under the auspices of Mutual-Biograph Studios, and starring Lillian Gish and Henry B. Walthall. The statistics of this pioneer epic were staggering at the time: six weeks in preproduction, nine weeks shooting, and the astronomical cost of $125,000 to produce. The film premiered amid raves and controversy in Los Angeles on February 18, 1915. The controversy was, and still is, over Griffith's racist handling of blacks in the Southern-set film, and especially in his positive portrayal of the Ku Klux Klan. The racial aspect still arouses harsh criticism (or praise, depending on point of view), and Griffith's name is forever linked in film history with racial bigotry.

LIVING IN THE PAST

The first historical/costume film is the early *Execution of Mary, Queen of Scots,* made by the Edison studios in 1895. Lasting about thirty seconds, the film shows the unfortunate Mary being led to the block by executioners, having her head placed on the block, and getting same lopped off. Since the audiences weren't as used to trick photography as today, they were probably amazed to see Mary's head go rolling across the stage, not knowing that the camera had been stopped and a dummy substituted before the fatal chop. This is the first known use of trick photography in film history.

SONG AND DANCE

The first musical film credit goes to *The Jazz Singer* (1927), starring Al Jolson and directed by Alan Crosland for Warner Bros. Though not a "musical" in the full sense of the term, it does have dialogue and a few songs mixed in with the silent portions.

The Broadway Melody of 1928 was the first full-talking musical, and it won the 1928–29 Oscar as Best Picture, launching thirty years of great screen musicals.

The first color musical was the immortal *The Wizard of Oz,* starring Judy Garland, Ray Bolger, Jack Haley, Bert Lahr, and Margaret Hamilton, and directed by Victor Fleming for MGM in 1939. *Wizard* very cleverly integrated black-and-white with color sections: The opening scenes in Kansas, credits and all, are black and white; as soon as Dorothy and Toto get to Oz, all is color. Fortunately, after treating the audiences to Oz in full color, the director had the courage to make the return to Kansas black and white, giving the film a somber, if happy, ending.

WAR GAMES

The first sound war film, and one of the best ever made, is the 1929 *All Quiet on the Western Front,* based on the Eric Maria Remarque antiwar novel, produced by Carl Lammle and directed by Lewis Milestone. The film, starring Louis Wolheim and Lew Ayres, won the Academy Award for Best Picture in 1929–30. *All Quiet* was the first film to depict war in all its horror, without glory, nobility, or patriotic fervor.

REEL LIFE

The first documentary film—and still one of the most famous—was Robert Flaherty's *Nanook of the North,* released in 1922. Newsreels had been produced continuously as introductory short "entertainments" for feature films as early as 1910. But Flaherty's pioneering film marked the first time a film had documented a single, real-life subject or situation with any depth and detail, and launched an important branch of filmmaking. What is not well-known about *Nanook of the North* is that the version seen today, revered as one of the classics of early film, is not the first version. Flaherty originally filmed Nanook, the Canadian Eskimo living on the frozen shores of Baffin Land, in three expeditions during 1910–16, while Flaherty was on an exploring expedition for a mining company. Back home, Flaherty experienced the worst fear of early filmmakers: The entire footage, shot under those difficult circumstances up north, was destroyed by fire (early nitrate-coated film stock was highly flammable); Flaherty himself was the culprit, when he dropped his cigarette ash into the packing crate containing the film.

Flaherty gamely decided to try again. He got backing from Revillion Frères furriers (the first example of industrial backing for a film, *à la* Mobil and Exxon), went back to Canada to reshoot the film, and completely reconstructed the film as we know it today. After the second time around, Flaherty commented that if the first version had survived, no one would remember the film today, so superior was the second version. "It was a bad film," he said, "it was dull."

Note: The first to use the word *documentary* to describe a nonfiction film was John Grierson, who has been called "the father of the documentary film." Grierson, a filmmaker, theorist, and writer, coined the word in a review of Flaherty's *Moana* (1926), a documentary about the Saruwan island of Savii.

EEK! ARGH! UGH!:
Famous First Monsters

As soon as men began capturing scenes on film, they learned that "movies" not only could entertain, educate, and amuse—they could frighten as well. Film, much more than stage or even fiction, can grip the beholder, make him part of another reality—the one on the screen. To their great credit, the first generation of filmmakers fell in love with the idea of horrifying or frightening their audiences, and their audiences loved it. So, in the early days of film, one of the most enduring and endearing—if uneven—genres of film was born.

The following roster of some of the most famous and popular scaries tells how they all got their start.

Frankenstein, probably the most famous of all screen monsters, has appeared in twenty to thirty films of wildly different merits; he has most often been in starring roles, but has made numerous appearances in supporting monster and stalk-on parts. The *Frankenstein* story, based on Mary Wollstonecraft Shelley's 1818 novel, was first filmed by none other than the Edison studios, probably in 1908 (some sources say 1910) with Charles Ogle as the monster.

The first important monster film, and one that was to have great influence on the classic *Frankenstein* films of the next decades, was *The Golem,* starring Paul Wegener, made in Germany in 1914. Wegener's monster, based on the European Jewish legend of a clay statue that comes to life, could be considered the first *physical* incarnation of Frankenstein as we know him, since his makeup and cos-

279

tume included the platform shoes and stony countenance so closely associated with the monster.

The first sound version of *Frankenstein* is the famous film produced by Universal Studios in 1931 and starring Boris Karloff in his greatest role. This classic version—and probably the greatest—was directed by James Whale and written by Henry Hull.

Dracula, the only rival to Frankenstein in the hearts of monster fans, has a filmography even longer than his rival's: almost forty films, ranging from the classic to the embarrassing. The first version of the Dracula story is the German *Nosferatu* of 1923, based very loosely on the Bram Stoker novel of 1898. This first screen vampire was played by Max Schreck, who, unlike his suave, sexual descendant as immortalized by Bela Lugosi, sported long, clawlike fingernails, a shaved head, and bulging, ghoulish eyes. He sucked blood all the same.

Like *Frankenstein,* the definitive *Dracula* is the Hollywood version produced by Universal in the early thirties; this first sound version starred Bela Lugosi and was directed by Tod Browning and released in 1931.

The Werewolf is the younger brother of cinema's unholy three, and didn't make his first full screen appearance until *The Werewolf of London,* starring Henry Hull, in 1934. Lon Chaney, the most famous screen lycanthrope, made his first appearance in face-fur under a full moon in Universal's *The Wolf Man* of 1941. The theme of man transformed to monster didn't make its first appearance with *Werewolf of London,* however; the bestial, befurred-man idea is closely linked to *Dr. Jekyll and Mr. Hyde,* and filmmakers borrowed liberally from the many earlier film versions of the Jekyll-Hyde story in creating the classic werewolf.

Dr. Jekyll and Mr. Hyde was another man-monster story that captured the imaginations of early filmmakers. The first version was a 1908 two-reeler made by Colonel Selig's Polyscope Company of Chicago, one of the pioneer film studios, and Richard Mansfield starred as the split-personality hero.

A curious sidelight of the Jekyll-Hyde saga is the color version made in 1913 (!) in England, utilizing the early and short-lived Kinemacolor process. This *Dr. Jekyll and Mr. Hyde* version gets the laurels for being the first horror film made in color.

The first sound version of the R. L. Stevenson novel of 1885 was made in 1931, produced by Paramount. Directed by Rouben Mamoulian in his first and only venture into the horror genre, *Dr. Jekyll and Mr. Hyde* is another first-sound version that has often been remade and sequeled, but never equaled. Frederic March received the Oscar for Best Actor, making him the first and only performer to be so honored for a performance in a horror film.

King Kong, the epitome of brute nature destroyed by brutal civilization, has, if anything, suffered more from remakes and sequels than he ever did from strafing biplanes swooping around him as he clutched the top of the Empire State Building: yet another example of a first version that has never been bettered. Based on the Edgar Wallace story, RKO produced *King Kong* in 1933, with special effects by Willis O'Brien (including twenty-seven different models for Kong and parts of Kong), starring Fay Wray, Bruce Cabot, and Robert Armstrong, with a score by Max Steiner.

The Hunchback of Notre Dame, based on Victor Hugo's famous novel, has two classic first versions to its credit. The 1923 silent version was produced by Universal Studios and starred Lon Chaney in what is probably his greatest screen role, and Patsy Ruth Miller as the gypsy girl Esmeralda. The first sound version of *The Hunchback* is the 1939 RKO production with Charles Laughton as Quasimodo, Maureen O'Hara as Esmeralda, and Cedric Hardwicke as Quasimodo's nasty brother.

The Mummy has been disinterred seven times. The first version by the same name, in 1932, starred Boris Karloff in the dual role of the 3,700-year-old Egyptian priest and Ardet Bey; the film was directed by Karl Freund, cinematographer of *The Golem*.

The Phantom of the Opera first played the organ in the deserted theater in the 1925 silent version starring Lon Chaney, Sr., as the hideously amorous denizen of the backstage; May Philben was the object of his affections, and Rupert Julian directed. This is one silent first version that is superior to all sequels.

The first sound version of *The Phantom of the Opera* was the 1943 vehicle with the unlikely cast of Claude Rains (the Phantom) and Susanna Foster and Nelson Eddy as the romantic couple threatened by Mr. Rains.

The Zombie—or living corpse—has stalked his (or her) way through numerous films, from *I Walked with a Zombie* to *Night of the Living Dead.* What is probably the first appearance of a zombie-like character—a physically dead body manipulated from without by magic or voodoo—is in the famous *Cabinet of Dr. Caligari* (Germany, 1919).

The Invisible Man was first not seen in *The Invisible Man,* based on the H. G. Wells story, in 1933. Claude Rains was the star under wraps, and James Whale of *Frankenstein* fame directed. The film, which made Rains famous, was turned down by Karloff, who didn't like the idea of not being seen until he was shot at the end of the film. Like most classic horror films, the first version was the best: Somehow, *The Invisible Woman* and *The Invisible Man's Revenge* just didn't make it.

Apes. Though not monsters in the strict sense, the civilized, talking simians of *Planet of the Apes* share one common trait with the great film monsters. Though not human or "normal," they manage to be more sympathetic and interesting than the humans they're pitted against. And, once again, the first film is superior to the sequels. *Planet of the Apes,* starring Charlton Heston as the displaced astronaut, and Kim Hunter, Roddy McDowall, and James Whitmore as the apes, and based on the Pierre Boulle novel *Monkey Planet,* appeared in 1967.

Fu Manchu, one of the all-time bad cookies (not a monster in the physical sense, but in the spiritual), made his screen debut in the 1932 *Mask of Fu Manchu,* produced at MGM by Irving Thalberg, based on the Sax Rohmer novel, and starring Boris Karloff.

(Last but not least) Godzilla. The most famous of the giant, red-eyed, scaly-backed, multi-winged, -footed, -headed, and eminently devastating creatures (usually from the bowels of the earth), Godzilla first wrought havoc on a miniature set of Tokyo in *Gigantis, the Fire Monster,* produced by Toho studios (Japan) in 1955. The 100-yard high reptilian apparently didn't like his first name, so changed it to *Gojira* a year later—which of course became the English *Godzilla, King of the Monsters,* released in 1956.

GOLD-PLATED FIRSTS

THE FIRST GOLD RECORD

In 1941 Glenn Miller's RCA recording of "Chattanooga Choo-Choo," from the film *Sun Valley Serenade,* sold in excess of one million copies, and RCA execs hit on the idea of gold-plating a master disc of the record and presenting it to Miller as an award and as a promotional gimmick (it was presented on a live Chesterfield cigarette program on February 10, 1942).

The idea caught on, and for the next fifteen years recording artists were given gold records for their single records that sold a million copies, and for their albums that tallied a million dollars in sales.

Beginning in 1958, the Recording Industry Association of America (RIAA) began certifying gold records—that is, auditing sales figures from the various record companies to verify gold disc status.

In 1975, mainly because many double-LP albums were being awarded gold records with relatively low sales figures because their high selling price racked up a million dollars in sales quickly, the requirements for an RIAA-certified gold record were again changed. Since 1975 a single record hits gold when it sells a million copies, and a long-playing album hits gold at half a million copies. Platinum discs are awarded for singles that hit the two million mark in sales, and for albums that sell one million copies.

No encore, Enrico!: Enrico Caruso was not only the first singer to sell a million records, he was the first opera star to "go Hollywood." In 1918 the great tenor made two full-length films for Paramount Studios. The first, *My Cousin,* shown here, was a flop. The second was so bad the studio never even released it. Perhaps the films would have come off better had they had the benefit of sound.
THE BETTMANN ARCHIVE, INC.

A MILLION OR TWO

Al Jolson's "Ragging the Baby to Sleep," released by the Victor Talking Machine Company in 1912, was reputed to have sold 2 million copies within two years, making it the first million- and first two-million-selling record.

SING IT, AGAIN, ALMA

According to *The Book of Golden Discs,* the first female artist to hit gold status is probably Alma Gluck, the famed opera star, with her recording of "Carry Me Back to Old Virginny" written by James Bland, a black songwriter. "Virginny" was recorded some time between 1911 and 1912 and released on a single-faced twelve-inch disc, then re-released in 1915 on a double-faced disc paired with "Old Black Joe." It's the second version that has been reputed to have sold a million copies by 1918.

THE MILLS' MILLION

The Mills Brothers' recording of "Tiger Rag" and "Nobody's Sweetheart" in 1930 on the Brunswick label was the first recording by a vocal group to hit seven-figure sales.

I AM CALLING YOOOOU . . .

"Indian Love Call," recorded in 1936 by Jeanette MacDonald and Nelson Eddy, gets honors as the first show tune to sell a million. The tune was from the 1924 Harbach, Hammerstein, and Friml musical *Rose Marie,* though the disc's success was due mainly to the MacDonald-Eddy film version of 1936.

BOOGIE WOOGIE BEST SELLER

"Bei Mir Bist du Schön," recorded by the Andrews Sisters—Patti, Maxine, and Laverne—in 1937 made them the first female group to rack up a million.

THE "POPS' " TOPS

"Jalousie," recorded by Arthur Fiedler and the Boston Pops Orchestra in 1935, and released on Victor in 1938, became the first light orchestral million seller—though it took until 1952 to do so.

RED, WHITE, AND GOLD

Kay Kyser and his orchestra's disc of "Praise the Lord and Pass the Ammunition," recorded for Victor in 1942, became the first patriotic million-selling record.

O-KAY!

In 1943 *Oklahoma!* (Rodgers and Hammerstein) became the first Broadway musical sound track to be recorded complete (on 78 r p m 's), and half a million sets were sold by 1945. When the complete score was re-released in 1949 in long-play, sales reached 2½ million.

MAMMY!

The souvenir set of *The Jolson Story,* containing a collection of Jolson's greatest hits, released on Decca in 1946, was the first multi-record album to hit gold status.

A MILLION LAUGHS

Kermit Schafer's *Radio Bloopers* (Jublilee Records, 1954) was the first comedy album to strike gold.

GOLD ROCK

A landmark in rock, Bill Haley and the Comets' "Shake, Rattle, and Roll," recorded on Decca on April 12, 1954, became the first rock 'n' roll smash hit.

THE FIRST LP BY A SOLO ARTIST TO SELL A MILLION

Harry Belafonte's *Calypso* on Victor, released in 1956, was reported to have sold a million by 1959, and was certified a gold record in 1963.

MANCINI WITH THE GOLDEN GUNN

Peter Gunn by Henry Mancini on RCA Victor was the first TV sound track to sell a million. The album collected twelve pieces written by Mancini from thirty-nine weeks of the filmed series. Released in 1958, it was certified gold in 1959.

HIGH CLASS

The Van Cliburn/Kiril Kondrashin recording of the Tchaikovsky Piano Concerto No. 1, released in 1958, became the first classical long-playing record to sell a million copies, in 1961.

GOLD GARLAND

The first female artist to get a certified gold disc, and the first double LP to sell a million was *Judy Garland at Carnegie Hall,* released in May, 1961, on Capitol. The two-LP album was certified a gold record in 1962.

GOLD SOUL

"Oh Happy Day" by the Edwin Hawkins Singers, released in 1969, was the first black gospel million seller.

THE FIRST GOLD TAPE CARTRIDGE

Carole King's *Tapestry* album, which sold a whopping 12 million records worldwide from 1971 to 1973 (six million in the United States alone), was the first recording to receive a gold tape award, in 1971.

GOLD SUPERSTARS AND THEIR FIRST MILLION-SELLERS

BING CROSBY

The great crooner made his first record "I've Got the Girl" in 1926; the first of his 22 million-selling records was "Sweet Leilani" on Decca, recorded February 23, 1937. Crosby, whose estimated record sales are a staggering 400 million, also has the distinction of recording "White Christmas" (May 29, 1942) from the film *Holiday Inn,* the best-selling record of all time, estimated at more than 30 million in Crosby's version and 68 million in all versions.

FRANK SINATRA

"Ol' Blue Eyes' " first record was "From the Bottom of My Heart/ Melancholy Mood," recorded July 13, 1939, with the Harry James Orchestra. The same year he recorded "All or Nothing at All," which sold about eight thousand copies. By 1943 Sinatra had become a star, and Columbia Records re-released the disc, which hit the million mark.

ELVIS PRESLEY

"The King" began his recording career with a private recording made for his mother's birthday. The cut got him a contract with Sun

Records, and his first disc for them was "That's All Right, Mama" backed with "Blue Moon of Kentucky" in 1954. The first of Elvis's 60 million-selling records was "Heartbreak Hotel/I Was the One" on RCA (who bought his contract from Sun for $35,000), recorded on February 10, 1956. The disc actually got two gold records—one for each side.

THE BEATLES

The first record by the group (then consisting of five members, minus Ringo and plus Stuart Sutcliffe and Pete Best) was made in Germany in 1961, on Polydor: "My Bonnie" and "When the Saints Go Marching In." Their first disc as the famous four was "Love Me Do" and "P.S. I Love You" on Parlophone in Britain, 1962.

Their first million-seller was "She Loves You" in 1964, and their album *Help!* in 1965 was the first LP in history to have sold a million copies in orders before being released—an instant gold record.

THE ROLLING STONES

The Stones' first disc was "Come On" in 1963; their first gold record was the huge smash "Satisfaction," released on London Records in 1965, and selling 4.5 million and getting a gold award the same year.

STEVIE WONDER

Little Stevie Wonder (as he was then known) was only twelve years old when his record "Fingertips, Part 2" passed the million mark and hit number one on the charts in 1963. Wonder was also the first recording artist to have both a single and an LP (*That 12-Year-Old Genius*) in the number one chart position in the United States at the same time.

THE BEE GEES

The group that was to break industry records with their 26 million worldwide sales figure for their *Saturday Night Fever* album in 1977 had a million seller in their first single release in Britain, "New York Mining Disaster," Polydor, April, 1967.

ELTON JOHN

The bespectacled wonder made his first recording "From Denver to L.A." in 1969 for the Michael Winner film *The Games.* The first of his 22 million-selling records (60 million sold) was the LP *Elton John,* released in 1970 and hitting seven figures by 1972.

DIANA ROSS AND THE SUPREMES

The Supremes' first record was "I Want a Guy" on Motown, and they had the first of their 26 million-selling discs with "Where Did Our Love Go?" in 1964. They're also the first and only female group to have twelve number one records in the United States.

Diana Ross left the group in 1970, and her first solo (on Motown) was "Reach Out and Touch." The same year "Ain't No Mountain High Enough" became her first million seller.

BARBRA STREISAND

Though she has had a remarkable twenty-three gold albums during her career, Barbra Streisand didn't have a gold single disc until 1973 with "The Way We Were." Barbra's first single was "My Coloring Book" on Columbia in 1963, and her first album, from the same year, was *The Barbra Streisand Album,* which was a gold record.

HIGH FREQUENCY FIRSTS

THE AMPLIFIER TUBE

Lee De Forest, a thirty-three-year-old American inventor, produced the first three-electrode vacuum amplifier tube in 1906. The tube revolutionized electronics because it allowed for the first time the easy amplification of signals received over radio waves: When combined with the Marconi wireless invention of 1895, radio as we know it was born.

THE FIRST REGULAR RADIO BROADCASTS

Were made by Lee De Forest from a building on Fourth Avenue, New York City, in February, 1907. The first broadcast was entirely of phonograph records provided by Columbia Records (shades of today's D.J. programs). The early De Forest programs were experimental—commercial receiving sets had yet to appear on the market, and the principal audience would have been ships' wireless technicians in the New York area.

THE FIRST LIVE MUSICAL PERFORMER ON RADIO

Eugenia Farrar, a Swedish soprano, sang "I Love You Truly" in a De Forest broadcast in September, 1906, the first live song to be broadcast over the ether as part of the regular De Forest programs.

THE FIRST SPEECH BROADCAST ON RADIO

Was given by Lee De Forest's mother-in-law, the noted women's rights advocate Harriet Stanton Black, who spoke on women's suffrage in 1909.

THE FIRST DAILY RADIO STATION

The Charles Herrold School of Radio Broadcasts in San Jose, California, which began on a once-a-week broadcast schedule in January, 1909, became the world's first daily station in 1910, and now qualifies as the world's oldest continuously operating radio station. It is now station KCBS in San Francisco.

THE FIRST COMMERCIAL RADIO RECEIVERS

Receivers were sold in a shop in the Metropolitan Life Insurance Building on Madison Square in New York by Lee De Forest in 1910. The De Forest sets, which were sold by the Radio Telephone Company, were kits which had to be assembled by the purchaser. Like all early radios, they had an earphone rather than a speaker to amplify the sound.

THE FIRST "MODERN" RADIO STATION

The golden age of radio, the three decades from 1920 to 1950, began in earnest on November 2, 1920, when station KDKA in Pittsburgh began broadcasting. KDKA was the first station in the world to be organized and licensed as a fully commercial radio station broadcasting regularly to the public. (The earlier stations, including the De Forest and Herrold stations, were pretty much experimental, one-man operations broadcasting to a small group of pioneer "ham" operators.) With KDKA, true public broadcasting was born, and manufacturers began widespread sale of radio sets to the public.

GATHER ROUND, FOLKS:
Familiar Radio Firsts

THE ADVENTURES OF OZZIE AND HARRIET

October 8, 1944, on CBS, starring Ozzie Nelson and Harriet Hilliard, with Tommy Bernard as David and Ricky Blair as Ricky.

AMOS 'N' ANDY

March 19, 1928, on WMAQ, Chicago, starring (whites) Freeman Gosden and Charles Correll as Amos Jones and Andrew H. Brown.

THE BOB HOPE SHOW

Tuesday nights beginning in 1934 on NBC Blue network, sponsored by Pepsodent, and featuring Jerry Colonna.

THE BURNS AND ALLEN SHOW

Started out on CBS in 1932 as *The Robert Burns Panatela Hour,* with Gracie's gimmick of walking onto other radio shows looking for her missing brother.

THE ED SULLIVAN SHOW

On CBS, early in 1931. Among the stars who made their first appearances on Sullivan's show: Jack Benny, Irving Berlin, Flo Ziegfeld.

THE EDDIE CANTOR SHOW

September, 1931.

THE EDGAR BERGEN AND CHARLIE McCARTHY SHOW

Starring Charlie, Mortimer Snerd, and Effie Klinker, beginning on the *Chase and Sanborn Radio Hour* on NBC in 1936.

FIBBER MAGEE AND MOLLY

Starring Jim and Marian Jordan and their famous closet at 79 Wistful Vista, sponsored by Johnson's Wax on NBC starting in 1935.

THE FRED ALLEN SHOW

Began October 23, 1932, on CBS as *The Linit Bath Show,* starring the famous comedian, who became one-half of the famous Jack Benny-Fred Allen feud.

THE GOLDBERGS

"Yoo-hoo! Is anybody home?" began on the Blue network, November 20, 1929, with Gertrude Berg and James R. Walters. First title: *The Rise of the Goldbergs.*

THE GRAND OLE OPRY

Began on November 28, 1925, in Nashville as the *WSM Barn Dance*.

THE GREEN HORNET

Began in Detroit in 1936, with Al Hodge as the Hornet, broadcast over the National Mutual network in 1938. Raymon Hayashi was Kato.

JACK ARMSTRONG, THE ALL-AMERICAN BOY

Began on CBS from Chicago in 1933, with St. John Terrell as Jack.

THE JACK BENNY PROGRAM

Jack debuted on *Ed Sullivan,* May 2, 1931, and had his own first broadcast on CBS in 1932. On hand: Eddie Anderson, Dennis Day, Don Wilson, Verna Felton, and Bea Benaderet.

THE KATE SMITH SHOW

"Hello, everybody" began on CBS in 1936.

KAY KYSER'S KOLLEGE OF MUSICAL KNOWLEDGE

The first term, Wednesday nights on NBC, began in 1938, with Kyser as The Old Professor and Mervyn Brogue as Ish Kabibble.

KRAFT MUSIC HALL

Premiered in 1934 with Al Jolson, Deems Taylor, and Paul Whiteman's Orchestra.

Famous first feuds: Radio comedy stars Fred Allen and Jack Benny carried on a legendary on-the-air "feud" beginning on December 30, 1936, when Fred Allen, hosting a child prodigy fiddler on his program, made a remark about "a certain alleged violinist," referring to Benny. The two milked the "feud" for laughs for more than a decade.   THE BETTMANN ARCHIVE, INC.

LITTLE ORPHAN ANNIE

"Leapin' lizards" was first exclaimed by Shirley Bell as Annie on the Blue network in 1931. Henry Saxe was Daddy Warbucks.

THE LONE RANGER

"Hi-yo, Silver" was first heard on January 30, 1933, with George Seaton as the Ranger and John Todd as Tonto.

MA PERKINS

Debuted on December 4, 1933, on NBC, with Virginia Payne, who was Ma for the entire twenty-seven-year run of the show.

THE MERCURY THEATRE ON THE AIR

Began in 1938 on CBS, hosted by Orson Welles and produced by Welles and John Houseman. Most famous for the "War of the Worlds" broadcast on October 30, 1938, when thousands thought Martians really *had* landed in Grovers Mills, New Jersey.

ONE MAN'S FAMILY

The longest running radio serial began April 29, 1932, on NBC in San Francisco with J. Anthony Smythe as Henry Barbour and Minetta Ellen as Fanny Barbour. They played the roles until well into the 1950's.

THE SHADOW

Lamont Cranston, alias the Shadow ("Who knows what evil lurks in the hearts of men?") began in 1936 on Mutual network with Robert Hardy Andrews. The Shadow had originally been just the narrator of mystery stories, and in that version was played first by James LaCurto, ca. 1932.

UNCLE DON

The most famous children's program began in September, 1928, with Don Carney as the host.

WALTER WINCHELL

"Good evening, Mr. and Mrs. America and all the ships at sea" was heard for the first time on December 4, 1932.

HIS MASTER'S VOICE:
Recorded Firsts

MARY HAD A LITTLE WHAT?

Thomas Alva Edison demonstrated the first sound recording device on November 29, 1877, at Menlo Park. He shouted "Mary Had a Little Lamb" into a hand-cranked machine, which etched grooves into tinfoil-wrapped metal cylinders, then played back his voice to himself. The machine was developed in part by Edison's assistant engineer, John Kreusi. The first commercial machines were produced beginning April 24, 1878, by the Edison Speaking Phonograph Company at 203 Broadway, New York City, and were leased mainly to traveling showmen who charged a fee to the curious who wanted to hear a talking machine.

PLAY IT AGAIN, JULES

The first known musical recording—Edison didn't sing "Mary Had a Little Lamb"—was made by Jules Levy, who played "Yankee Doodle" into the horn of one of the leased Edison Machines in New York in 1878. (The lack of originality in material chosen for these early recordings is astonishing.)

LOOK, MA, NO HANDS

The machine-driven phonograph was invented by Edison in 1887. It featured a wax cylinder to replace the old foil-covered ones (the wax cylinder, which gave far better sound quality, was patented by Winchester Bell and Charles Sumner Tainter in 1886), and was put into production in 1888. Before this, the phonos had to be continuously cranked by hand. Edison's machine was wound up—with a spring mechanism.

THE MUSIC GOES ROUND AND ROUND

The phonograph disc was invented by Emile Berliner (a German living in Washington, D.C.) in 1887, the same year as the Edison wax cylinder models. The Berliner disc would give engineers their first problems with tone-arm tracking distortion, but the convenience and durability of discs would eventually root out the cylinder system of Edison's machines. Berliner's disc machines, which went into production in Germany in 1889, were intended as toys, though within a few years the Berliner Company recognized the serious market value of disc players.

HIGH BROW

Child prodigy pianist Josef Hofmann made the first classical recordings at the Edison labs at West Orange, New Jersey, in 1888; the first symphonic recording was made by Edison at the (old) Metropolitan Opera House on Broadway in New York City the same year. Edison recorded conductor Hans von Bülow and the New York Philharmonic in a performance of the Beethoven "Eroica" Symphony (No. 3), Wagner's *Die Meistersinger* overture, and the Haydn "London" Symphony No. 102 in B-flat major. (Edison, besides being an inventor of great genius, also had considerable talents as a commercial promoter. The success of many inventions was due in no small part to his using "names" to promote them.)

SIMPLY ELECTRIFYING

Introduced in 1929 by Western Electric, the Orthophonic Phonograph developed by engineer H. C. Harrison was the first commercial electric phonograph. It replaced the wind-up mechanical phono introduced by Edison in 1887, and relieved music buffs of having to periodically wind up their phonographs.

THE FIRST FIFTH

The first long-playing 33⅓ records were introduced in 1931 by RCA Victor in a demonstration at the Savoy Plaza Hotel in New York. The first LP disc was a recording of Beethoven's Fifth Symphony by Leopold Stokowski and the Philadelphia Orchestra. The high price of the new LP recorders during the Depression, followed by the diversion of technological resources during the war, kept LP's from being commercially successful (or even commonplace) until 1948, when the microgroove record developed by Peter Goldmark of the Columbia Broadcasting System was introduced.

IN ONE EAR AND IN THE OTHER

Stereophonic recording techniques were pioneered in the late 1930's and early '40's by German sound engineers, but stereo records weren't commercially available until 1958 when Audio Fidelity of the United States released their first "stereo" discs.

REEL REALITY

The first magnetic tape recorder was invented in 1929 by Louis Blattner, a German film producer, who magnetized steel tape with his machine, then replayed it synchronously with his films as a sound track. By 1935 German inventors introduced the Magnetophone, using plastic tape for the first time, and they would continue to work on the magnetic recording machine through World War II.

THE GRAMMY AWARDS

The National Academy of Recording Arts and Sciences (NARAS) was founded in 1957, and in 1958 it began to hand out awards, patterned after film's "Oscars" and theater's "Tonys" for "artistic achievement within the recording field." Among the first winners were "Nel Blu Dipinto di Blu" by Domenico Modugno as Record of the Year and Song of the Year; Album of the Year was Henry Mancini's *The Music from Peter Gunn;* Best Classical Performance, Soloist with Orchestra, went to Van Cliburn & Kondrashin in the *Tchaikowsky Concerto No. 1;* Best Female Pop Vocal, Ella Fitzgerald, *The Irving Berlin Song Book;* Best Male Pop Vocal, Perry Como, "Catch a Falling Star"; Best Record for Children, David Seville, "The Chipmunk Song."

The Best New Artist of the Year was Bobby Darin.

BOOB TUBE:
Televised Firsts

TEST PATTERNS

Television became theoretically feasible in 1884 with the invention
of the Nipkow scanner by Paul Nipkow, a twenty-four-year-old
German inventor. By 1925 two men working independently, J. L.
Baird of Scotland and Charles Francis Jenkins of the United States,
were able to transmit fuzzy pictures by wire. The Baird and Jenkins
televisions (the word apparently appeared in print for the first time
in *Scientific American* in 1907) were developed enough for the first
intercity transmission (by wire) in 1927, when Secretary of Commerce Herbert Hoover, in Baltimore, was seen on a two and one-half-
inch screen in the office of the president of A.T. & T, Walter Gifford,
in New York. The two men spoke to one another by telephone.
Station WGY in Schenectady, New York, inaugurated the first regular TV broadcast on May 11, 1928.

This infant television broadcasting used the Nipkow scanning
principle, which depended on mechanical means—a rotating wheel
—to break down and reconstruct the image, and it soon became clear
that the system was inherently limited.

THE TURNING POINT

Television as we know it began in 1930 when Philo T. Farnsworth,
a twenty-one-year-old inventor, patented his cathode-tube scanner,

The idiot box: This unidentified woman, who seems to be much in need of a good TV dinner, is being mesmerized by the early television built by Dr. E.F.W. Alexanderson of the General Electric laboratories in 1927–28. This photo, taken early in 1928 at the G. E. labs, shows the revolving wheel, or Nipkow scanner, used to transmit images in television's infancy. Within months, the first public broadcast would be made by station WGY, New York, and by 1930 the mechanical scanner shown here would be replaced by the electronic scanning tube that is the basis of modern television tubes. THE BETTMANN ARCHIVE, INC.

and Vladimir Zworykin of the Radio Corporation of America invented his iconoscopic camera and kinescopic tube. So important were these inventions that RCA for the first time was forced to pay royalties to an outside inventor—the youthful Farnsworth. RCA began its experimental station W2RBX in New York on July 30, 1930.

BUT HOW DID IT DO IN THE RATINGS?

Tuesday night, July 21, 1931: the historic, first scheduled TV program. Mayor Jimmy Walker of New York introduced the proceedings; George Gershwin played "Lisa"; the Boswell Sisters sang "Heebie-Jeebie Blues"; Henry Burbig did a comic "Little Red Riding Hood"; Helen Gilligan and Milton Watson sang current musical comedy hits; and, yes, folks, Kate Smith sang "When the Moon Comes Over the Mountain" on television for the first, but not the last, time.

EARLY RETURNS

Presidential elections were covered on television for the first time by CBS in 1932: Franklin D. Roosevelt versus Herbert Hoover. CBS—as is the norm today—predicted the winner early in the broadcast before final returns were in.

WHAT DO YOU THINK ABOUT . . . ?

One of television's less ingratiating habits began in 1938 when NBC corralled pedestrians in Rockefeller Center and asked them the first "man-on-the-street" questions.

TV-SIDE CHATS

Franklin D. Roosevelt became the first President to appear on TV when he attended the opening ceremonies of the New York World's Fair, Flushing Meadows, New York, 1939.

PLAY BALL

The first major-league baseball telecast took place on August 26, 1939, the Brooklyn Dodgers against the Cincinnati Reds at Ebbets Field, broadcast on NBC.

"THEY LOOKED JUST LIKE POSTAGE STAMPS"

King George VI and Queen Elizabeth were the first royalty to appear on the tube, at the World's Fair, June 10, 1939.

PIGSKIN PARADE

The first football game on TV was broadcast on September 30, 1939, Fordham versus Waynesburg, in New York City.

TARA-IFFIC!

The first movie premiere to be televised was for *Gone With the Wind* at the Capitol Theatre, New York City, 1939.

PROUD AS A PEACOCK

Bell Lab scientists produced a color image as early as 1929, but it wasn't until August 27, 1940, that CBS demonstrated color TV to members of the FCC and the press at the Chrysler Building, where their transmitter was installed. The first public demonstration of color television was, again by CBS, on January 9, 1941.

THE FIRST WORD FROM OUR SPONSOR

On July 1, 1941 (on station WBNT, New York), the giant industry of television advertising was born when Bulova sponsored the first commercial—a camera focusing on one of their wristwatches with the announcer reading the time: "ten minutes after ten." The commercial cost nine dollars.

WHICH WAY TO SESAME STREET?

Educational television began January 23, 1942, when NBC started a training program for air raid wardens in the New York area.

AND NOW FOR THE BAD NEWS

Another demonstration of television's potential, for better or worse, came on July 26, 1938, with the first coverage of a suicide. John Warde jumped from a building ledge in New York City.

PRIME TIME:
First Broadcasts of
the Fourteen Longest-Running Programs

1. *THE TONIGHT SHOW*—26 SEASONS

Premiered September 27, 1954, on NBC with Steve Allen as host, after running since June, 1953, as a local program on WNBT-TV, the NBC flagship station in New York. The original format was not unlike the show's today—informal chatting, entertainment, guest stars. Among the early regulars were Gene Rayburn, Eydie Gorme, Steve Lawrence, and Andy Williams. Ernie Kovacs took over as host on October 1, 1956. After a change of title to *Tonight! America After Dark,* with a news-oriented format, which ran from January 28, 1957, to July 26, 1957, the show became *The Jack Paar Show.* Paar, along with Hugh Downs, hosted the program from July 29, 1957, to March 30, 1962. After Paar's much-publicized and emotional departure, the program again became *Tonight.* From April 2, 1962, to September 28 of that year, the show featured guest hosts, including Merv Griffin, Groucho Marx, and Art Linkletter. Johnny Carson, with sidekick Ed McMahon, made their debut on *The Tonight Show Starring Johnny Carson* on October 2, 1962. Carson and crew moved from New York to Burbank in May, 1972.

On May 6, 1980, the announcement was made that Carson had signed a three-year contract with NBC, for an amount reputed to be in excess of 5 million dollars a year. For those bucks, the Carson show would be trimmed from ninety minutes to sixty minutes, and Johnny would be required to appear in person four nights a week, with guest hosts the other evenings. In addition, the king of late night

TV would be required to participate in the "development of new projects" with his employers.

2. *THE WONDERFUL WORLD OF DISNEY*—26 SEASONS

Premiered October 27, 1954. Originally titled *Disneyland,* this pioneering series, a mixture of cartoons, documentaries, nature, and adventure stories with a family-entertainment slant was a big gamble for NBC, but proved to be their first major hit show. The series—which ran until 1981—was variously titled *Walt Disney Presents, Walt Disney's Wonderful World of Color,* and *The Wonderful World of Disney.* The program was introduced each week by Disney himself until his death in 1966.

3. *THE ED SULLIVAN SHOW*—24 SEASONS

Premiered June 20, 1948, on CBS, under the title *Toast of the Town.* The first program was budgeted at $1,375, with a whopping $375 spent on talent. The guests on the first broadcast were concert pianist Eugene List, songwriters Richard Rodgers and Oscar Hammerstein II, and Dean Martin and Jerry Lewis, who received $100 each for their talents. The June Taylor dancers—then called the Toastettes—were also on hand.

4. *GUNSMOKE*—20 SEASONS

This television institution premiered as a half-hour "adult" Western (as the producers billed it) on September 10, 1955. Matt Dillon, played by James Arness; Kitty, portrayed by Amanda Blake; and Doc, played by Milburn Stone, continued with the series until its demise on September 1, 1975.

5. *THE RED SKELTON SHOW*—20 SEASONS

Premiered on NBC, September 30, 1951. Skelton, who had been a big radio star, endeared himself to television audiences with his comic characters: Clem Kadiddlehopper, Freddie the Freeloader, and The Mean Widdle Kid. The last telecast was August 29, 1971.

6. *MEET THE PRESS*—18 SEASONS

If both nighttime and daytime broadcast years are combined, *Meet the Press* is by far the longest running series on television. It was originated as a radio program for *American Mercury* magazine by Martha Rountree and Lawrence Spivack in 1945, and was first aired on local television on November 6, 1947. Later that month (November 20) it moved to "network," which at that time consisted of exactly two stations. The show, with its format of a panel interviewing a public or political figure still intact, made its last nighttime broadcast August 29, 1965. It has been an old standby of Sunday afternoon programming ever since.

7. *WHAT'S MY LINE?*—18 SEASONS

This institution of a quiz show premiered February 16, 1950, on CBS, with John Daly as moderator. The first panelists were Dorothy Kilgallen, Harold Huffman, Louis Untermeyer, and Dr. Richard Hoffman. (Arlene Francis didn't make her appearance until the second show.) The show ended its long and dependable history on September 3, 1967.

8. *LASSIE*—17 SEASONS

Starring one of the most successful female impersonators in show business (the real Lassie was a boy dog), this spin-off from the successful movie series premiered September 12, 1954, and remained a Sunday night institution until September 12, 1971. Tommy Rettig was the original Jeff Miller, Lassie's boy companion.

9. *THE LAWRENCE WELK SHOW*—17 SEASONS

Welk's famous champagne bubbles first floated across the screen on July 2, 1955, on ABC, when it originated as a summer replacement show. The program continued as *Lawrence Welk's Dodge Dancing Party* (eventually acquiring the present name) until September 4, 1971. The show was dropped by the network because its audience was considered too old, but the show is still bubbling away as a popular syndicated weekly program, and neither the show nor its audience shows signs of dying off.

10. *KRAFT TELEVISION THEATRE*—16 SEASONS

This prestigious showcase for television drama premiered Wednesday, May 7, 1947, with a play called *Double Door* starring John Baragrey. The series originated on NBC, but from October, 1953, to January, 1955, Kraft sponsored a second drama series on ABC, which ran simultaneously with the competing network's program.

11. *I'VE GOT A SECRET*—15 SEASONS

CBS was able to duplicate its success with *What's My Line* when it premiered *I've Got a Secret* (with Garry Moore as moderator) on June 19, 1952. Among the first panelists were Bill Cullen, Henry Morgan, Faye Emerson, and Jayne Meadows. The show ran until April, 1967.

12. *THE JACK BENNY SHOW*—15 SEASONS

After becoming a household word in radio, Benny moved to TV on October 28, 1950, with a special which eventually developed into his long-running series. Eddie "Rochester" Anderson and Don Wilson were with Jack from the first to the last and, of course, Jack was still thirty-nine at the time of the last broadcast, September, 1965.

13. *THE JACKIE GLEASON SHOW*—15 SEASONS

Gleason was lured away from the Dumont network by CBS, along with Art Carney and the June Taylor dancers, and premiered his show with Columbia Broadcasting on September 20, 1952. "The Honeymooners" was originally a sketch done along with a variety of other Gleason bits, but it proved so popular that the variety format was dropped and the show became *The Honeymooners* on October 1, 1955, with Audrey Meadows as Alice Kramden, Art Carney as Ed Norton, and Joyce Randolph as Trixie. The series was dropped September 22, 1956 (though it is still regularly rerun), and *The Jackie Gleason Show* continued until September, 1970, in a variety format.

14. *THE PERRY COMO SHOW*—15 SEASONS

Premiered on NBC, Friday, December 4, 1948, as *The Chesterfield Supper Club.* Originally not much more than a filmed fifteen-minute radio show, *The Perry Como Show* expanded considerably in both time and sophistication during its long run until June 12, 1963.

STAGESTRUCK FIRSTS

OPENING NIGHT

Theater as we know it began in the fifth century B.C. when Aeschylus (525–456 B.C.) changed the Greek theater from Dionysian religious celebration to true dramatic art.

FOR MEN ONLY

Because Greek theater was rooted in religious ceremony, the men who performed in plays—the first actors—occupied a high place in the society. In more primitive societies (even today) an "actor" in religious ceremonies is virtually indistinguishable from a priest or shaman (little wonder that some of the best performances are still to be seen on pulpits).

Ancient Rome, however, had a different approach. Most actors were slaves, a custom that modern impresarios no doubt would love to revive, and one that many modern actors would insist has indeed been revived.

The first professional actors appeared in the sixteenth century in England, Italy, France, and Spain, with the rise of secular theater.

ACTRESS LIB

Sexism in the theater can be measured not in centuries, but millennia. Women weren't allowed on the Greek stage, and in Rome "actresses" were confined pretty much to the "live sex act" end of the Roman theatrical spectrum. The first professional actresses appeared in Italy in the sixteenth century, and the first one of any stature was Isabella Andreini (1562–1604), who managed a successful career with her actor husband, as well as mothering seven children, all of whom went onto the stage.

MASS APPEAL

The first true indoor public theater was at the Hotel de Bourgogne, Paris, which was converted from a conventional hall in 1548 by adding a stage, a pit for standing patrons, and raised tiers and boxes for more affluent patrons. Prior to the existence of this theater, public plays had been confined to religious mystery or passion plays performed in churches, or to secular plays performed privately in homes or schools, though there is evidence that in the decades before 1548 Italian theater troops may have operated from semipermanent theatrical halls.

A NIGHT AT THE THEATER

The first public theater in England was built just outside the London city limits in Shoreditch by James Burbage, an actor, in 1556, and aptly named "Theatre." Little is known about the building, but it probably followed the plan of the famous later Elizabethan theaters, such as Shakespeare's Globe. Burbage would later be Shakespeare's partner in the famous Blackfriar's Theatre.

THE CLASS PLAY

Ralph Roister Doister, a comedy written by Nicholas Udall, headmaster of Eton, ca. 1534–41, and performed by the boys of the school, is usually considered the first true play in English. The plot concerns the efforts of a vain fool to win the heart of a wealthy widow —rather grown-up stuff for schoolboys.

INAUSPICIOUS DEBUT

All the female roles in Shakespeare (and his contemporaries) were performed by boys and young men. (The Elizabethan audience apparently didn't find any dubious overtones in watching two males act the balcony scene in *Romeo and Juliet.*) The first actress to appear on the English stage was Mrs. Edward Coleman in 1656. Mrs. C. appeared in a work written by her husband and, according to Bricker's *Our Theatre Today,* "was so inept an actress that she never got her head out of the book during the entire performance and, apparently, retired from acting immediately afterward."

LIGHTING AND THUNDER

In 1566, Serlio, an Italian architect who addressed himself to theater design, wrote the first treatise on stage lighting in which he recommended putting bottles of wine in front of torches to give colored light: red wine for red light; white wine for amber light; and a solution of aqua vitae, vernis, and sulfuric acid for blue light.

Special effects were apparently used much earlier, in the outdoor performances of the passion and mystery plays, where angels and devils could throw thunderbolts, appear in flashes, and generally make an impression on the audience.

TREADING COLONIAL BOARDS

The first theater in America was built in 1716 in Williamsburg, Virginia, by William Levingston. The site of the historic building has been preserved by the Colonial Williamsburg Foundation, but lack of information about the design of the theater has prevented its reconstruction.

AMATEUR NIGHT

The first amateur performance of a play by an American author was given in 1690 by Harvard students in Benjamin Coleman's *Gustavus Vasa;* Coleman was born in Boston in 1673 and died there in 1747. *Gustavus* is the first known play written in America.

ALL-AMERICAN ACT

American theater can be said to have begun in 1787 with the production at the John Street Theatre, New York, of Royall Tyler's *The Contrast,* the first play with an American theme and setting and by a native-born author.

THE BIRTH OF BROADWAY

The great New York theater tradition began on December 6, 1732, with the first known appearance of professional actors in North America, in a performance of George Farquhar's comedy *The Recruiting Officer.* This event took place at what was called the "New" Theatre—the first known reference to a theater in New York City. A newspaper correspondent for the *New England and Boston Gazette* reported, "The new Theatre in the building of Rip Van Dam [then acting Governor of New York] was opened with the comedy of 'The Recruiting Officer,' the part of Worthy acted by the ingenious Mr. Thomas Heady, barber and peruque maker to his honour."

CAN I HAVE YOUR AUTOGRAPH?

The first in a long line of American matinee idols was John Henry (1738–94), who made his debut on December 7, 1767, at the John Street Theatre in *Beaux Strategem.* Henry set the tone for his genre —the irregularities in his private life caused as much talk as his acting technique.

THESPIAN ROOTS

The first company of black actors was organized in New York in 1821 by James Brown. The troupe appeared at The African Grove, an outdoor theater-garden, and at indoor theaters. Their repertory included *Othello* and *Richard III,* and starred James Hewlett, a native of the West Indies. The troupe also performed the first known American play by a black author, Brown's *King Shotaway.*

TIME FOR A CIGARETTE

Greek playwright Horace (65–8 B.C.) was the first to advocate dividing plays into acts. The first English author to use acts was Ben Jonson (1572–1637). Historians agree that the acts in Shakespeare were added later by the posthumous publishers of the plays.

BRING ON THE DANCING GIRLS

The Black Crook is considered to be the first musical comedy, though it is a distant relative of the twentieth-century productions bearing the name. Opening in 1866, *The Black Crook* was a harbinger of things to come in its lavish use of elaborate sets, scantily clad chorus girls, singing and dancing, and general spectacle.

The first musical which acheived the status of a true musical play —with integration of book, music, and lyrics into a convincing theatrical whole—was *Show Boat,* which opened at the Ziegfeld Theater, New York, in 1927, based on the Edna Ferber novel, with music by Jerome Kern.

ON THE WAY TO THE GREAT WHITE WAY

Gaslights were installed for the first time in a theater by Frederick Winser, a German, in the Lyceum Theatre, London, in 1803. The first American theater with gaslighting was the Chestnut Street Opera House in Philadelphia, 1816.

FRENCH FIRST

In 1880 the Paris Opera was the first theater to have incandescent lights installed—only one year after the invention of the light bulb by Swan and Edison.

THE ENVELOPE, PLEASE

Named after Antoinette Perry (1888–1946), actress, director, and chairperson of the Board of Directors of the American Theater Wing, the Tony Awards were given for the first time in 1947. They quickly became the highest honor in the American theater. Among the illustrious first-year winners were José Ferrer for *Cyrano de Bergerac* and Fredric March for *Years Ago;* Ingrid Bergman for *Joan of Lorraine* and Helen Hayes for *Happy Birthday;* Patricia Neal for *Another Part of the Forest;* Elia Kazan for directing *All My Sons;* and choreographers Agnes de Mille (for *Brigadoon*) and Michael Kidd (for *Finian's Rainbow*).

O'NEILL NOBELED

The first American to win the Nobel prize in Literature for drama was Eugene O'Neill (1888–1953), who received the award in 1936 for *Anna Christie* and *Mourning Becomes Electra.*

WITH A LITTLE BIT OF LUCK:
First Plays that Made It Big

Theater is traditionally one of the toughest arenas in which to achieve success, yet some of our best-known stage writers have hit the top on their first try. Here are ten of them.

1. SAMUEL BECKETT (b. 1906), *Waiting for Godot*
One of the most famous plays of this century, written 1952–55 and produced in London in 1956.

2. ABE BURROWS (b. 1910) and JO SWERLING (b. 1897), *Guys and Dolls*
This was Burrows's first attempt, and it netted him the Tony Award and the New York Drama Critics Circle Award in 1950.

3. LORRAINE HANSBERRY (1930–65), *A Raisin in the Sun*
The gifted, young, black playwright achieved fame with her first Broadway play in 1959.

4. LILLIAN HELLMAN (b. 1905), *The Children's Hour*
A powerful and controversial first play, produced in 1934.

5. CHRISTOPHER MARLOWE (1564–93), *Tamburlaine the Great*
Marlowe would have rivaled Shakespeare had he lived longer: He was killed in a barroom brawl at age twenty-nine.

6. CLIFFORD ODETS (1906–63), *Awake and Sing!*
The socially conscious writer had a one-acter, *Waiting for Lefty,* produced in 1935. His first full-length play, *Awake and Sing!* written in 1935, is considered his finest work.

7. EUGENE O'NEILL (1888–1953), *Beyond the Horizon*
O'Neill wrote earlier short dramas, but his first full-length play, originally written for the Provincetown Players, won him the 1929 Pulitzer prize.

8. JOHN OSBORNE (b. 1929), *Look Back in Anger*
The Concise Oxford Companion to the Theatre describes the opening night of Osborne's first play "a landmark in the modern theatre," May 8, 1956. The play also received the New York Drama Critics Circle Award as Best Foreign Play of 1958.

9. WILLIAM SHAKESPEARE (1564–1616), *Henry VI, Parts 2 and 3*
Shakespeare was about twenty-six when he penned his first plays, the last two parts of the *Henry* historical series. They were produced in 1591, followed by the first part in 1592. Though not on the incomparable level of the later plays, they are remarkable first efforts from the most remarkable dramatist of all.

10. GEORGE BERNARD SHAW (1856–1950), *Arms and the Man*
Shaw had *Widower's Houses,* his first effort, produced privately in 1892, but his first public production, *Arms and the Man,* launched his long and important career (April 21, 1894, London).

FIRST
WORDS

He does give a damn: Margaret Mitchell, author of the most successful first novel of all time—*Gone with the Wind*—gloats with Clark Gable and Vivien Leigh on the opening night of the film version of the book, 1939.

FIRST EDITIONS

STILL IN PRINT

The oldest printing comes from China, where illustrations and writing were printed from wood blocks at least as early as the ninth century A.D. The earliest surviving example is a Buddhist scroll known as the *Diamond Sutra,* dating from A.D. 868. The Chinese were also the first to use movable type, possibly as early as A.D. 1317.

Most experts agree that printing developed independently in Europe. The first printer to work with movable type was Johann Gutenberg (ca. 1397–1468) at Mainz. The first dated work is a papal indulgence from 1454, printed at Mainz where Gutenberg did all his printing work with movable type. Two pages of a Latin grammar survive, which may date from as early as 1451, and there were no doubt numerous experiments with the cast metal type before the earliest surviving examples from the 1450's.

The first complete book printed in Europe, marking the beginning of the publishing industry, and still remaining one of the great achievements in the art of printing and book design, is Gutenberg's justly famous Bible (the so-called Mazarin or forty-two-line Bible) printed in Mainz between 1451 and 1455. Gutenberg's great project was financed by Mainz lawyer Johann Fust—who lost his investment when Gutenberg went broke printing the book.

BLOCKBUSTER!

Without question, the Holy Bible is the first and biggest best seller. From the first edition printed by Gutenberg in 1455 there have been more than 2 *billion* copies of the Bible printed in every current written language.

IN THE BLOCKBUSTING TRADITION OF *SHŌGUN*

The first novelist was Murasaki Shikibu, who lived ca. A.D. 978 to 1031 at the Japanese court during the Heian period. Her famous novel of Japanese court life and romance is *Genji Monagatiri, or The Tales of Genji. Genji* is one of the oldest works of fiction still widely read today, and the first by a woman novelist.

DEFOE'S DEFIRST

There are several candidates for the honor of the first English novel, all written within thirty years of one another: Daniel Defoe's *Robinson Crusoe* (1719), Samuel Richardson's *Pamela* (1740), and Henry Fielding's *Tom Jones* (1749). The three books, while dealing with realistic settings and characters that are the backbone of the modern novel, introduce types that would be seen time and again in later literature: Crusoe, an ordinary man suddenly thrust into adventure and struggle against nature; Pamela, a virtuous heroine battling the evil world around her; and Tom Jones, the first antihero.

WHO DUNNIT?

The detective story genre originated with "The Murders in the Rue Morgue" by Edgar Allan Poe, 1841.

ONCE UPON A TIME

The first historical novel was Sir Walter Scott's *Ivanhoe,* 1820.

MIGHTIER THAN THE SWORD

Harriet Beecher Stowe's *Uncle Tom's Cabin,* serialized in the abolitionist newspaper *National Era* in 1852, and published in book form in 1852, became the first best-selling American novel. The famous novel, which contributed significantly to the growing anti-Southern, abolitionist movement, sold 300,000 copies the first year alone, had big foreign sales, and made Mrs. Stowe an international celebrity.

MAKE THE LISTS

According to Alice Payne Hackett and James H. Burke, authors of *Eighty Years of Best Sellers,* the first use of the word "best seller" appeared in *Publishers Weekly* in connection with a "New York bookseller, who, returning to his house on Staten Island, asked a newsstand dealer in the ferryboat terminal what his best-selling books were."

The first best-seller list appeared in *The Bookman,* a literary magazine, in 1895; the first best-seller list that is still being published is in *Publishers Weekly,* which first appeared in 1912.

Of the ten novels listed on the first list in *The Bookman,* only two are even remotely familiar to modern readers: *The Prisoner of Zenda* by Anthony Hope, and *Trilby* by George du Maurier.

The first *Publishers Weekly* list of 1912 listed ten fiction and ten nonfiction titles separately—the first breakdown by category. While the novels of 1912 are mostly forgotten and forgettable, the titles in nonfiction include *The Montessori Method* by Maria Montessori; *A New Conscience and an Ancient Evil* by Jane Addams; *Woman and Labor* by Olive Schreiner; and *Your United States* and *How to Live on 24 Hours a Day,* both by Arnold Bennett, the first author to have two nonfiction best sellers the same year.

The first author to have two best-selling novels the same year was Ian Maclaren, whose *Kate Carnegie* and *Beside the Bonnie Brier Bush* made the 1896 list in *The Bookman.*

LEWIS THE LAUREATE

The first American novelist to win the Nobel prize was Sinclair Lewis in 1930 for *Main Street, Babbitt,* and *Arrowsmith.*

MAIN SELECTIONS

The Book-of-the-Month Club was founded in 1926 by Maxwell Sackheim, Harry Scherman, Charles and Albert Boni, and Robert Haas, who mailed out their first selection on April 16 to 4,750 charter members. The first selection was the novel *Lolly Willowes* by British author Sylvia Townsend Warner. There are now over 150 book clubs in the United States, and BOMC alone has sold over 300 million discount books by mail.

FORTY FAMOUS FIRST NOVELS

1. Jane Austen, *Sense and Sensibility,* 1813.
2. James Baldwin, *Go Tell It on the Mountain,* 1953.
3. Pearl S. Buck, *The Good Earth,* 1931.
4. Charlotte Brontë, *Jane Eyre,* 1847.
5. Emily Brontë, *Wuthering Heights,* 1847.
6. James M. Cain, *The Postman Always Rings Twice,* 1934.
7. Lewis Carroll (Reverend Charles L. Dodgson), *Alice's Adventures in Wonderland,* 1865.
8. Agatha Christie, *The Mysterious Affair at Styles,* 1920.
9. Daniel Defoe, *The Life and Strange Times of Robinson Crusoe,* 1719.
10. Theodore Dreiser, *Sister Carrie,* 1900.
11. Alexandre Dumas, *The Three Musketeers,* 1844.
12. Henry Fielding, *Joseph Andrews,* 1742.
13. F. Scott Fitzgerald, *This Side of Paradise,* 1920.
14. William Golding, *The Lord of the Flies,* 1954.
15. John Hersey, *A Bell for Adano,* 1944.
16. James Joyce, *A Portrait of the Artist as a Young Man,* 1916.
17. Thomas Mann, *Buddenbrooks,* 1901.
18. Norman Mailer, *The Naked and the Dead,* 1948.
19. Carson McCullers, *The Heart Is a Lonely Hunter,* 1940.
20. Herman Melville, *Typee,* 1846.
21. James Michener, *Tales of the South Pacific,* 1947.
22. Henry Miller, *Tropic of Cancer,* 1934.
23. Margaret Mitchell, *Gone with the Wind,* 1936.

24. Boris Pasternak, *Dr. Zhivago,* 1957.
25. Sylvia Plath, *The Bell Jar,* 1962.
26. Katherine Anne Porter, *Ship of Fools,* 1962.
27. Eric Maria Remarque, *All Quiet on the Western Front,* 1929.
28. Samuel Richardson, *Pamela, or Virtue Rewarded,* 1740–41.
29. J. D. Salinger, *The Catcher in the Rye,* 1951.
30. Jean-Paul Sartre, *Nausea,* 1938.
31. Sir Walter Scott, *Waverly,* 1814.
32. Mary Wollstonecraft Shelley, *Frankenstein,* 1818.
33. Aleksandr Solzhenitsyn, *One Day in the Life of Ivan Denisovich,* 1962.
34. Lawrence Sterne, *Tristram Shandy,* 1760–67.
35. Bram Stoker, *Dracula,* 1897.
36. Harriet Beecher Stowe, *Uncle Tom's Cabin,* 1852.
37. J.R.R. Tolkien, *The Hobbit,* 1937.
38. Jules Verne, *Five Weeks in a Balloon,* 1863.
39. Evelyn Waugh, *Decline and Fall,* 1928.
40. Virginia Woolf, *The Voyage Out,* 1915.

FLASH IN THE PAN:
One Novel Novelists

MARGARET MITCHELL (1900–49)

Mitchell began writing her first novel while recuperating in the hospital. Eight years later, in 1936, *Gone with the Wind* was published, setting all kinds of book sales records: fifty thousand copies in a single day, 2 million in the first year. What is not widely known is that Mitchell wrote a second novel, set in the South in the twentieth century, but the eccentric and secretive author burned the manuscript, preferring to let her first success be her only success. She was killed in her hometown of Atlanta in 1949 when struck by a taxicab.

J. D. SALINGER (b. 1919)

Jerome David Salinger gained critical and popular acclaim for *Catcher in the Rye,* published in 1951, and became something of a cult figure among students in the 1950's and '60's, who found Holden Caulfield, the novel's hero, a voice in the wilderness of hypocritical American society. Since *Catcher,* Salinger has published only short stories, and has adopted an extremely reclusive life-style, shunning publicity and interviews.

EMILY BRONTË (1818–48)

The most gifted of the three Brontë sisters, Emily published her classic, one-and-only novel, *Wuthering Heights*, in 1847, along with those of her sisters: Charlotte's *Jane Eyre* and Anne's *Agnes Grey*. In September of 1848 Emily's alcoholic, tubercular brother, Branwell, died. Emily contracted a cold at his funeral—then refused medical care. She died of tuberculosis in December of that year.

TEN FAMOUS FIRST LINES FROM BOOKS...OR YOU *CAN* TELL A BOOK BY ITS FIRST LINE

Though Winston Churchill thought it was not the first battles in wars that counted, but the last, with his literary capabilities Churchill surely would have agreed that books aren't war. What better way to launch a successful and winning book campaign than with a memorable first line? Here are some of the most famous first lines of all time, fiction and nonfiction.

1. "In the beginning God created the heaven and the earth."
　　　　　—Genesis, King James version of the Old Testament

Many an author wishes he'd written this one, probably the most famous first line of all. A model of brevity, stateliness, and simplicity, in a mere ten words it sets out the canvas for the biblical panorama to come: the conflict between heaven and earth, God and man.

2. "Call me Ishmael."
　　　　　—*Moby Dick*, Herman Melville

A famous and puzzling first line, from a famous and puzzling book. Why not, "My name is Ishmael"? or, "I am Ishmael"? Is Ishmael maybe somebody else, but he's not telling? The evasiveness of the line does inaugurate the air of mystery that pervades the famous opening chapters.

3. "It was the best of times, it was the worst of times, it was the age of wisdom, it was the age of foolishness, it was the epoch of belief, it was the epoch of incredulity, it was the season of light, it was the season of darkness, it was the spring of hope, it was the winter of despair, we had everything before us, we had nothing before us, we were all going direct to Heaven, we were all going direct the other way—in short, the period was so far like the present period, that some of its noisiest authorities insisted on its being received, for good or for evil, in the superlative degree of comparison only."

—*A Tale of Two Cities,* Charles Dickens

One of the great sentences of literature, and justly famous. It's got a catchy premise (with no little understanding of Enlightenment thinking), is eminently quotable, and fun to boot. Of course, today the author could tell us we are all going straight to Hell. Thank you, Mr. Dickens, for such a terrific first line.

4. "Last night I dreamt I went to Manderley again."

—*Rebecca,* Daphne du Maurier

The most famous line from the Queen of Romance, a brief but skillful introduction to the mysteries to come. Even the name Manderley has just the right exotic touch.

5. "Once upon a time and a very good time it was there was a moocow coming down along the road and this moocow that was coming down along the road met a nice little boy named baby tuckoo. . . ."

—*A Portrait of the Artist as a Young Man,* James Joyce

This opener makes one wish Joyce had written children's stories. In case you're unfamiliar with the book, *Portrait of the Artist* doesn't go on in this vein. It's just "the artist" remembering his dad telling him stories when he was a kid. But it is a wonderful first line (of course, remember that Joyce began his third and last novel in the middle of a sentence, the beginning of which is the half-finished last sentence of the book). But the adventures of baby tuckoo and the moocow *would* have been a delight.

6. "Lolita, light of my life, fire of my loins."

—*Lolita,* Vladimir Nabokov

This line says it all, in another children's story of sorts. Anyone who has ever been lustfully in love knows *exactly* what Humbert Humbert is talking about.

7. "In the second century of the Christian Era the empire of Rome comprehended the fairest part of the earth and the most civilized portion of mankind."

—The History of the Decline and Fall of the Roman Empire, Edward Gibbon

The opening line of Gibbon's epic history introduces us to the felicities of this great historian's writing style. Gibbon's beautiful language continues through this long, long work, but the story of Rome is all downhill from here.

8. "When I wrote the following pages, or rather the bulk of them, I lived alone, in the woods, a mile from any neighbor, in a house which I had built myself, on the shore of Walden Pond, in Concord, Massachusetts, and earned my living by the labor of my hands only."

—Walden, or Life in the Woods, Henry David Thoreau

A straightforward opening line that sets out in a few phrases the premise of the book to come: the joys of solitude, contemplation in the beauty of unspoiled nature, the rewards of simplicity, even the advantages of bachelorhood. But did he *really* build that house himself?

9. "It is a truth universally acknowledged that a single man in possession of a good fortune must be in want of a wife."

—Pride and Prejudice, Jane Austen

One of the more neatly turned-out phrases in literature, and a snappy introduction to a great novel about the joys of eliminating bachelorhood.

10. "Scarlett O'Hara was not beautiful, but men seldom realized it when caught by her charm as the Tarleton twins were."

—Gone with the Wind, Margaret Mitchell

A famous beginning for Ms. Scarlett and her story. Eight hundred pages later the Tarleton twins aren't on the scene, but Scarlett is still charming the readers. Who could resist a belle who utters one of the great *last* lines in literature: "Tomorrow is another day."

YOU *CAN'T* TELL A BOOK BY ITS FIRST LINE: A Quiz

The opening line of any book is vital—it has to set the mood, tone, and style; establish characters, dates, times, and places; and most important, grab the reader's attention. Over the last two centuries, novelists have risen admirably to the challenge, giving us such famous first lines as "It was the best of times, it was the worst of times," and "Call me Ishmael." But not every opening line is all *that* memorable, and to prove a point, here are ten famous novels, listed alphabetically by author, along with their first lines, listed in random order. See just how many lines are worth remembering.

_____ George Eliot, *Silas Marner*

_____ F. Scott Fitzgerald, *The Great Gatsby*

_____ Oliver Goldsmith, *The Vicar of Wakefield*

_____ Henry James, *The Portrait of a Lady*

_____ Somerset Maugham, *Of Human Bondage*

_____ Marcel Proust, *Remembrance of Things Past* (trans. by C. K. M. Scott)

_____ Harold Robbins, *The Adventurers*

_____ Philip Roth, *Portnoy's Complaint*

_____ John Steinbeck, *The Grapes of Wrath*

_____ Jacqueline Susann, *The Valley of the Dolls*

1. To the red country and part of the gray country of Oklahoma, the last rains came quietly, and they did not cut the scarred earth.

2. In my younger and more vulnerable years my father gave me some advice that I've been turning over in my mind ever since.

3. For a long time I used to go to bed early.

4. I was ever of opinion, that the honest man who married and brought up a large family, did more service than he who continued single and only talked of population.

5. Under certain circumstances, there are few hours in life more agreeable than the hour dedicated to afternoon tea.

6. In the days when spinning-wheels hummed busily in the farm-houses—and even great ladies, clothed in silk and thread-lace, had their toy spinning-wheels of polished oak—there might be seen in districts far away among the lanes, or deep in the bosom of the hills, certain pallid undersized men, who, by the side of the brawny country-folk, looked like the remnant of a disinherited race.

7. She was so deeply embedded in my consciousness that for the first year of school I seem to have believed that each of my teachers was my mother in disguise.

8. The day broke gray and dull.

9. It was ten years after the violence in which he died.

10. The temperature hit ninety-degrees the day she arrived.

ANSWERS: 6, 2, 4, 5, 8, 3, 9, 7, 1, 10.

COLLECTOR'S ISSUES:
Famous Magazine Firsts

THE SATURDAY EVENING POST

Founded by Charles Alexander and Samuel C. Atkinson in Philadelphia, 1821.

The common misconception that Benjamin Franklin "founded" the *Post* stems from the fact that Alexander and Atkinson set up their operation in the two-story brick building at 53 Market Street, Philadelphia, where Ben had once published his *Pennsylvania Gazette*.

LIFE MAGAZINE

The most successful modern picture magazine was published by Henry R. Luce in November, 1936. The first issue had ninety-six pages, cost a dime, and featured a photograph of a doctor slapping the buttocks of a newborn baby, captioned "Life begins."

LOOK MAGAZINE

Look grew out of the rotogravure section of the *Des Moines Register and Tribune* when a Gallup survey revealed the newspaper's readers preferred pictures to text. The first issue was published by Cowles Newspapers (who owned the Des Moines paper) in January, 1937, as a monthly. The magazine promised its readers: *"Look* gives you a thousand eyes to see 'round the world." The first issue sold 700,000 copies, reaching almost 2 million circulation within a year.

SPORTS ILLUSTRATED

First published on August 12, 1954, circulation the first year reached 600,000, and the first "Sportsman of the Year" was Roger Bannister for running the four-minute mile.

BETTER HOMES AND GARDENS

In July, 1922, Edwin Thomas Meredith, a retired Secretary of Agriculture and gardening enthusiast, published a pet project of his: a 52-page illustrated magazine called *Fruit, Garden, and Home.* The small magazine flourished (with articles like "What $50 Will Do in the Backyard"), and became *Better Homes and Gardens* with the April, 1937, issue of 184 pages. By 1940 the magazine had surpassed 3 million circulation.

TV GUIDE

Founded by Walter Annenberg in Philadelphia in April, 1953, it reached a circulation of 1,500,000 the first year, and 19,547,763 by 1980. It is now the largest circulated magazine in the U.S.

TIME

Twenty-four-year-old Henry R. Luce and former Yale classmate Briton Hadden, who had resigned the year before as newspaper reporters on the *Baltimore News,* published Volume 1, number 1 of *Time* magazine, on March 3, 1923. Haddon was responsible for the magazine's style, and coined such words as *tycoon* and *socialite.*

NEWSWEEK

English newspaperman Thomas J.C. Martyn published a rival for *Time* on February 17, 1933, called *News-Week.* The magazine had financial troubles until it merged with *Today* (founded by Vincent

Astor and Averill Harriman), in February, 1937, and published the first issue of dehyphenated *Newsweek* in October, 1937.

NATIONAL GEOGRAPHIC MAGAZINE

The National Geographic Society was founded in Washington, D.C., in 1888 by Gardiner Greene Hubbard (father-in-law of Alexander Graham Bell) and published the first quarterly issue of *National Geographic* the same year. The first monthly issues of the magazine, and the first photos, appeared in 1896; the first color photos in 1906; and the famous yellow border cover in February, 1910.

LADIES' HOME JOURNAL

High school dropout Cyrus Curtis, thirty-two, published the first issue of his fourth magazine, *Ladies Journal* in Philadelphia in 1896. Mrs. Curtis was the editor.

READER'S DIGEST

In February, 1922, DeWitt Wallace, a Presbyterian preacher's son, and his wife, Lila Acheson Wallace, used $5,000 savings and a borrowed $1,300 to edit and publish 5,000 copies of the first issue of *Reader's Digest* in the basement of a Greenwich Village speakeasy. The *Digest,* now the world's largest magazine in circulation, publishes in excess of 18 million copies in the United States, read by an estimated 45 million readers, and a staggering 31 million copies a month worldwide (in fifteen languages) with an estimated 100 million readers.

ESQUIRE

Former ad copywriter Arnold Gingerich, twenty-nine, published the first issue of what was intended to be a men's fashion quarterly, in October, 1933. However, the good writing (by the likes of Hemingway, in the first issue), adult cartoons, and drawings of seminude women soon pushed circulation into the millions, in spite of a stiff fifty-cent cover price.

THE NEW YORKER

Fleischmann's Yeast heir Raoul Fleischmann provided financing for a thirty-two-page, fifteen-cent first issue of *The New Yorker*, edited by Harold Wallace Ross, on February 19, 1925. The first cover featured a drawing by Rhea Irvin of a Regency dandy, complete with monocle and top hat, contemplating a butterfly. He was eventually named Eustace Tilley.

Ross's prospectus for the magazine has become something of a classic. In it he says (among other things) that the *The New Yorker* "will be human. Its general tenor will be one of gaiety. It will not be what is commonly called sophisticated, in that it will assume a reasonable degree of enlightenment on the part of its readers. It will hate bunk . . . *The New Yorker* will be the magazine which is not edited for the old lady in Dubuque."

PLAYBOY

Former eighty-five-dollar-a-week *Esquire* staff member Hugh Hefner scraped up seven thousand dollars (including a loan against his Studebaker) to start an indoor sports magazine for men, called *Playboy,* in December, 1953. The undated magazine (there might never have been a Volume 1, number 2!) sold 51,191 copies, and featured a soon-to-be-famous nude calendar photograph of Marilyn Monroe, for which Hef paid the calendar printer two hundred dollars in rights.

PLAYGIRL

The first *Playboy*-type magazine for women, *Playgirl* was published by Douglas Lambert and edited by Marin Scott Milam, June, 1973. The first center-spread nude was Ryan MacDonald, one of the stars of the NBC soap opera *Days of Our Lives;* the first four-page foldout was Lyle Waggoner of *The Carol Burnett Show. Playgirl* also became, in a later issue, the first magazine to have frontal nude male centerfolds.

WHO SAID IT FIRST?

Below are eight famous sayings that are often misattributed, or used without knowing who said them in the first place. Now, to set the record straight:

1. *A little revolution now and then is a good thing; the tree of liberty must be refreshed from time to time with the blood of patriots and tyrants.*

No, it wasn't Lenin, or Robespierre, or Oliver Cromwell, but good old Thomas Jefferson. He penned the line on hearing that a group of Massachusetts farmers had formed an armed rebellion against the young United States Government in 1797 to protest high taxes that were destroying their livelihood.

2. *The Almighty Dollar, that great object of universal devotion throughout the land.*

Not Karl Marx, or Alexander Hamilton, or an economist, but Washington Irving, condemning the materialism of Americans in his book *The Creole Village,* written in 1837.

3. *Now is the time for all good men to come to the aid of their country.*

This call to arms was not shouted by a Thomas Paine or an Abraham Lincoln, but was actually written, believe it or not, as a typing test. The author was Charles Weller, a friend of C. L. Sholes, inventor of the first practical commercial typewriter, in 1868.

4. *Let them eat cake!*

Poor Marie Antoinette, saddled with this callous statement, when she probably never said it. The line *"Qu'ils mangent de la brioche"* appears as early as Jean Jacques Rousseau's *Confessions* of 1766, where he used it to describe a noblewoman's attitude toward the poor who complained of not having enough bread. Marie was only eleven at the time, but a few years later the line made good propaganda for the revolution, and the misattribution of the line to the queen helped to keep the heads rolling.

5. *I have nothing to offer but blood and toil and tears and sweat.*

A memorable line from the author of many such lines: Winston Churchill. This one's from his address to the British Commons on succeeding Neville Chamberlain as Prime Minister in 1940.

6. *Don't give up the ship!*

Commodore Perry usually gets credit for this one, urging his men aboard the *Niagara* to stick it out in a battle with the British during the War of 1812. Perry did apparently use the line, but he got it from Captain James Lawrence, who is said to have uttered the words as he lay dying of wounds aboard *his* ship, the *Chesapeake*, off Boston, after an encounter with the British in 1813. The heroic death of Lawrence made the words a popular battle cry, though some historians credit Lawrence's words to Benjamin Russell, editor of the *Boston Centinel.*

7. *Power tends to corrupt, and absolute power corrupts absolutely. Great men are almost always bad men.*

This popular saying, usually corrupted to "Power corrupts" is seldom credited to anyone. So, to British historian Lord Acton for saying this in *Historical Essays and Studies* (1907), his due.

8. *To the memory of the man, first in war, first in peace, and first in the hearts of his countrymen.*

Most folks know this was said about George Washington, but the author seldom gets credit. It was uttered by General "Light Horse Harry" Lee, Revolutionary officer and grandfather of Robert E., in his eulogy for the Father of Our Country in 1799.

FIRST THINGS LAST:
Prehistoric and Progressive Firsts

Two touching firsts: The *Graf Zeppelin,* the first dirigible to fly around the world, noses in to the tower of the Empire State Building, the world's first skyscraper with more than 100 floors and more than 1,000 feet in height. The Empire State's tower was designed expressly for dirigible docking, but the idea didn't work, and the closest the *Graf* ever came to docking above the canyons of Manhattan was this composite photograph from the period, showing New Yorkers what they might have seen overhead.   THE BETTMANN ARCHIVE, INC.

FROM ATOM TO ADAM:
The First 15 Billion Years of the Universe

THE COSMIC EGG: THE FIRST THING EVER

More than 15.5 billion years ago the universe as we know it did not exist. All matter, or so most astronomers believe, was compressed together into a superdense core at the center of an empty universe. This core is known as the Cosmic Egg. Science has yet to propose a Cosmic Chicken.

THE FIRST EVENT, EVER

And it was a big one. The Cosmic Egg exploded, hurling the compressed matter out into the emptiness of space. This "Big Bang" signaled the start of the universe as we know it, about 15.5 billion years ago.

A STAR IS BORN

About 12 billion years ago matter from the Big Bang began to condense into clusters of hundreds of billions of stars—the first galaxies. A galaxy is usually a flat spiral with dense concentrations of stars near the center of the spiral, thinning out along the arms. The whole thing rotates as it hurtles through space, and astronomers estimate there are hundreds of billions of them out there.

Our own galaxy, the Milky Way, is 100,000 light-years across, 30,000 light-years thick at the center, and is moving at 170 miles per second.

TERRA FIRMA

About 10 billion years ago our sun had a star companion (or, some theories go, a nebula companion), which was finally pulled apart 5½ or 6 billion years back by the tidal forces between the two objects. The remnants of this destroyed companion began collecting into the first planets about 5 billion years ago.

HOT ROCKS

When the earth was first formed it was about one thousand times larger and five hundred times heavier than the planet we know. The earth spent the first half billion years or so of its existence cooling down and settling in. The heavier elements (iron, nickel, cobalt) settled to the earth's core, while the lighter elements (hydrogen and helium) moved up into the atmosphere, with large amounts escaping the planet's gravity altogether. By 4.5 billion years ago the molten planet had cooled down enough for the first basaltic rocks to form, making a crust on the planet.

WATER, WATER, EVERYWHERE

The molten, volcanic conditions in the primordial earth created huge amounts of water vapor which, along with poisonous methane and ammonia, made up the atmosphere. When the crust cooled sufficiently about 4 billion years ago, the water vapor began condensing, forming the first oceans, which cover 71.43 percent of the surface.

OUT OF THE PRIMORDIAL OOZE

In 1979 a rock from Australia was found to have wavelike layers that are believed to be the fossils of threadlike bacteria that were alive 3.5 billion years ago in the ocean of the Precambrian era. The bacteria represent a fairly complex state of evolution, and indicate that the formation of organic molecules by the interaction of the oceans and atmosphere, which evolved into the first life, began soon after oceans were formed.

THE FIRST LAND ANIMAL

The scorpion (like spiders, an arachnid, and part of the phylum Arthropoda, which includes true insects and crustaceans) evolved during the Silurian period, 405–425 million years ago; it was possibly the first animal to live on land and to take oxygen directly from the atmosphere. Amphibians had yet to evolve.

WHEN DINOSAURS RULED THE EARTH

During the Jurassic period, 150 million years ago, small animals evolved that gave birth to live young and nourished them with secretions from the female's skin. Reptiles, especially dinosaurs, dominated the animal world at the time, and these first mammals remained relatively inconspicuous for millions of years.

VERY HANDY

Fifty to sixty million years ago, the first primates—small lemurs and tarsiers—evolved. The arboreal, nocturnal mammals developed binocular stereoscopic vision and five-fingered hands to cope with their environment. Their great-great grandchild, *Homo sapiens,* would eventually rule the earth.

PLANET OF THE APES

Thirty million years ago the first apes began to evolve from their primate ancestor, the monkey. The apes, who would eventually evolve into the modern gibbon, orangutan, chimpanzee, gorilla, and man, developed brachiation—locomotion by overarm swinging, a high ratio of brain volume to spinal cord volume, and complex social and child-rearing behavior.

CIVILIZED FIRSTS:
From Caveman to Cuneiform

Ca. 3,000,000–1,000,000 B.C.

Australopithecines, apelike predecessors of man, begin using tools, probably for simple tasks like cutting open fruit or breaking shells.

Ca. 1,000,000 B.C.

As *Australopithecus* begins developing into *Homo erectus* and into a hunter-scavenger as well as a fruit and plant eater, he first begins using language to communicate with his hunting and gathering companions.

Ca. 400,000 B.C.

Homo erectus begins using fire to cook meat, which has become an increasing part of his diet during the last million years. He probably learns about the pleasant taste of cooked meat after scavenging scorched animal carcasses from brush fires.

Ca. 100,000–50,000 B.C.

Neanderthal man, who practices cannibalism on occasion, paints the bodies of his dead, the first indication of the concept of an afterlife.

Ca. 50,000–30,000 B.C.

The first boats and rafts are built by *Homo sapiens,* enabling man to cross large rivers, lakes, and even oceans, to colonize places like Australia and New Guinea.

Ca. 12,000 B.C.

The Asian wolf is domesticated into the dog by nomadic hunters living in Asia Minor. Man's first "pet" is used to help track and kill game.

Ca. 10,000 B.C.

Goats are domesticated by nomads living in Asia Minor, the first domestic animal to provide dairy products for human consumption, as well as provide a source of meat.

Ca. 8,000 B.C.

As the last glacial period comes to a close, men living in Asia Minor begin planting seeds gathered from edible wild grasses like *Triticum dicoccum*—wild wheat, the first domesticated plant.

Ca. 7,000 B.C.

The first permanent agricultural settlements spring up in fertile areas of the Tigris-Euphrates Valley and the Jordan Valley, Asia Minor.

Ca. 7,000 B.C.

As settled agricultural centers evolve, a need for written records arises, and early pictographs evolve into the first writing.

Ca. 6,500 B.C.

The Sumerians of the Tigris-Euphrates Valley invent the first wheel, which soon spreads over the Middle East. However, the wheel remains unknown to the great Maya and Inca civilizations that grow up in later centuries in the Western Hemisphere, except occasionally in wheeled children's toys.

Ca. 6,700–6,300 B.C.

The auroch is domesticated into the cow, the first large domestic animal capable of providing work power as well as food and raw materials.

Ca. 6,000 B.C.

The first pottery is made in the Near East.

Ca. 3,500 B.C.

Copper, which has been mined for about two thousand years and used for jewelry and ornaments, is smelted with tin to make the first metal alloy hard enough to take and hold a cutting edge. The Bronze Age is born, and tools and weapons are made with the new substance.

Ca. 3,000 B.C.

The first "literature" evolves with the epic of Gilgamesh, written in Sumerian cunciform, which tells how man saved himself from a great flood by building an ark.

GIMME SHELTER:
Firsts from Rock Pile to Rockefeller Center

OUT OF AFRICA

The oldest known man-made structure was discovered in 1960 at Olduvai Gorge, Tanganyika. The structure consisted of a circle of piled lava stones enclosing a flat area probably used as a work area (as evidenced by bones and tool artifacts). It was dated to the lower Paleolithic period, perhaps as early as 1,750,000 years ago, or during the time when *Australopithecus* was evolving into *Homo erectus*.

A ROOF OVER OUR HEADS

The first known covered buildings date from about 120,000 B.C. at Terra Amata, near Nice, France, and were probably built by Cro-Magnon man of the Acheulean culture. The twenty-one structures from the site have pebble-lined fire pits and stake holes indicating a roofed structure supported by wooden beams.

BUILT TO LAST

The first large stone structure in the world is the stepped pyramid of Zoser, built by Imhotep, counselor to Zoser, ca. 2900 B.C. The Pyramid of Zoser launched the great age of pyramid building, culminating in the three great pyramids at El Giza (Giza), built ca. 2680–2565 B.C. Imhotep is also the first doctor known to history.

PRE-PARTHENON

After the decline of the Minoan and Mycenaean cultures in the Greek islands by 1100 B.C. (possibly brought on by the eruptions of the volcanic island of Thera between 1520 and 1430 B.C.), the Greek peninsula was invaded by the Dorians (before 1000 B.C.), who marked the beginning of true Hellenistic culture. The Dorians seem to have borrowed little of their distinctive architectural style from other cultures, and the famous temples with their Doric orders were developed between the tenth and seventh centuries, and reached the highest statement in the Parthenon, completed in 438 B.C. The first known major temple built by the Dorian Greeks is the Heraeum at Olympia, which was probably built around the time of the first Olympiad 776 B.C. (perhaps earlier), and was remodeled in the early Doric stone style in the seventh century. The Greek temple became the single most influential architectural style in the world, being copied, reinterpreted, and bastardized for two thousand years.

CONCRETE EVIDENCE

Concrete—in its simplest form a mixture of gravel or stones with sand, cement, and water—was first used in the ancient world as a quick way to thicken and fill walls and fortifications without the time-consuming process of making mud or kiln-dried bricks. Its use was sporadic until the Romans, who were the first to use it extensively as a major building and structural material. After the second century B.C. the Romans used a combination of volcanic earth (called pozzolana), lime, broken stones, and tuff; this durable concrete was suitable for building roads, forums, basilicas, and baths. In buildings like the immense Baths of Caracalla they used concrete to build vaulted arches over large indoor spaces; the famous Pantheon is also a concrete structure. Most of these buildings were then faced with marble to give them the appearance of solid stone structures.

POSITIVE REINFORCEMENT

The use of concrete disappeared after Roman times, and it was lost as a structural material for centuries. Modern use of concrete began about 1830, and the most important development was that of reinforced concrete (or ferroconcrete). The process of reinforcing concrete by introducing steel rods was invented by the Frenchman Joseph Monier, and first was used in a house in Port Chester, New York, in 1857. The great tensile strength given to concrete by the steel rods has made it a rival to steel in the construction of bridges and large buildings.

HIGH POINTS

The Romanesque style, which had evolved slowly out of Roman architecture influenced by Byzantine styles during the ninth to eleventh centuries, gradually gave way to the Gothic style, characterized by its pointed arch, lively ornamentation, and emphasis on verticality. The first major monument of Gothic architecture is generally considered to be the ambulatory of the Abbey of St. Denis, on the Île de France, completed in 1144; the first major cathedral in the High Gothic style is Chartres, begun in 1194.

BORN AGAIN

The rediscovery of the classical architecture of Greece and Rome naturally took place in Italy, where the Gothic style never really took hold. The first important architect to reinterpret classical elements in the new Renaissance style was Filippo Brunelleschi (1377?–1446) of Florence, who designed the final version of the Florence Cathedral (ca. 1407) with its famous dome (built 1420–61), and the churches of Spirito Santo and San Lorenzo, ca. 1420. Brunelleschi's designs launched the great age of Renaissance building, and had great influence on Michelangelo.

THE FIRST AMPHITHEATER

The Greeks were famous for their semicircular theaters, built into hillsides, and Romans and Greeks both built U-shaped stadiums for racing events. But the granddaddy of today's football stadiums and bullrings is the famous Coliseum in Rome. Though the Romans had built circular public amphitheaters of wood, the Coliseum is the first one built of stone. With its 617-foot-long axis, 4-story height, and 45,000-seat capacity, it was of unprecedented size and scale. The Coliseum was begun ca. A.D. 75 by Vespasian and completed in A.D. 80 by his son Titus. It was used for lavish, excessive, and often brutal public entertainment.

THE IRON IS CAST

The first major innovation in building construction after the Middle Ages was the introduction of cast iron during the nineteenth century. Cast iron was first used about 1840 for structural columns and beams (both in Europe and America) because it was cheaper and faster to work with than conventional stone or stone and wood construction. It found its first applications in commercial and industrial buildings. (The use of structural metal had been pioneered in bridge building between 1779, when Abraham Darby III built the first iron bridge across the Severn River in England, and 1840, when the first iron truss bridge was built in the United States by Earl Trumbull at Frankfort, New York.) The first important European use of iron in a building was the Bibliothèque Sainte-Geneviève, built in 1841 by Henri Labrouste (1801–75), which pioneered the "modern" use of cast iron supporting columns and arched beams. Another major first came in New York in 1849 when James Bogardus (1800–74) built the first cast iron front building for the Laing stores at the corner of Washington and Murray streets. The Bogardus system of casting interchangeable, repeating sections of building fronts from iron, allowing for maximum window area, revolutionized the construction of commercial buildings in rapidly growing American cities, and contributed greatly to the development of the true skyscraper a few decades later.

SKY HIGH

Men have been building tall structures for a long time, though until modern times these "skyscrapers" were almost invariably for ceremonial or observational use. The Pyramid of Cheops, the largest of the three pyramids at Giza, Egypt (ca. 2500 B.C.), was 482 feet, 6 inches tall when completed—the equivalent of a modern 40-story building. And during the Middle Ages, European cities and towns were dominated by the spires of their cathedrals, many of which reached heights above 300 feet. (The taller spire of Chartres Cathedral, for example, is 375 feet tall).

The first skyscraper in the modern sense—that is, a tall building with a steel frame construction and an interior devoted to commercial (and later residential) use—is the Home Insurance Building in Chicago, designed by William Le Baron Jenney and completed in 1883. The building, a modest 10 stories high, was the first in the world to employ steel frame construction and the other characteristics of modern skyscrapers.

The first skyscraper to exceed 50 stories in height was the Woolworth Building, completed in 1913 at Broadway between Park Place and Barclay Street, New York City. The 792-foot Gothic-detailed building, dubbed the "Cathedral of Commerce," contained 60 stories, and remained the tallest building in the world until 1931.

The first skyscraper to exceed 100 stories was the Empire State Building, completed May 31, 1931, on the site of the famed Waldorf-Astoria Hotel, Fifth Avenue and 34th Street, New York City. The Empire State originally stood 1,250 feet, with 102 floors; a radio and television transmission tower later raised the height an additional 222 feet.

CITY SLICKERS:
Urban Firsts

HOW YA GONNA KEEP 'EM DOWN ON THE FARM?

The *Columbia Encyclopedia* defines a city as a "densely populated urban center, larger than a village or town, whose inhabitants are engaged primarily in commerce and industry." By this definition, the first cities evolved in Egypt and Mesopotamia in the period from 3500 to 3000 B.C. In Mesopotamia, in the vicinity of the Tigris and Euphrates rivers, cities like Ur, Kish, and Erech grew up; farther to the north were Nineveh and Samarra. In Egypt, King Menes, the traditional first ruler of Egypt, founded Memphis, ca. 3100 B.C. By 3000 B.C. the Indus valley civilization had evolved in what is now West Pakistan. At Mohenjo-Daro, for example, houses of several stories are found, with drainage and irrigation systems, and planned streets.

ONE MILLION STORIES IN THE NAKED CITY

In 1811 a census showed that London had 1,009,546 inhabitants, the first city in history with a seven-figure population. London remained in first place until 1957, when she was overtaken by Tokyo. New York City became the first in the United States to exceed 1,000,000. In the census of 1900, Manhattan had a population of 1,850,093, and the five boroughs—which had been incorporated into New York City in 1898—had a total population of 3,437,202. Thus, even before

356

the incorporation of the five boroughs, Manhattan—then what was all of New York City—had a larger population than second-rated Chicago, with a population of 1,698,575 in 1900.

TEN MILLION STORIES IN THE NAKED CITY

By January, 1972, Tokyo reported a population of 10,000,000, up an estimated 7,333,000 after World War II. Thus there were *twice* as many men, women, and children living in Tokyo in 1972 than inhabited the entire earth in 9000 B.C. at the beginning of the New Stone Age. The Tokyo-Yokohama metropolitan area now contains in excess of 17,000,000 people.

GASLIGHT GAIETIES

On February 17, 1817, gaslights were installed on a street in Baltimore, Maryland, by the Gas Light Company, organized the same month in that city.

In 1829 Paris became the first gaslit city in Europe when the old oil burning reflectors, or reverberes, were replaced with lamps fed by gas lines.

NO RIGHT TURN ON RED

In 1868 a gas-powered red and green traffic signal was installed at Bridge Street and New Palace Yard in London. The signal, mounted on top of a twenty-two-foot iron pole, was manually operated by a constable on the street.

The first American city with a traffic light, and the first signal designed to handle traffic going in two directions, was installed at Euclid Avenue and 105th Street in Cleveland, Ohio, on August 5, 1904. It had red and green lights, with a warning buzzer as the color changed.

The classic red-yellow-green lights were installed in New York City in 1918, and have become the standard for most cities. Curiously, the three-light system was later changed to a two-light one on most New York signal lights, though in recent years the three-signal lights have been replaced by the city on many streets.

CLANG, CLANG, WENT THE TROLLEY

The first horse-drawn trolley began service in New York City on November 14, 1832. The tracks for the service ran along Fourth Avenue from 14th Street to Prince Street, and the carriages held ten passengers. These trolleys were derived in part from the familiar wheeled stagecoaches and from mining cars, which were horse drawn along tracks. The fare was twelve and one-half cents.

The first electric trolleys were installed in Baltimore, Maryland, by the British-American electrical engineer, Leo Daft, on August 10, 1885. The electrical supply, carried in overhead wires, was picked up by the carriage through a rolling wheeled contact called a troller.

A POTHOLE IS BORN

Many ancient sites show evidence of paving of public areas, especially around temples, palaces, and marketplaces. The first city with evidence of any extensive paving is Babylon, ca. 2000 B.C. Large sections of Roman cities (as well as the extensive Roman highway system) were paved with concrete or stone and concrete. It was not until the nineteenth century, however, that city streets became almost exclusively paved, and even today some of the largest urban areas—Mexico City and Cairo, for example—have large sections with dirt streets.

TAKE THE "A" TRAIN

The London Metropolitan Railway, the first subway, which ran from Paddington Station to Farringdon Street, was opened on January 10, 1863. The four-mile trip, in gaslit cars, took thirty-three minutes.

The first subway in the United States was developed and built in New York City by Alfred Beach and known as the Beach Pneumatic Underground Railway. The system featured round tunnels and bullet-shaped cars that were propelled by air forced through the tunnel and against the back of the car by means of a rotary fan. The tunnels were 9 feet in diameter, and the twenty-two-passenger cars slightly less so. The line opened in 1870 and ran 312 feet from Broadway and Warren Street to Broadway and Murray Street. The Beach system was not a long-range success.

The first conventional underground railway in the United States, and one that is still running virtually unchanged except for newer cars, is the Interborough Rapid Transit in New York City. The first line of the IRT opened on October 27, 1904, and ran from Brooklyn Bridge, in downtown Manhattan, to 145th Street in upper Manhattan. The cars, then as today, were driven by electric motors powered by a third, electrified rail. The ride cost five cents.

CAN METER MAIDS BE FAR BEHIND?

On July 16, 1935, 150 parking meters were installed in Tulsa, Oklahoma. The idea for charging drivers for parking on city streets via meters came from Carlton Magee, a newspaper editor who was appointed to a commission to study traffic control in the city. The first meters were manufactured by Dual Parking Meter Company founded by Magee.

EL CITY

On July 2, 1867, Charles T. Harvey opened his elevated railway in New York City. The first stretch of tracks went from Battery Place to Dey Street, Manhattan, along Greenwich Street. The single track, supported on T-shaped columns set in a single line along the curb, was operated by cables. The line was a flop and went bankrupt. However, the tracks and equipment were bought by another developer, who extended the line to 29th Street and Ninth Avenue and put steam engines on the line (1871). New York soon became famous for its "Els," which were considered great boons to urban living. Unfortunately, in the twentieth century the Els, with their noise and the gloom created on the streets below, contributed significantly to the decline of the once-flourishing streets they were built over.

THE PRIVY PUBLIC

According to tradition, the emperor Vespasian (ruled A.D. 69–79), had the first public conveniences installed in Rome. Historians, however, insist that the facilities had existed in Rome for some time, and Vespasian was merely the first to charge the public for their use.

Vespasian gave his name to the *vespasienne,* the famous Parisian *pissoirs* which first appeared in the city of light in 1841 when they were installed under the orders of the prefect of the Seine Department, Claude-Philibert de Rambeteau, one of the first sanitation engineers in the modern world.

BUT IS IT FOUR STAR?

Restaurants, in the modern sense of an establishment in an urban area that serves food and drink at set hours and at set prices, with separate tables provided for individual groups, are surprisingly recent. The first restaurant was opened in Paris in 1765. Prior to that date, there had been public places where one could buy food: An *auberge* was a country inn which sold food to travelers, along with lodging; *tavernes* were places that sold wine along with some food served offhandedly from the bar; and *traiteurs* were food shops that delivered food prepared on their premises to private homes, much like today's Chinese takeout. Finally, in 1765, a gentleman named Boulanger (meaning baker) opened a place where one could sit at a table, order a meal and wine, pay the tab, and go on one's way. Over the door Boulanger hung the sign (in amateur Latin) *"Venite ad me omnes qui stomacho laboratis, et ego restaurabo vos"* (Come to me all you whose stomachs are distressed, and I will restore you). So the word *restaurant* was born—originally *restaurat*—derived from the Latin "to restore."

FAITHFUL FIRSTS:
The Beginnings of Major Religions

CHRISTIANITY

Origins: With the birth of Jesus Christ, now calculated in the summer of 4 B.C., in Bethlehem, and beginning especially with Christ's ministry in Palestine beginning ca. A.D. 26 in his thirtieth year, and ending with his crucifixion during the procuratorship of Pontius Pilate in A.D. 29.

Records: The New Testament, especially the gospels of Sts. Matthew, Mark, Luke, and John, telling of the ministry of Christ. The first complete manuscript of the New Testament, written in Syrian-Aramaic, dates from ca. A.D. 350; the earliest gospel, that of St. Mark, dates from about A.D. 65.

Establishment: Soon after Christ's death the disciples began spreading the Christian religion throughout the Middle East and the Mediterranean; Paul went to Rome ca. A.D. 42 and was martyred in A.D. 67. The Church became established in Rome and the provinces, but Christians were prosecuted at various times, especially by order of Emperor Diocletian in A.D. 303. The true establishment of the new religion came in A.D. 313 when Emperor Constantine embraced Christianity and proclaimed it the official religion of Rome.

Current estimates: 1 billion, 50 million Christians in Catholic, Eastern Orthodox, and Protestant groups.

ISLAM OR MUHAMMADANISM

Origins: July 16, A.D. 622, when Muhammad (ca. A.D. 575–632), a caravan conductor and shopkeeper in Mecca who had begun preaching in 616, began praying to the god Allah in Mecca instead of the Israeli god Jehovah in Jerusalem.

Records: The Koran (or Qur'an), a collection of revelations of Allah made to the Prophet, Muhammad, during the prophet's life, principally at Mecca and Medina. Without doubt the second most influential book in the world after the Bible, the Koran was collected by Zaid ibn Thabit, Muhammad's secretary, and was codified during A.D. 651–52 (about twenty years after the Prophet's death) by the caliph, Uthman, who had all collections of the Koran except Zaid's destroyed, thus establishing the only text for the book.

Establishment: During the century after the hegira (A.D. 622) the spread of Muhammadanism was rapid, even phenomenal. This was due in part to the Islamic concept of holy war—that he who dies fighting for Allah will go to paradise—during a period when the Arabic empire was expanding rapidly and militantly throughout the Near East and the Mediterranean.

Current estimates: 600 million followers.

HINDUISM

Origins: With the nomadic Aryan tribes of south Russia and Turkestan during the second millennium B.C., who invaded the Indian subcontinent ca. 1500 B.C., where their religious concepts mingled freely with those already existing in the Indus culture. Hinduism is unique in that there is no one founder as in the other major religions, and in that it is even today loosely organized and permits a wide range of personal and local deities along with the general concept of caste.

Records: The Vedas, dating from the Aryan invasions of 1500 B.C., are a collection of hymns, verses, spells, and treatises written and compiled over the millennium, ending in about 500 B.C. and culminating with the Upanishads, metaphysical and philosophical speculations, first begun ca. 900 B.C.

Establishment: After 1500 B.C. with the rise of the Brahman (or priest) caste in India. The Brahmans, even today, are the only Hindus permitted to interpret the Vedas.

Current estimates: 437 million followers.

CONFUCIANISM

Origins: with the teaching of Confucius (551–479 B.C.) and other members of a group of teacher-philosophers called *Ju* or meek ones. An accountant in the province of Lu, K'ung Fu-tzu (as he's more accurately named), was the first Chinese teacher to teach all ranks of people the six arts: history, numbers, ceremonies, music, archery, and charioteering.

Records: The Wu Ching (Five Classics), traditionally attributed to Confucius as author or compiler, were compiled during the Chou dynasty (ca. 1027–256 B.C.) and further codified by the Han dynasty, 202 B.C.–A.D. 220.

Establishment: More a religious philosophy and code of ethics than an organized religion, by the first century A.D. sacrifices were being offered to Confucius; from the third to seventh centuries the philosophy was almost eclipsed, but was revived and made the state religion in the T'ang dynasty, A.D. 618–906.

Current estimates: 312 million followers.

BUDDHISM

Origins: With the Indian prince, Siddhartha (ca. 563–483 B.C.), a member of the Gautama clan of the Sakyas. Ca. 534 B.C. Siddhartha began a six-year wandering of self-examination and introspection. After the wandering he meditated for forty-nine days until he achieved Nirvana, or enlightenment. For the rest of his life he taught the path to enlightenment in Bengal. Prince Siddhartha became known as Gautama Buddha, or Gautama, the enlightened one.

Records: The enormous Buddhist canon was orally transmitted during the second to first centuries B.C., and first collected in three main sections, the Vinaya, the Sutra, and the Abhidhamma, written in the Pali language, in 29–17 B.C.

Establishment: In the third century B.C. the Indian emperor, Asoka, provided official encouragement for Buddhism, and sent missionaries throughout southern Asia; ironically, though Buddhism became firmly entrenched in places like Tibet, Ceylon, China, and Japan, it was displaced in its home country by Hinduism.

Current estimates: 160 million followers.

SHINTOISM

Origins: The ancient native religion of Japan, involving the worship of numerous deities closely related to the forces and forms of nature.

Records: The oral tradition was first set down by imperial order in two books, the Kojiki (records of ancient matters) in A.D. 712 and the Nihongi (chronicles of Japan) in A.D. 720.

Establishment: The emperors of Japan were said to be descendants of the Ruler of Heaven, the sun goddess, beginning with the first Japanese emperor, Jimmu, in 660 B.C. This concept made Shinto the state religion of Japan until Emperor Hirohito formally renounced his divinity in 1946 at the end of World War II.

Current estimates: 60 million followers.

TAOISM

Origins: With Lao-tzu, Chinese philosopher born ca. 600–500 B.C., who taught that the ultimate being could be reached through the practice of compassion, thrift, and humility.

Records: The Tao-te-Ching is traditionally ascribed to Lao-tzu but was probably set down in the third century B.C.

Establishment: Though originally a philosophical system, by the fifth century A.D. Taoism had acquired an organized religious system complete with a pantheon of gods, monastic orders, and lay followers. In the eighth century A.D. the Master of Heaven became the secular leader of Taoists.

Current estimates: 52 million followers.

JUDAISM

Origins: Traditionally, with Abraham, a native of Ur in Mesopotamia, who moved to Canaan ca. 1700 B.C. and founded a religion based on worship of Jehovah, the one God, with animal instead of human sacrifices, and with circumcision of males signifying the covenant with God.

Records: The Torah—the book of law, or the Pentateuch—the first five books of the Old Testament, traditionally handed down by Moses to the Jews after he received them from God on Mount Sinai ca. 1250 B.C. The Torah was written down by Israeli scribes in the seventh century B.C.

Establishment: Though almost seven hundred years old, the worship of Jehovah became firmly entrenched in 1005 B.C. when David of Hebron conquered Jerusalem and began his reign of thirty-three years. His son Solomon built the Great Temple ca. 970 B.C. Christians later traced the lineage of Christ through twenty-seven generations on his father's side to King David.

Current estimates: 14,600,000 followers.

'TIS THE SEASON:
Firsts for Famous Holidays

CHRISTMAS, DECEMBER 25

First celebrated: In Rome, from the first century B.C. through A.D. 313. December 25 was *Natalis Solis Invicti*—Birthday of the Unconquerable Sun—a major holiday for Mithra, the sun god whose cult was the major rival to Christianity at the time.

First celebrated as a Christian holiday: In A.D. 336, the year before Constantine's death. With Christianity now the official religion of Rome, Church authorities appropriated the sun god's holiday in order to popularize the new state religion.

First celebrated in America: December 25, 1492, when Columbus's ship the *Santa Maria* was grounded on a reef off Haiti and had to be abandoned.

First celebrated by the Pilgrims: Like most conservative Protestant groups, the Pilgrims considered Christmas celebrations a pagan frivolity. The first Christmas in the New World (1620) found the Pilgrim fathers going ashore, "some to fell tymber, some to saw, some to rive, and some to carry; so no man rested all the day."

First decorated with trees: Tree worship was practiced by the ancient Druids, and seems to have been taken into Christian practice by the German Druids when they were converted. By the fifteenth century, in the Rhine area, mystery plays included decorated "Paradise" trees.

First tree in America: Mentioned in the diary of Matthew Zahm of Lancaster, Pennsylvania (a German settlement), December 20, 1821.

First Christmas cards: Created in 1843 in England by John Calcott Horsley. One thousand copies were printed showing a family group feasting, with the inscription "Merry Christmas and a Happy New Year to You." Price: one shilling.

First American Christmas cards: Printed by Louis Prang, an emigrant German printer, in 1875.

First made a legal holiday: Alabama, 1836—it took until 1890 for all the states and territories to follow suit.

HANUKKAH, EIGHT DAYS BEGINNING THE TWENTY-FIFTH DAY OF THE LUNAR MONTH KISLEV

First celebrated: 165 B.C. in Palestine to celebrate the rededication of the Temple of Jerusalem after the Jewish victory in the Maccabean revolt, when Jews who supported traditional religion and lifestyles revolted against the hellenizing of the Jewish religion and society under the Syrian ruler, Antiochus III.

THANKSGIVING, FOURTH THURSDAY IN NOVEMBER

First celebrated: 1621, Plymouth, Massachusetts, attended by survivors of the winter of 1620 to celebrate their first successful harvest. On hand for the celebration were Chief Massasoit and ninety braves of the Wampanoag tribe.

First menu: Venison (brought by the guests), duck, goose, fish, eels, corn bread, wheat bread, watercress, leeks, wild plums and berries, and wine made from wild grapes.

First official celebration: Proclaimed Thursday, November 26, 1789, by the newly inaugurated George Washington, to celebrate, in part, "the great degree of tranquility, union and plenty which we have enjoyed."

First made a regular national holiday: By proclamation of Abraham Lincoln, 1863, due in no small part to the intensive campaign of Sarah Josepha Hale, editor of *Godey's Lady's Book.*

INDEPENDENCE DAY, JULY 4

First celebrated: Philadelphia, 1777, one year after the Declaration of Independence and during the height of the Revolution. Entertainments included church bell ringing, bonfires, fireworks, and music provided by the Hessian band that had been captured at Trenton on December 26. The local Quakers complained about the windows broken during the celebration.

First official celebration: Made a state holiday in Massachusetts, 1781.

NEW YEAR'S DAY, JANUARY 1

First celebration: Various dates in various societies, since the beginning of civilization, usually having to do with the end of one harvest and the beginning of another crop cycle.

First January 1 celebration: During the Middles Ages, March 25 was the usual Christian New Year; with the adoption of the Gregorian calendar in 1582 the holiday was moved to January 1, though when the British took over New Amsterdam from the Dutch in 1674, the British still observed March 25 and adopted the Dutch holiday out of necessity.

HALLOWEEN, OCTOBER 31

First celebrated: By ancient Celts in Britain as their New Year's feast when human or animal sacrifices were offered to the god Samhain to release the souls of the sinful dead trapped in animal's bodies.

First celebrated as a Christian holiday: Eighth century A.D. when Pope Gregory III moved All Saints' Day to November 1. The night before, All Hallows' Eve, remained associated with witches and demons, in part due to Celtic custom.

First celebrated in America: Mainly by Irish Catholic immigrants during the nineteenth century.

First trick or treat: In ancient celebrations, villagers dressed as demons and ghosts and paraded through their town to the outskirts to lead away real demons that lurked near houses. The night also became associated with tricks and pranks in pre-Christian times— the mischief could always be attributed to spirits that were about.

APRIL FOOLS' DAY, APRIL 1

The origins are obscure, but April Fools' Day probably dates from the calendar reform to the present Gregorian calendar in 1582.

The Julian calendar, used before 1582, was 365 days, 6 hours long —a bit too long in comparison to the Earth's actual period of revolution around the sun. The extra time each year accumulated to the point that by the sixteenth century the spring equinox came on March 11, instead of the correct day of March 22. To rectify this, in 1582 Pope Gregory XIII instituted a corrected calendar—the one we use today—but it was necessary to take ten days out of that year to make up for the time accumulated under the old, incorrect Julian calendar. With the reform, many holidays were displaced, including the old New Year's of April 1, when the French had customarily exchanged gifts and entertained one another.

With the new calendar, New Year's became January 1, and the old holiday was left "high and dry"—a kind of "fool's holiday" that was celebrated by conservative diehards who refused to give up their old holiday. These "April fools" were probably treated to mock gifts and invitations by their younger and more progressive friends and relatives, hence the custom of tricking on April 1.

SAINT PATRICK'S DAY, MARCH 17

First celebrated: In Ireland, as a religious holiday honoring the arrival of St. Patrick in A.D. 432; the origin of the March 17 date is not known.

First celebrated in America: March 17, 1737, when the Charitable Irish Society (a Protestant group founded that year), organized a nonreligious celebration honoring St. Paddy.

GROUNDHOG DAY, FEBRUARY 2

First celebrated: In Germany, where farmers would watch for a badger to emerge from winter hibernation underground. If the day was sunny, the sleepy badger would be frightened by his shadow and duck back in for another six weeks' nap; if it was cloudy, though, he'd stay out, knowing that spring had arrived. The farmers would take this as a cue to plant their crops.

First celebrated in America: By German farmers who emigrated to Pennsylvania. Finding no badgers to speak of in Pennsylvania, they chose the groundhog as a reasonable substitute.

MOTHER'S DAY, SECOND SUNDAY IN MAY

First celebrated: May 10, 1908, in Grafton, West Virginia. Miss Anna M. Jarvis (1864–1948), a spinster extremely devoted to her mother, Mrs. Anna Reeves Jarvis, was concerned about the neglect shown mothers by their grown children (a sin of which she was decidedly not guilty). When Anna Reeves Jarvis died in Philadelphia in 1905, her daughter began campaigning for a special observance for her mother, and by extension, all mothers. Finally, on May 10, 1908, Dr. H. C. Howard held a memorial service honoring Anna's mother at his church in Grafton, West Virginia, while another service was held at Mrs. Jarvis's church in Philadelphia.

First decorated with carnations: Mrs. Jarvis's favorite flowers had been carnations, so faithful Anna chose them for the first observance.

First officially celebrated: West Virginia, 1910; by 1911 all the states in the union had Mother's Day proclamations.

SAINT VALENTINE'S DAY, FEBRUARY 14

First celebrated: In ancient Rome, as the Lupercalia, a February 15th feast in honor of the pastoral deity Lupercalis and the goddess Juno Februata. During the celebration, the names of young Roman women were put on slips of paper in a box, and the names were drawn by young men. The random couples would then be "going steady" for the upcoming year.

First celebration by Christians for St. Valentine: When the early Christians came into power in Rome ca. A.D. 313, they appropriated many "pagan" holidays to encourage Romans to join the Church. The feast day of St. Valentine, a martyr of A.D. 269 (though his origins are hazy—there were possibly as many as eight Valentines martyred by the Romans, and all may have been combined into one saint), was February 14—very close to the Lupercalia. The Christians retained the "valentine box" custom, but instead of having youths draw the names of eligible girls, they drew the names of Church saints from the box. The fortunate youths were then supposed to spend the year emulating the particular virtues of that saint. Though the custom still lingers on in some religious orders, the youth of Rome found it hard to give up *their* matchmaking custom. They reverted to the old matchmaking valentine box and the custom has continued for almost two thousand years with valentine boxes in schoolrooms and at children's parties—not to mention some interesting variations at wife-swapping clubs.

The first valentines: Credit for the valentine often goes to Charles, duc d'Orléans, who sent his wife "poetical or amorous addresses" which he called valentines while he was imprisoned in the Tower of London after the Battle of Agincourt in 1415. Charles's valentines were merely rhymed love letters. The custom of sending "home-made" love remembrances was traditional in Europe and the Colonies. In 1723, the first "commercial" valentines appeared—with decorated papers on which men (and women) could inscribe various amorous verses conveniently provided for them by the card makers. From there, it was only a short step to the printed valentine card, which originated in the United States in 1840 with Esther Howland. Of course, the custom of wooing one's lover with homemade valentines is still popular with romantics today.

EASTER, THE SECOND SUNDAY FOLLOWING THE FIRST FULL MOON AFTER THE VERNAL EQUINOX, OR SOMETIME BETWEEN MARCH 20 AND APRIL 25

First celebrated: The early Christian Church celebrated Pascha (second century A.D.) during the season of the vernal equinox, with Paschal Sunday a special observance of the Resurrection of Christ. However, almost all societies celebrate rebirth holidays during the spring equinox, and the early Christian celebration has links with the Roman sun-god cults which celebrated the rebirth of the sun and the new year.

First use of the word Easter: The Venerable Bede (672–735), an early English historian, claimed that Easter derived from Eostre, the Anglo-Saxon goddess of spring, who was celebrated by the pre-Christian English during the vernal equinox. Eostre, according to legend, opened the gates of Valhalla (heaven) to the murdered sun god Baldur, who was reborn (or resurrected) and ascended to heaven.

First Easter celebration in America: The Puritans discouraged any kind of celebration concerning Easter (except for the usual Sunday service), and it wasn't until after the Civil War that the holiday became what it is today.

The first Easter parade: Ancient New Year's celebrations (which took place in the spring until the Gregorian calendar reform) included the custom of putting on new clothes to symbolize a new beginning. This still carries over, and by the nineteenth century, wealthy Americans decided that it was a good idea to show off their new clothes after the Easter church service.

The first Easter bunny: The rabbit of Easter is technically a hare, which was linked in Anglo-Saxon mythology with Eostre, and rebirth; the hare was also linked in ancient cultures with the lunar cycle because of its nocturnal habits, and therefore with the lunar cycle of female fertility. German immigrants brought the Easter bunny to America, where their children would anticipate visits from the bunny on Easter evening. The kids built nests in hidden places for the rabbit, who paid a Santa-like visit during the night to lay colored eggs in the nests if the children had been good.

The first White House egg roll: Actually took place at the U.S. Capitol during the term of James Madison (1809–17), at the suggestion of wife Dolley.

THE BEST MEDICINE: Fads, Failures, and Famous Successes in Medical History

WHAT'S UP, DOC?

In prehistoric cultures the administration of medicines—usually herbs or brews—was accompanied by chants, dances, and the general carryings-on associated with the medicine man, whose "magic" was considered to be part and parcel of his "medicine." Thus the first doctors were sorcerers and witch doctors.

OOPS!

The Babylonian code of Hammurabi, ca. 3000 B.C., contains the first known penalties for doctors who botch things. If a physician killed a patient while opening and draining an abscess, his hands were cut off. If the patient were a slave, however, all the doctor had to do was buy the owner a new slave.

LOOKS SERIOUS TO ME

Greek historian Herodotus, in his famous *History,* recorded the first medical consultations: Babylonians customarily put their sick on beds in the street so that passersby could offer medical advice.

LAB TESTS: POSITIVE

The Babylonians (as well as numerous other ancient cultures) would diagnose the nature of a patient's illness by sacrificing an animal and examining the animal's liver to see what kind of shape the patient was in.

HE MADE HOUSECALLS

Imhotep, adviser to King Zoser of Egypt (2980–2900 B.C.), is the first doctor whose name has come down to us. The versatile Imhotep also designed the first stone pyramid, built by his boss.

THE HIPPOCRATIC OATH

The beginnings of modern medicine can be traced to Hippocrates the Great, physician of Athens, a survivor of the great plague of 429 B.C. which killed Pericles and at least one-third of the city's population. Hippocrates gave us the oath that set the first standards for medical practice: among them, "I will use treatment to help the sick according to my ability and judgment, but I will never use it to injure or wrong them"; and "whatsoever in the course of practice I see or hear . . . that ought not to be published abroad, I will not divulge, but consider such things to be holy secrets."

THE THIGH BONE'S CONNECTED TO THE HIP BONE

Herophilus of Chalcedon, a physician and scholar at the Museum of Alexandria, in 275 B.C. founded the first school of anatomy, dissected cadavers, and was the first to notice the difference between sensory and motor nerves. In spite of Herophilus's progressive attitude, as late as the nineteenth century British physicians still had to resort to grave robbers to obtain (illegally and secretly) bodies for dissection.

YOU WON'T FEEL A THING

In A.D. 1236 the Dominican friar, Theodoric of Lucca, was the first to recommend using opiates to ease pain during surgery. His method was to soak sponges in opium or mandagora (a narcotic) and place them over the patient's nose.

CUT UPS

Though the ancients studied internal anatomy by dissection, it was prohibited by the Catholic Church by an edict of the Council of Tours in 1163. However, in 1275 William of Saliceto wrote in his *Chirugia* of dissection for medical study, the first known reference to dissection in Europe since the ban. The *Chirugia* marked the beginning of new interest in scientific study of the workings of the body. Ironically, the Church ban of 1163 had not really been aimed at doctors who wanted to dissect cadavers. The Holy See had really meant to stop the Crusaders from their grisly (but practical) habit of cutting up the bodies of their fallen comrades, boiling them down, and packing the stew in casks to be sent home to Europe from the Holy Land for burial on Christian ground.

RATS!

The bubonic plague that killed one-third of Europe's population in the first half of the fourteenth century was brought from Asia by a group of Genoese merchants who were attacked by infected Tatar bandits at the Crimean trading outpost of Capha. The Tatars, whose own men were dying of the black death, catapulted their corpses over the town walls where the Italian merchants were holed up; many of the merchants got the disease and died, but those who survived returned home and brought the plague with them. The first European city to have an outbreak was Constantinople in 1334.

YOU'RE NOT GOING ANYWHERE

The world's first quarantine was imposed by the doge of Venice in 1403, who decreed that all travelers wishing to enter the city must wait for a clean bill of health to reduce the plague risk in the city. In 1485 the quarantine was standardized at forty days.

THE BEST THINGS IN LIFE

The world's first free clinic opened for the treatment of the poor of Paris in 1635, under the direction of Dr. Theophraste Renaudot.

LUB-A-DUB-DUB, LUB-A-DUB-DUB

English physician William Harvey made public his famous discovery of the circulatory system in 1628 with "Essay on the Motion of the Heart and Blood." Harvey was the first to point out that the heart is a muscle, and that it pumps the blood through the vessels.

O-POSITIVE

The first blood transfusion was performed in 1667 by French physician Jean Baptiste Denis, who transfused lamb's blood into the veins of a young boy. The experiment was a success insomuch as the patient didn't die, probably because the foreign blood quickly clotted.

The first successful transfusion of human blood wasn't made until 1818 by Dr. James Blundel at Guy's Hospital, London.

HOW SWEET IT IS!

Thomas Willis of Oxford, Charles II's personal physician, wrote in 1674 that the urine of diabetics was "wonderfully sweet as it were imbued with Honey or Sugar." Though Willis may have made the discovery that diabetics excrete excessive amounts of sugar (rather than metabolizing it) by observing flies drawn to sample vials, his almost ecstatic description causes one to wonder just how he *did* test for sweetness.

BACTERIAL FIRSTS

Dutch microscope inventor Anton van Leeuwenhoek built his first microscope in 1675, which magnified enough for him to see red blood cells and spermatozoa. With an improved model in 1683 he became the first to see bacteria in scrapings taken from his own teeth.

NINETY-EIGHT POINT SIX

The first workable thermometer invented by Gabriel Daniel Fahrenheit of Germany in 1709 used alcohol instead of mercury; mercury was introduced in 1714.

A POX ON YOU

In 1718 Lady Mary Wortley Montagu, wife of the British minister in Constantinople, observed inoculation against smallpox, a practice that had been in use in the East for centuries. The process involved taking a small amount of pus from a smallpox sore and putting it in a scratch made in the skin, causing a mild case of smallpox. The minor infection prevented full-scale, serious cases during epidemics. Her paper, "Innoculation against Smallpox," was the first public description of the process (though some European doctors had heard of the practice) and during the London epidemic of 1721 Lady Mary became the first European parent to have her child vaccinated.

BUT I THOUGHT IT WAS GAS!

The first successful appendectomy was performed in 1736 by British doctor Claudius Aymand.

BAD NOSE

In 1761 Dr. John Hill of London noted that patients who used an excessive amount of snuff developed nasal polyps more often than nonsnuffers. Hills's observation was the first link between tobacco use and cancer.

377

HO! HO! HO!

Nitrous oxide, or laughing gas, was made for the first time in 1799 by British chemist Sir Humphry Davy, who soon discovered the delightful properties of the gas, and recommended it for anesthesia.

I HEAR YOU LOUD AND CLEAR

Made in 1819 by French physician René Laennec, the first stethoscope was merely a roll of paper which could be placed against the breasts of female patients to avoid the embarrassment of the doctor's ear being placed against her flesh.

OUT LIKE A LIGHT

Though doctors were familiar with the value of narcotics for subduing pain during surgery, it wasn't until 1842 that Crawford Williamson Long of Jefferson, Georgia, performed the first surgery under general anesthetic. During the early nineteenth century, the effects of "laughing gas" and other chemical highs were known, and were occasionally used at parties. Long and a few friends tried ether at one bash instead of old-hat nitrous oxide, and Long found that the sulfurous ether was a stronger sensation killer than laughing gas. He then used the ether (not at the party, though) to put out his patient James Venable while he removed a cyst from Venable's neck.

Long's wife became the first woman to deliver under ether, in 1844, during the birth of their second child.

IT'S ALL THEIR FAULT

When Leeuwenhoek first saw bacteria in 1683 he didn't make a direct connection between the invisible living organisms and disease. It wasn't until 1861 that Louis Pasteur laid the foundation for modern disease treatment with his *"Memoire sur les corpuscles organisés qui existent dans l'atmosphere"*—the first germ theory of disease.

CLEAN HANDS IN A CLEAN BODY

British surgeon Joseph Lister, working in Glasgow, read Pasteur's germ theory paper of 1861 and discovered the germ-killing properties of carbolic acid. Lister performed the first antiseptic surgery in 1865.

IT'S A GALLSTONE

The first successful gallstone operation was performed on June 15, 1867, by Dr. John S. Bobbs on Mary Wiggins of McCordsville, Indiana.

SIMPLY DRILLING

The first electric dental drill was patented in 1875 by George F. Green of Kalamazoo, Michigan, and sold to Samuel S. White Company of Philadelphia, who began manufacturing "electro-magnetic dental tools."

A WEIGHT OFF MY MIND

Though the Egyptians were performing cranial surgery four thousand years ago and drilling through the skull and installing metal plates under the scalp—possibly as a cure for aneurisms, possibly to release evil spirits—it wasn't until November 25, 1884, that the first operation to remove a brain tumor was performed, by Dr. Rickman John Goodell of England.

HIS BITE WAS BIGGER THAN HIS BARK

The first rabies vaccination was administered beginning July 9, 1885, by Louis Pasteur to nine-year-old Joseph Meister, who had been severely bitten by a rabid dog, and would have died without the vaccine. The Pasteur vaccine had never been tried on humans, though it worked on test animals. Meister survived.

MY HEART'S AN OPEN BOOK

In Chicago in 1893, Dr. Daniel Hale Williams operated on a man with an arterial wound near his heart from a knife stab incurred in a street fight. It was the first open heart surgery—that is, an operation involving an incision (in this case, the knife wound) through the wall of the heart or a major connecting blood vessel. Before this, no person is known to have survived a punctured heart.

I'LL BE SEEING THROUGH YOU

X rays were discovered accidentally by Wilhelm Conrad Roentgen, a Bavarian physicist, on November 8, 1895, when he noticed that a cathode-ray tube caused a barium-plated paper to fluoresce, even when shielded by black paper.

FOLLOW YOUR HEART

In 1903 Dutch physiologist Willem Einthoven of Leiden built a "string galvanometer," which developed into today's heart-monitoring electrocardiograph.

SAFE AT LAST!

In 1910 Paul Erlich introduced his arsenic compound number 606, which killed syphilis bacteria. It was the first antibacterial drug. Marketed under the name Salvarsan, it reduced the incidence of syphilis in England and France by 50 percent within five years.

YOU'RE UNDER CARDIAC ARREST

It is remarkable that medical science didn't recognize the true nature of heart attacks until 1912, when Dr. James B. Herrick of Chicago described the classic attack in a banker patient (even then, certain types were more prone to coronaries!). Before Herrick's work, which revealed that clots entering the heart caused myocardial infarction and, frequently, death, doctors had laid these "attacks" to indigestion, heartburn, or food poisoning.

CAUSE AND EFFECT

The first induced cancers were produced by Japanese research chemists Katsusaburo Yamagiwa and Koichi Ichikawa in 1915, when they painted rabbits' ears with coal tar, causing skin cancers in the animals. The danger of carcinogenic chemicals wasn't to be fully realized for another fifty years.

THE GIRL IN THE IRON LUNG

Harvard professor Philip Drinker built the first Drinker respirator in 1927 using two old vacuum cleaners and other spare machine parts. Nicknamed the "iron lung," the machine was used for the first time in October of 1927 to maintain a young girl whose respiratory muscles were paralyzed due to polio. The machine operated by alternating high and low air pressure in the sealed chamber to force air in and out of the victim's lungs.

A FUNGUS AMONG US

The *Penicillum notatum* fungus has been around for millions of years, but its bacteria-killing property was first discovered accidentally in 1928 by Alexander (later Sir Alexander) Fleming, a British bacteriologist, at St. Mary's Hospital, London. Fleming noticed that no bacteria grew around bits of the fungus that happened to fall into a bacterial culture in his laboratory.

Penicillin was introduced commercially in 1945, and was being prescribed for 60 percent of all patients in the United States by 1950.

SPEAK UP!

Various ear horns and amplifying devices have been used for centuries to help the hard of hearing, but the first true, portable, wearable electronic hearing aid was made in 1935 by A. E. Stevens of England, who started his own company, Amplivox, to manufacture his two-and-one-half-pound invention.

PLASTERED

Plaster casts for fractures were used for the first time during the Spanish Civil War (1936–39) by Dr. José Trutta of Barcelona, who developed the casting method from principles discovered by Dr. Winnett Orr of Lincoln, Nebraska. Though arm and leg casts seem routine today, prior to their development a high percentage (often 50 percent) of fracture victims either died from complications or were subject to amputations.

A SMEAR CAMPAIGN

The pap test was developed in 1928 by Dr. George N. Papanicolau of Cornell University. The medical establishment didn't recognize the value of Dr. "Pap's" test for cervical cancer until 1943; it soon caused a sharp drop in the number of deaths among American women from cervical cancer.

LIFE SUPPORT

The kidney machine was developed in 1944 by Dutch physician Willen Kolff, who used the machine in secret to help save lives of Dutch partisans during the Nazi occupation. Though the first Kolff kidney machine was good only for filtering wastes during temporary kidney failure, it would eventually be able to support patients with nonfunctioning kidneys on a permanent basis.

THE BLUES ARE GONE

The first blue-baby operation was performed November 9, 1944, at Johns Hopkins Children's Hospital by Dr. Alfred Blalock. The operation corrects a congenital arterial defect in infants that ordinarily dooms them to early death or severe invalidism. The operation was developed by Dr. Helen Taussig.

A CRIPPLER CRIPPLED

In 1952 Dr. Jonas Salk developed the first polio vaccine based on virus culture techniques perfected by Drs. John Enders, Frederick Robbins, and Thomas H. Weller, all of Boston Children's Hospital. The Salk vaccine, and the Sabin oral vaccine, first publicly administered in 1961, virtually eliminated polio in Europe and North America, except Mexico.

NO MORE MEASLES

In 1962 Dr. John Enders (of Salk vaccine fame) developed the first successful measles vaccine. It was released for public use in 1966.

THE THALIDOMIDE TRAGEDY

In 1960 Frances Kelsey, a Food and Drug Administration researcher, prevented Thalidomide from being marketed in the United States, noting that in West Germany, where the drug had been widely used for several years, there had been a marked increase in infants born with phocomelia, or flipperlike limbs. The Thalidomide tragedy was to be the first—but not the last—case of delayed effects from improperly researched drugs being prescribed by doctors and marketed by pharmaceutical companies in the drug boom following World War II.

UNCLE SAM WANTS YOU TO BE HEALTHY

Medicare, the first U.S. Government-operated health program, went into effect July 30, 1965, against the objections of the AMA, and provided health benefits for 20 million elderly Americans.

SPARE PARTS

On December 3, 1967, in Capetown, South Africa, Dr. Christiaan Barnard, age forty-four, and a team of thirty associates performed the first heart transplant. In the five-hour operation the heart of Denise Ann Darval, age twenty-five, an auto accident victim, was transplanted into the body of Louis Washansky, a fifty-five-year-old wholesale grocer. Washansky lived for eighteen days before succumbing to pneumonia.

We hope you have enjoyed *The First of Everything.* If you have any comments, suggestions, or firsts that you would like to share with us, please write to: *The First of Everything,* P.O. Box 352, Key West, FL 33040.

INDEX